The Real World of EU Accountability

The Real World of EU Accountability

What Deficit?

Edited by

Mark Bovens, Deirdre Curtin, and Paul 't Hart

OXFORD
UNIVERSITY PRESS

OXFORD
UNIVERSITY PRESS

Great Clarendon Street, Oxford OX2 6DP

Oxford University Press is a department of the University of Oxford.
It furthers the University's objective of excellence in research, scholarship,
and education by publishing worldwide in

Oxford New York

Auckland Cape Town Dar es Salaam Hong Kong Karachi
Kuala Lumpur Madrid Melbourne Mexico City Nairobi
New Delhi Shanghai Taipei Toronto

With offices in

Argentina Austria Brazil Chile Czech Republic France Greece
Guatemala Hungary Italy Japan Poland Portugal Singapore
South Korea Switzerland Thailand Turkey Ukraine Vietnam

Oxford is a registered trade mark of Oxford University Press
in the UK and in certain other countries

Published in the United States
by Oxford University Press Inc., New York

British Library Cataloguing in Publication Data
Data available

Library of Congress Cataloging in Publication Data
Data available

Typeset by SPI Publisher Services, Pondicherry, India
Printed in Great Britain
on acid-free paper by
MPG Books Group, Bodmin and King's Lynn

ISBN 978–0–19–958780–3

1 3 5 7 9 10 8 6 4 2

Acknowledgements

The editors are deeply grateful to the other members of the project team: Gijs Jan Brandsma, Madalina Busuioc, Marianne van de Steeg, and Anchrit Wille. Amidst the pressures of dissertation deadlines, book contracts, and teaching obligations, they gave this project their all. They put up with our less than subtle nudging towards the systematic application of a uniform analytical framework. They cheerfully delivered comments on our and one another's work. And each in their own right made a range of outstanding contributions to the empirical study of accountability in European governance during the four-year lifetime of this project.

The research for this book project was funded by the Nederlandse Organisatie voor Wetenschappelijk Onderzoek (NWO), the Netherlands Organization for Scientific Research, under the *Shifts in Governance* programme (project number 450-04-319). The research for Chapter 4 on the Commission, by Anchrit Wille, was also funded by NWO, under its SARO programme (number 014-24-740). Earlier versions of Chapters 3–7 were presented as papers at a variety of academic conferences and seminars in Europe, the United States, and Australia. Of these various occasions for scholarly exchange, accountability, and learning, the meetings of the Connex network have been extraordinarily helpful for the development and refinement of our analysis. An earlier version of Chapter 3 was published as EUROGOV-paper C-06-01 and in the *European Law Journal* (Bovens, 2007). In addition, several of the contributors participated actively in specific workshops related to accountability in the EU and published work in progress relating to the subject matter of this book in a number of special issues of journals (*European Law Journal* and twice in *Western European Politics*).

Early drafts of Chapters 1, 2, and 8 were conceived at the Research School of Social Sciences of the Australian National University, where Paul 't Hart holds a full-time, and Mark Bovens an adjunct, appointment. They were taken further in an exceptionally fruitful stay of the three editors at the Netherlands Institute for Advanced Study (NIAS) in

Wassenaar in April 2009. The stay in Wassenaar facilitated progress greatly, and we were able to bring together the whole team for the crucial brainstorming and refinement of the overall project. In addition, the project and its various components have been discussed regularly with our colleagues at the Utrecht School of Governance (USG) at Utrecht University. Their incisive, helpful comments have been invaluable. In particular, we would like to thank other Europeanists and accountability researchers within USG for their collaboration and encouragement: Femke van Esch, Karin Geuijen, Albert Meijer, Ank Michels, Sebastiaan Princen, Thomas Schillemans, and Kutsal Yesilkagit. At the end of the day, however, responsibility for the text lies with us alone.

This project has also been a genuinely European project, in that almost all of its participants have benefited a great deal from their intensive engagement with the EU-funded Connex network. In particular, we have received very useful feedback on precursors of this project as well as on some draft chapters from Connex colleagues Morten Egeberg, Walter van Gerven, Carol Harlow, Beate Kohler-Koch, Peter Mair, Ioannis Papadopoulos, Richard Rawlings, and Antje Wiener.

In Canberra, Karen Tindall edited the final manuscript in her usual rigorous style – a necessary and much appreciated rod for our backs. In Oxford, we had a supportive and patient editor in Dominic Byatt, as well as the certainty of a dedicated and competent production team. In Amsterdam, Angela Moisl provided trojan help in finalizing the bibliography and coordinating the proofreading, as did Carlijn Ruers.

Contents

List of Boxes

List of Figures

List of Tables

List of Abbreviations

AAR	Annual Activity Report
ABB	Activity-Based Budgeting
ABM	Activity-Based Management
AMP	Annual Management Plan
APS	Annual Policy Strategy
AWF	Analytical Work Files
BSE	Bovine Spongiform Encephalopathy
CDR	Career Development Review
CEDEFOP	European Centre for the Development of Vocational Training
CEPOL	European Police College
CFSP	Common Foreign and Security Policy
CIE	Committee of Independent Experts
CLWP	Commission's Legislative and Work Programme
CPVO	Community Plant Variety Office
DG	Directorate-General
EAC	European Affairs Committee
EASA	European Aviation Safety Agency
EC	European Community
ECJ	European Court of Justice
ECSC	European Coal and Steel Community
EEA	European Environment Agency
EEC	European Economic Community
EMCDDA	European Monitoring Centre for Drugs and Drug Addiction
EMEA	European Medicines Agency
ENVI	Environment, Public Health, and Food Safety Committee
EP	European Parliament
ETF	European Training Foundation

List of Abbreviations

ETI	European Transparency Initiative
EU	European Union
EU-OSHA	European Agency for Safety and Health at Work
IAS	Internal Audit Service
IMCO	Internal Market and Consumer Protection
JHA	Justice and Home Affairs
JURI	Legal Affairs Committee
LIBE	Civil Liberties, Justice and Home Affairs Committee
MEP	Member of the European Parliament
MP	Member of Parliament
NAFTA	North American Free Trade Agreement
NGO	Non-governmental Organization
NIAS	The Netherlands Institute for Advanced Study
OHIM	Office for Harmonization in the Internal Market
OJ	*Official Journal of the European Union*
OLAF	European Anti-fraud Office (in French: Office Européen de Lutte Anti-fraude)
OMC	Open Method of Coordination
SPP	Strategic Planning and Programming
TEU	Treaty on European Union
TFEU	Treaty on the Functioning of the European Union
TRAN	Transport and Tourism Committee

List of Contributors

Mark Bovens is professor of public administration and research director at the Utrecht University School of Governance and adjunct professor at the Australian National University. His research interests include public accountability, success and failure of public governance, democracy and citizenship, and political trust. Web page: www.uu.nl/staff/m.bovens

Gijs Jan Brandsma is a postdoctoral researcher in public administration at the Utrecht University School of Governance. His research interests include European governance, accountability, democracy, and politics. Email: g.j.brandsma@uu.nl

Madalina Busuioc is a postdoctoral researcher at the Amsterdam Centre for European Law and Governance (ACELG), at the University of Amsterdam. Her research interests include European governance, European agencies, accountability, and aspects of constitutionalism in the EU. Email: e.m.busuioc@uva.nl

Deirdre Curtin is professor of European law at the Faculty of Law of the University of Amsterdam and Director of the Amsterdam Centre of European Law and Governance (ACELG). She is also professor of international and European governance at the Utrecht University School of Governance. Her research interests include public accountability of EU (executive) actors, open government of the EU, as well as the constitutional and institutional evolution of the EU more generally. Web page: http://home.medewerker.uva.nl/d.m.curtin

Paul 't Hart is professor of political science at the Australian National University and professor of public administration at the Utrecht University School of Governance. His research interests include public leadership, crisis management, policy analysis, European governance, and public accountability. Web page: http://polsc.anu.edu.au/staff/hart

Marianne van de Steeg is postdoctoral researcher at Free University, Berlin, and is affiliated to the Utrecht University School of Governance and to the political science department at Amsterdam University. Her research focuses on the European Union: democracy in the European Union, public accountability and European governance, European public sphere, and processes of Europeanization. Email: m.w.vandesteeg@uva.nl

Anchrit Wille is associate professor at Leiden University's Institute of Public Administration. Her research interests include political administrative leadership, executive–legislative politics, accountability, citizen politics, trust, and European governance. Email: wille@fsw.leidenuniv.nl

1

The EU's Accountability Deficit: Reality or Myth?

Mark Bovens, Deirdre Curtin, and Paul 't Hart

EU Governance Matters – a Lot

This book rests on a simple premise: since European governance matters a lot in a growing number of domains, questions about how European governance should, could, and is being accounted for are increasingly salient. The contribution we seek to make is to shed light on how such accountability for European governance is currently organized, how it occurs in practice, and how such practices can be evaluated. Few active observers of contemporary politics and public policy in Europe will need to be convinced of the validity of our premise. But to be on the safe side, let us at least illustrate the scope and significance of European governance in a number of policy areas.

First, let us look at environmental policy. Europe's nature is protected by two key pieces of legislation, the Birds Directive and the Habitats Directive. The latter obliges member states to maintain a number of designated habitat types and species at favourable status at selected sites agreed with the Commission. Together with sites from the Birds Directive, these sites form part of Natura 2000, the biggest ecological network in the world. In total, the Natura 2000 network contains over 25,000 sites (Birds and Habitats Directives combined) and covers around 17 per cent of the European Union (EU) territory. The regulation makes it an offence to kill or significantly disturb protected species or to accidentally damage or destroy their breeding sites and resting places. This applies even if such action is the result of an otherwise lawful activity. For example, if consent is given by the council to manage a tree protected by a tree preservation order and if there are bats in the tree while work is carried out, the person carrying out the work could be guilty of an offence. Likewise, if planning permission is given for a site that included a pond containing great crested newts and if the pond is damaged by the building process, the site manager and person carrying out the work could be guilty of an offence.

The impact of these directives has reverberated throughout the member states, down to the local level. An example of this (in a long line of others) is that the Canary Islands' regional government recently stopped the construction of a controversial port in Tenerife in an area protected by the Habitats Directive, after a Spanish high court ruled the site could not be declassified to allow the project to go ahead. Moreover, at around the same time, the European Commission sent a final written warning to Spain for failing to comply with a European Court ruling on a Segarra-Garrigues irrigation project in Catalonia, which the Court had ruled as being in breach of EU nature protection directives.

Clearly, when it comes to environmental protection, the Commission often takes a hard line in enforcing European policies, and member state governments at all levels cannot afford to ignore it. However, it occasionally also softens its stance – yet selectively so. For example, on 2 July 2009, it issued decisions addressed to nine member states (Austria, Belgium, Denmark, France, Germany, Greece, Hungary, the Slovak Republic, and Spain) concerning their requests for temporary exemptions in ninety-four zones or agglomerations from the EU's air quality standards for airborne particles (the so-called particulate matters, PM_{10}, standard). Under the 2008 EU Air Quality Directive (2008/50/EC), member states may, under strict conditions and for specific parts of the country, extend the time for meeting the PM_{10} standard until June 2011. The Commission decisions approved the time extensions for nineteen air quality zones in Austria, Germany, and Hungary, yet they also contained objections to requested exemptions in all other zones.

We see European legislative and executive power at work here. From an accountability perspective, we want to know how this power is constituted, legitimated, and, above all, how it is being subject to checks and balances. Many questions thus arise. Who designed these directives? Who decided which areas to include and exclude from Natura 2000? To what extent were national governments and parliaments involved in this process? What principles does the Commission follow in policing member state compliance with these directives? How does it make decisions? On what grounds does it grant exemptions? What, if any, possibilities do local and regional governments (who have to implement these decisions) have to influence or appeal them? To whom is the Commission accountable for its decisions, its exemptions, and its formal and informal policing principles?

Let us look at a second area, competition policy. A Commission press release in April 2007 announced the following:

> The European Commission has fined the Dutch brewers Heineken, Grolsch and Bavaria a total of €273 783 000 for operating a cartel on the beer market in The Netherlands, in clear violation of EC Treaty rules that outlaw restrictive business practices (Article 81). The Commission's decision names the Heineken group, Grolsch and Bavaria, together with the InBev group which also participated in the cartel. Beer consumption is around 80 litres per capita in The Netherlands. Between at least 1996 and 1999, the four brewers held numerous unofficial meetings, during which they coordinated prices and price increases of beer in The Netherlands. InBev received no fines as they provided decisive information about the cartel under the Commission's leniency programme.... After the Commission, on its own initiative, uncovered a cartel on the Belgian beer market, InBev provided information under the auspices of the Commission's leniency policy that it was also involved in cartels in other European countries. This led to surprise inspections on brewers in France, Luxembourg, Italy and the Netherlands. (European Commission, 2007)

This was just one of a range of high-profile, high-impact enforcement activities undertaken by the Commission. Another example is the long and bitter war fought with Microsoft. In February 2008, the Commission fined Microsoft €899 million for abusing its dominance of the market. Small beer, some would say. But it sent a strong signal: in August 2009, it was announced that Microsoft had agreed to open up Windows to different Internet browsers to fend off further European Union litigation.

Controlling competition between companies is an area where the EU is particularly powerful and where its decisions are clearly felt by European citizens. The EU's control over competition policy gives it the power to rule on mergers, takeovers, cartels, and the use of state aid. The EU has been able to develop competition regulation into a key area of EU leadership. It has had wide success in imposing its vision of open market competition on member states and has a direct effect on European citizens' daily lives, with actions being taken against big names like Microsoft. Yet, it has also been criticized for going beyond its accepted remit and for pursuing a free market policy that might undermine parts of the social market model that has operated in many European countries. And so again, questions arise about the degree to which the Commission's powers in this area are counterbalanced effectively by its obligations to account for its use of these powers.

The Commission is the best-known example of an EU institution exercising significant power vis-à-vis other governments and private actors. But it is by no means the only EU body that does. Some of the EU's lesser-known 'backstagers', such as the comitology committees (Brandsma, 2010), and 'outposts', such as the European agencies (Groenleer, 2006, 2009; Busuioc and Groenleer, 2008; Busuioc, 2010) have perhaps less conspicuous but no less significant roles to play in shaping and implementing policies and decisions that bind the governments, businesses, and private citizens of its member states.

Take the comitology committees, which are a critical pivot in approving the implementation of European public policy. By the latest count (Brandsma, 2010) they number 233, covering a huge range of issues areas, and making sometimes momentous decisions. Brandsma (2010) recounts numerous instances, and describes how this decision-making proceeds. Let us look at one:

> Two days before a meeting of one of the committees related to the seventh Research Framework Programme [for stimulating cooperation between and involving university and research institutes in member states], I met Sandra Tol and several of her colleagues – including people from executive agencies – at the Dutch education and science ministry in a pre-meeting. Lots of specific points were raised about the discussion papers that the Commission sent to them, mainly because they were unclear. They resulted in a short list of questions to be asked to the Commission. There were also discussions about a programme budget...that the committee was due to approve. Still everyone agreed that the Dutch could vote in favour of this programme budget anyway.
>
> Sandra was joined to the actual committee meeting by a colleague from another ministry. The meeting consisted mainly of presentations. Two professors who had been contracted by the Commission to do a policy review had been invited to make a speech and there were several points where the Commission gave the member states an update of the latest developments. Finally, there was the official vote. As nobody replied to the question of the chairman 'Do we have unanimity?', this was taken as a vote in favour. The committee had just approved 57 billion Euros of public spending.

The example highlights not just the scope of comitology decision-making, but also the multilevel nature of comitology committee governance. National public servants prepare for and attend meetings that result in decisions concerning the implementation of European programmes or legislation. National comitology members do not necessarily operate under much scrutiny from their hierarchical superiors, let alone the responsible ministers or the national legislature. However, the European Parliament (EP), which may have a much bigger interest in scrutinizing comitology processes, has very limited powers in doing so. Does this mean that comitology operates in the 'grey zone' of exercising public power without public accountability (Van Schendelen, 2006; Brandsma, 2007, 2010; Brandsma, Curtin, and Meijer, 2008)?

These examples and the questions they raise form part of a much bigger debate. As the EU has grown in size and as the shift of policy-making competences from the national level to the level of the EU has become more pronounced in the last twenty years or so, debate about its alleged democratic deficit has become louder and more vehement. This debate has many dimensions and elements – far too many to discuss in one single study. This book focuses, therefore, on one particular aspect of democratic governance: accountability. Proponents on both sides of the claim that Europe suffers from a democratic deficit do agree that one of the key indicators for the democratic quality of the EU is the extent to which both European and national actors who populate EU institutions can be – and are – held to account by democratic forums.

Aims and Scope

Across the globe, accountability has come to be considered a hallmark of democratic governance (Mulgan, 2003). It should therefore come as no surprise that, as the EU is turning more and more into a genuine polity (Van Gerven, 2005), issues of accountability have increasingly found their way onto the political and academic agendas (Bergman and Damgaard, 2000; Arnull and Wincott, 2002; Harlow, 2002; Curtin, 2004; Fisher, 2004). There is a growing concern that the shift from national, state-based policy-making to transnational and multilevel European governance is not being matched by an equally forceful creation of appropriate accountability regimes (Schmitter, 2000; Fisher, 2004: 496). Accountability deficits are said to be a key cause of the low public visibility and legitimacy of the EU (Scharpf, 1999; Arnull and Wincott, 2002: 1).

In the past years, much discussion has been focused on the relative merits of various proposals to institutionalize accountability in the complex, multilevel web of European governance structures. However, other than a few descriptions of existing formal accountability arrangements, there have been almost no efforts to describe and evaluate how existing accountability mechanisms regarding the major EU institutions actually operate. This study begins to fill that gap. It examines whether there are any accountability mechanisms at all, how they operate in practice, and whether they have the necessary 'bite'. In shorthand, our aim is to assess if, where, and how the EU suffers from an accountability deficit.

This book reports the findings of a major empirical study into patterns and practices of accountability in European governance. It is the product of a four-year project involving four senior and three junior scholars all affiliated with the Utrecht School of Governance of Utrecht University. It assesses to what extent and how the people who populate the key arenas where European public policy is made or implemented are held accountable. Using a systematic analytical framework, it not only examines the formal accountability arrangements but also describes and compares how these operate in practice. In doing so, it provides a unique, empirically grounded contribution to the pivotal but often remarkably fact-free debate about democracy and accountability in European governance.

In short, the present book does not contain yet another suite of general arguments about 'democracy in Europe'. Instead, it seeks to make a much needed empirical contribution to these sweeping normative debates. It is the first study to systematically cover

- how accountability is organized in and around the key institutions where European public policy is made and implemented,
- how these accountability arrangements operate in the day-to-day practices of European governance, and
- how the current formal and de facto accountability arrangements can be evaluated.

With four empirical chapters each covering a pivotal EU institution – the Commission, its agencies, the Council, and the comitology committees – the study shows that a web of formal accountability arrangements has been woven around most of them. However, it also shows that the extent to which the relevant accountability forums actually use the oversight possibilities offered to them varies markedly. Some forums lack the institutional resources, others the willingness, yet others appear to possess both. In those cases where both are on the increase, as in the EP's efforts vis-à-vis the Commission, fundamentally healthy accountability relationships are developing. Although ex post accountability is only part of the larger equation determining the democratic quality of European governance, this study suggests that, at least in this area, the EU is slowly but surely reducing its 'democratic deficit'.

Outline of the Book

Chapter 2 situates the study within the ongoing debate about legitimacy and democracy in European governance. Deficits, in both democratic and accountability terms, are not self-evident truths: they depend on perspectives. Different perspectives on the nature and purpose of EU governance will produce different deficits and locate them in different places. Chapter 2, therefore, provides us with the necessary lenses to evaluate the nature of the European project.

Chapter 3 sets out a conceptual framework for the systematic description and evaluation of accountability structures and practices in European governance. Few students of public accountability or European governance take the trouble of doing so. Much of the existing literature on accountability is high on big normative vistas, but low on conceptual consistency and empirical rigour. Chapter 3 instead provides a parsimonious framework for the analysis and assessment of accountability mechanisms. Chapters 4–7 use this framework to analyse and assess the accountability regimes that have developed regarding the major institutions of EU governance.

Chapter 4 paints a picture of how political and administrative reforms in the Commission have altered the mechanisms and operation of accountability at the top of the Commission. Drawing on documentary evidence of Commission accountability politics during the Prodi (1999–2004) and Barroso years (2004–present) and on more than fifty in-depth interviews held with senior Commission officials during the Barroso years, the chapter shows how strengthened accountability mechanisms, changed role expectations, and a shift in the dominant types of accountability feature in the modernization of executive accountability at the apex of the Commission.

Chapter 5 focuses on European agencies, the most novel and proliferating institutional entities at the EU level. Given the powers of these agencies and their impact on the implementation of European policies, the extent to which they are accountable becomes an increasingly important issue. The chapter zooms in on two key aspects of agency accountability: managerial and political accountability. The investigation focuses on five European agencies: the European Aviation Safety Agency (EASA), European Medicines Agency (EMEA), the Office for Harmonization in the Internal Market (OHIM), Europol, and Eurojust. The extensive insights into the practice of agency accountability are based on both documentary sources as well as over forty expert interviews with agency practitioners and with members of the relevant forums holding them to account, such as members of the management boards, respondents from the Council structures, and members of the EP.

Chapter 6 evaluates the accountability regime for the European Council, the major arena for EU decision-making. The main difficulty for democratic accountability on European affairs is that decision-makers in the European Council wear two hats – they are both European and national leaders – and that there are two types of venue available for accountability: the EP and the national parliaments. As a European leader, the European Council Presidency appears before the EP. As national and European leaders, they might be held to account by the various parliaments of the member states. This chapter reports on a qualitative analysis of parliamentary sessions in which the European Council Presidency appeared before the EP, and the Dutch delegation to the European Council appeared before the Dutch Parliament. The selected parliamentary debates took place immediately after a European summit in which a new treaty was negotiated or in which the European response to a crisis was discussed.

Chapter 7 focuses on the comitology committees which concern themselves with the implementation of European policies. In total, about two-thirds of all implementation measures first pass through comitology. Several hundreds of these committees exist, and their competences range from juridical aspects of cableways to preventing animal diseases. They are composed of civil servants from the member states who are specialized in the topics under discussion. The chapter analyses who, if anyone, monitors and assesses their performance and to what extent the current accountability regimes and practices in this area of EU governance are appropriate. It uses new survey and interview data collected from Dutch and Danish participants of 225 active committees, and their direct superiors.

Chapter 8 recapitulates and compares the main findings of the empirical studies reported in Chapters 4–7 in light of the analytical frameworks set out in Chapters 2 and 3. Based on this analysis, it goes full circle and examines this study's implications for the ongoing debates about the alleged 'accountability deficit' in European governance. It concludes by setting out areas for future research as well proposing areas of institutional development and reform that should be considered as the EU moves towards further integration.

The research for the empirical chapters was carried out prior to the entry into force of the Treaty of Lisbon on 1 December 2009.

2

The Quest for Legitimacy and Accountability in EU Governance

Mark Bovens, Deirdre Curtin, and Paul 't Hart

'Brussels, We Don't Trust You'

'Why does nobody seem to like us?' It is not difficult to imagine the odd European commissioner or commission official exclaiming this from time to time. Nor does it take much imagination to assume that heads of government and ministers in France, the Netherlands, Ireland, and various other EU member states were perplexed why they failed to convince their electorates that they should trust their judgement that treaty reform would strengthen the Union in a desirable fashion. While the elites that 'do' European governance on a daily basis may overwhelmingly agree that having a strong, inclusive, expansive system of Europe-wide governance is a good thing, the proverbial man in the street is either not interested or retains considerable scepticism.

The former is not new, but the latter is. When six European states started coordinating some of their industrial and agricultural policies towards the end of the 1950s, few objections were raised. With memories of two world wars uppermost in the collective mind, and the continent divided, it seemed yet another welcome step towards building bridges between former enemies in what was now Western Europe. But as the European Community grew in size and saw its remit greatly expanded in the decades that followed, slowly but surely its alleged technocratic, bureaucratic, non-transparent, non-democratic form of exercising public power came under more critical scrutiny. To be sure, the great mass of the citizenry still did not know or care that much about any of this. But a disparate, yet passionate, set of voices were raised, from nationalists, democrats, and academic experts, questioning the soundness of the deepening and widening EU fabric that was being woven.

By the time of the Maastricht, Amsterdam, and Nice treaty discussions in the 1990s, which were transforming what had begun as an economic union into a much more fully fledged and overt political union, 'Euroscepticism' had become a force to be reckoned with, in at least some member states (e.g. the United Kingdom and Denmark). While the elites in Brussels and in the national capitals were busy preparing the ground for further integration and widening of the EU's membership to the outer reaches of collective conceptions of 'Europe' (think Turkey, Ukraine, and Belarus), the sceptics were working on the 'hearts and minds' of the silent majority. And in 2005, the elites were stunned when popular referendums in the founder nations of France and the Netherlands rejected the proposed 'European Constitution' that they had presented as a crowning achievement of five decades of European integration. Today, it is safe to say that the EU has become a peculiarly contested international organization – both in theory and in practice. As we write this, the Treaty of Lisbon still reels from referendum defeat (Ireland), constitutional court challenges (Latvia, Germany, and, latterly, the Czech Republic), and form (attempted) executive rebellion (the Czech Republic).

How come? Much of the contestation revolves around the EU's legitimacy – whether and how the authority structures and governance practices of the EU are considered 'rightful'. This should not entirely surprise us. Today's EU covers many countries, regions, and hundreds of millions of people who have been at loggerheads in one way or another for considerable parts of their living memory. Naturally there will be disagreement, since there are real conflicts of interest, real cultural differences, and real scars. Eurosceptic forces can tap into these reservoirs without too much difficulty, and when their arguments are not countered persuasively by Euro-enthusiast political elites, accidents may, and do, happen. Moreover, member state citizens may keep their eyes on the bottom line even when their elites are captivated by a mood of enthusiasm about the benefits of transnational cooperation. When asked to vote in another referendum on yet another complex treaty reform (Treaty of Lisbon), a majority of the Irish people were confused as to what they were being asked to vote on, they did not trust the elite 'spin' and they, for a myriad of reasons, some imagined, some real, voted against it (Houses of the Oireachtas, 2008).

The Nature and Legitimacy of the EU: A Kaleidoscope

Preconceived ideas play a prominent role even in the somewhat less emotion-ridden world of expert discourse about European integration. It is this world that we will try to map in this chapter. We contend that different judgements about EU legitimacy are largely contingent upon underlying views of the nature of the EU as it has evolved in practice over the years. Different groups of scholars, often with particular disciplinary predilections, bring their own perspectives and biases to the often moving and changing images. Thus, some (realist) international relations scholars as well as those from public international law will tend to view the EU as essentially nothing more than an international organization (no matter how elaborate its remit or sophisticated its structure). In this image, the EU is a creature of its constituent member states through their national political and constitutional systems (Moravcsik, 2002; Dekker and Wessel, 2004; Magnette, 2005). Its legitimacy derives from the explicit or tacit consent of national parliaments (to the Ministers in the European Council and Council of Ministers) and in some rare instances from national referendum processes.

But what if the nature and intensity of the EU and its policies are such that a wide range of rights and interests of individual citizens are deeply affected by them, thus piercing the veil of national sovereignty? If this is one's perspective, then it can hardly be argued that the *indirect* legitimacy that heads and members of national governments confer upon the EU governance by virtue of being elected in their own national political systems is sufficient. Proponents of this view – often constitutional law scholars, European law specialists, and some comparative politics scholars – argue that there is a need to focus on the EU as an autonomous political force in its own right, requiring more *direct* legitimacy at the European level itself.

Such a view raises profound intellectual and practical challenges. After all, it is often argued that the EU can as such never be directly legitimate because it has no *demos*. In other words, on this understanding of legitimacy, a polity can only be built around a culturally homogeneous community. This is certainly the view of the German Constitutional Court (*Bundesverfassungsgericht*) in its judgment on the Lisbon Treaty of 30 June 2009 stressing the primordial role of the German *Volk* as defined in the German Constitution.[1] If we need to ensure that the EU as such enjoys a measure of direct legitimacy in its own right then we need to reach beyond the current institutional and constitutional design. This has significant implications, as we may need not only to reconstitute Europe (as a matter of institutional design) but rather to more radically reconstitute our under-standing of democracy (and of democratic theory) so that it 'fits' at the supranational level of governance (Bohman, 2007; Eriksen, 2009).

Regardless of these opposing views on the nature of the EU and the nature and level of democratization of its structures and processes (see also Kohler-Koch and Rittberger, 2007), we need to distinguish between two different types of legitimacy. The *formal* (legal) legitimacy of the EU goes relatively unchallenged for the simple reason that it is difficult to argue that the proper procedures and methods of authorization are not followed, in particular at the level of treaty reform. But formal legitimacy does not lead to legitimacy as a matter of fact, of feeling and accepting structures of authority. *Social legitimacy* refers to the affective loyalty of those who are bound by a structure of authority, on the basis of deep common interest and/or strong sense of shared identity (Habermas, 1976). The assumption made by integrationists was that the superior problem-solving capacity of supranational institutions would be sufficiently strong to induce the progressive transfer of the loyalties and political demands from the national to the European level (Haas, 1958). It is this progressive shift of this more empirical legitimacy to the European level that has not taken place. Or in Fritz Scharpf's much-used terminology (1999): the 'outputs' of EU governance have not been so highly appreciated by its citizens that they alone have been sufficient to overcome the nagging doubt about the lim-ited democratic legitimacy of its 'inputs'. This lack of social legitimacy is widely recognized, not only by scholars (Weiler, 1991; Beetham and Lord, 1998) but also in post-mortems on the 'shock' of the French and Dutch EU treaty referendum defeats of 2005 (Aarts and Van der Kolk, 2005; Toonen, Steunenberg, and Voermans, 2005).

However democratically legitimate the governance institutions of mem-ber states may be in their own jurisdictions, a sense of social legitimacy for the EU as a whole will not be created simply by the attribution of rule-making competences to European institutions. The welfare gains through integration, which should be made possible by the creation of those insti-tutions, can be expected to facilitate it, but never to deliver it in their own right. Social legitimacy is created over time simply by the practice, and habit, of doing things together. There is only so much that can be done to accelerate this process by symbol-building campaigns and communication strategies (Shore, 2000).

There are many reasons to expect social legitimacy in particular to be a pronounced problem for the EU, and remain so for the foreseeable future. The EU is, in the words of Lord (2000: 4), a new and unfamiliar political system; it has substantial powers to go into the nooks and crannies of member societies; its rules over-ride those made by national institutions; it takes decisions that affect ordinary lives; it demands sacrifices, sometimes with uncertain long-term reward; it takes from some in order to give to others; it affects deeply held values, including basic feelings of identity; and it is a large political system that often seems physically distant to its citizens.

Not only does the EU have a serious problem of social legitimacy vis-à-vis the citizens of the constituent member states, there are also very different views as to what should be done about what type of input at what level. Those who focus on the level of the (nation) state stress the structures and confines and guarantees of (representative) democracy at that level. This intergovernmental view will focus on government ministers and national parliaments (and civil servants) fitting within a national democratic hierarchy. The German *Bundesverfassungsgericht* echoed this view in its Lisbon judgment, claiming that democratic legitimacy as such is well-nigh impossible at the level of the EU anyway. Those, on the other hand, who stress the autonomy of the EU constitutional (and legal) order and the evolving patterns emerging in that context could not disagree more vehemently. It may be only a matter of time and of degree but the reflection that will resolve in the mirror from the national level is supranational (or, even more daring, postnational) democracy. The latter entails a focus also on issues of institutional and constitutional design that may either develop incrementally in practice or may leap forward.

In what follows, we explore further key perspectives on the nature of EU governance in order to identify, in a more precise way, the locus of the discussion on democracy and its possible content. In so doing, we also focus on where accountability comes into this debate, at what level, and in what form. We start with the basics: describing how the EU is constituted, what it actually does, and most importantly who does what. In many ways, different approaches to understanding the nature of the EU cast the spotlight on different *actors* at both the EU and national levels of governance. We will examine three different perspectives on the nature of the EU that dominate the scholarly literature. In each case, we tease out their accounts of who the central actors are, to whom they might be held to account, and for what. In this manner, we hope to be able to pinpoint much more precisely the relationship between holding a myriad of actors at various levels to (democratic and other forms of) accountability and the broader unsolved legitimacy problems of the EU (in the final analysis in Chapter 8).

How Europe is Run: Contending Perspectives

The EU as an Intergovernmental Bargaining Arena

Intergovernmentalism is a traditional school of thought in European integration theory with a long lineage (Hoffmann, 1995). It assumes that European integration and the institutional form of the EC and later that of the EU is sufficiently like other international organizations that it can be studied within a conventional interstate relations perspective. The classical, still popular yet often challenged, 'realist' theories of international relations assume that states are the central actors in international politics and that they act in a context of anarchy. States live on their capabilities and their wits in the absence of a centralized authority capable of enforcing political decisions. Policy-making in international politics is therefore viewed largely as a process of intergovernmental negotiations.

A variant to this approach is what has been termed *liberal intergovernmentalism*. This is a theory that has been specifically tailored to explain European integration processes (Moravcsik, 1993; Schimmelpfennig, 2004). It depicts states as unitary actors (via national governments driven by national preferences) on the European scene. It assumes that no actors other than national governments play a significant independent role in negotiations beyond the state. Through this lens, which organizes the autonomous role of international or supranational actors out of the picture (cf. Reinalda and Verbeek, 1998), the theory claims to explain the major steps towards European integration. These in particular comprise the intergovernmental conferences and treaty amendments that have changed the core policies and the institutional set-up of the EU (Moravcsik, 1993).

Intergovernmentalists assert that the key role in European governance is (and ought to be) played by the member states. Governments can express national preferences in various ways, for example during an intergovernmental conference leading up to the completion of a treaty revision process (by unanimity). But preferences also find prominent expression in the context of largely 'intergovernmental' institutions such as the Council of Ministers and the increasingly central and top-level European Council (deciding by – implicit – consensus).

The intergovernmentalist view claims that the EU is (simply) a sophisticated international organization, nothing more, nothing less. Seeing the EU through the lens of an international organization helps, in the words of Magnette, to 'avoid optical illusion, highlight its originality, and understand its proper value' (Magnette, 2005: viii). Intergovernmentalists do not necessarily deny the existence of strong supranational institutions but rather view them as strengthening the power of national governments in a number of ways (Moravcsik, 1993).

The fact that the member states are formally and de facto the 'masters of the treaties' as well as in control of key innovations in policy terms has led scholars to analyse the EU in terms of an international organization essentially comparable to other intergovernmental organizations (De Witte, 1994; Schermers and Blokker, 2003; Werner and Wessels, 2005). This approach does not generally deny that the EU may have certain specific (even *sui generis*) types of institutions when compared with other international organizations (e.g. the Commission and the Court). Yet it still analyses EU governance in formal terms as having been constituted by the member states and as being capable of revision only by virtue of processes of their specific and unanimous agreement (and according to their own national constitutional requirements).

Some scholars are more specific in their categorization of the EU as an international organization and describe the EU as an 'international integration-organization' (Virally, 1981). An essential feature of these integration organizations is that competences are transferred from the member states to the organization or that new competences of the organization are created, for example to set rules to harmonize the legal systems of the member states in certain areas (Dekker and Wessel, 2004). A number of international organizations have evolved into autonomous legal entities with competences to govern the behaviour of the member states. This may be not only at the level of the international legal order but also within the national legal orders of the member states. The EU is by no means the only international organization with such competences: the North American Free Trade Agreement (NAFTA), Mercosur, and the World Trade Organization (WTO) can all be placed along an integration continuum with the EU (Reinalda and Verbeek, 1998). But the EU is still in the vanguard. It is in particular such integrator organizations 'that are in need of a whole toolbox of governance instruments to steer, stimulate or enforce the cooperation between member states and to get a grip on the actions of their citizens ... this means that a larger number of legal acts in a variety of shades conceivably form part of the legal system of international organizations ... and thus of the national legal systems' (Dekker and Wessel, 2004: 236). This legalistic view of the nature and effects of the legal systems of international organizations complements and partly corrects classical (liberal) intergovernmentalism.

The EU as a Supranational (Federal) Polity

An alternative tradition of framing European integration is through the lens of federalism. Many old-style federalists plus European integrationists, dominated as a group by legal scholars passionate about the emerging federal constitutional system, insist that the federal idea is sufficiently broad that its relevance should not be restricted to the nation state. They argue that federalism can be used effectively as a means of structuring the relationship between different levels of government. It provides a tried and tested model that they feel the EU should emulate (Koopmans, 1992; Lenaerts, 1998) and one that is closely linked to a supranational model of European integration.

Looking though these lenses, the EU is a multilevel polity comparable to other polities in which authority is dispersed among constituent units at two or more levels. Federalism is a particular way of bringing together previously separate, autonomous, or independent territorial units to constitute new forms of union based upon principles that, broadly speaking, can be summarized in the dictum 'unity in diversity' (Burgess, 2004: 25). Integration can take place in a wide variety of ways, with the basic spectrum running from a confederation (Koopmans, 2008) – a union of states, rather than a single state – to a federation. A variety of federal and confederal polities share this characteristic, including Argentina, Belgium, Canada, Germany, India, and the United States. Conceptualized as a polity – with both territory and citizenship – the EU has been categorized as a (unique) 'supranational federation' (von Bogdandy, 2000).

Viewing the EU as an evolving (federal) state (at the supranational level of governance) obviously leads to quite different (and much more politically sensitive) conclusions than comparing it to an international organization. After all, it implies logically that the Commission may be considered as a type of supranational 'government' and the Court of Justice as a federalizing organ with central and binding authority. The political sensitivity lies in the fact that such supranational institutions are not embedded within an autonomous and democratically legitimate political system (Mair, 2005) and the national political systems are out of the loop when it comes to the EU institutions as such (as opposed to their respective national representatives).

The manner in which the EU has evolved in recent times certainly invites a comparison with a state-like development. An increasing number of political scientists and political philosophers discuss the EU in these terms (Christiansen, 2005). They argue that the EU is not just concerned with what can be termed Pareto-efficient interstate negotiation outcomes (i.e. with no clear losers), but rather that many EU regulatory policies have identifiable winners and losers as they allow choices with distributive or even redistributive effects. European competition policy and the Common Agricultural Policy provide many telling examples of EU decisions hitting certain regions, economic sectors, or firms harder than others, or indeed benefiting some much more conspicuously than others (Kay, 1998; Molle, 2006; Ackrill, Kay, and Morgan, 2008).

And so one can, these scholars argue, conceptualize the EU as a (supranational) *polity*: a regime responsible for authoritative decisions concerning the allocation of values in a society (Easton, 1953; Hix, 2005; Van Gerven, 2005; Magnette and Papadopoulos, 2008). In the supranational view, these decisions are taken largely through what is termed the 'Community method'. The Community method includes positive integration, namely legislative decisions taken by the Council (increasingly by qualified majority voting) and across a wide spectrum of policy areas in co-decision with the European Parliament (EP), on the initiative of the European Commission and subject to the judicial control of the Court of Justice. The 'Community method' also includes what is termed negative integration, meaning the removal of national restrictions hampering the application of primary Treaty rules, supervised by supranational actors such as the Commission and the Court of Justice (Majone, 2009).

An increasingly widely accepted perspective on the EU understands it as an evolving political system. Both lawyers and (comparative) political scientists have signed up to it (Hix, 2005; Mair, 2005; Van Gerven, 2005; Curtin, 2009). By using the conceptual language of a 'political system' rather than that of a (federal) state to frame the component parts of the EU, it is possible to 'encompass pre-state/non-state societies, as well as roles and offices that might not seem to be overtly connected with the state' (Finer, 1970). In the EU context, the use of these classic political science terms has the major advantage of allowing the EU to be treated as a political system comparable to other political systems. This theoretical framework enables an analysis of the EU in substantive terms as a 'would-be polity' (Lindberg and Scheingold, 1970). It follows from this perspective that it is possible to raise empirical and normative questions about EU governance that are being asked about any other polity, for example concerning its efficacy, legitimacy, and accountability.

The EU as a Regulatory Regime

A third key perspective on EU governance sees the emerging structure in Europe as a governance regime deeply embedded in extensive institutional arrangements of public (or semi-public) character (Eberlein and Grande, 2005: 97). It is grounded in the manner in which the EU has evolved as a matter of policy-making in day-to-day practice. We call it the regulatory perspective on the EU. Majone (1996), many years ago, referred to it as the 'regulatory state', but it is more appropriate to characterize it as a regulatory regime. It envisages the EU as a *functional* regime set up to address problems that the member states cannot resolve when acting independently. The EU not only adopts laws harmonizing national rules (positive integration) but also provides a framework for what is termed 'risk regulation' via more informal mechanisms than those of formally binding law and legal instruments. The focus on (risk) regulation has become a defining feature of EU governance (Majone, 1996).

The regulatory perspective designates actor configurations and problem-solving activities which do not necessarily fit into the institutional frameworks foreseen by European law but which have instead emerged as responses to functional exigencies. Such regulation is not achieved simply by passing a law but requires detailed knowledge of and intimate involvement with the regulated activity. As a result the trend has been for specific scientific/technical 'epistemic communities' to be established where non-political experts ensure that knowledge is enhanced and the information problems with regard to choice under conditions of risk are reduced (Haas, 1992). Inherent in notions and practices of regulation is decision-making (in one form or another) by actors other than politicians (and judges), namely by technocrats (either civil servants or scientific experts of one kind or another) and/or private actors.

Geuijen et al. (2008) call these people the 'New Eurocrats'. These are not the Commission officials who belong to the much-maligned 'Brussels bureaucracy'. They are the much more sizeable armies of national public servants and related 'experts' who piggyback on EU committee meetings to form and maintain networks of like-minded people working on the same issues in different countries. Veterinarians, crime fighters, radiation experts, epidemiologists, educators, industrial safety specialists, pharmacists, physicists: they see the value of agreeing on common product or safety standards, exchanging data and sharing experiences, and even actively collaborating to pragmatically solve common problems (e.g. jointly combating cross-border crime, aligning the handling of migrants and refugees) – even when the political bodies of the EU have not (yet) put in place the legal or policy frameworks authorizing and indeed legitimizing their doing so. They are in fact often keen to keep the politics out of their cooperation and 'get on with the job' without worrying much about national lobbies, negotiation mandates, and elusive package deals.

The transfer of governmental decision-making authority to outside actors occurs along a continuum. Thus, at one (far) end of the EU spectrum, it covers very loose coordination processes such as the so-called open method of coordination (hereafter OMC) involving stakeholders and other nongovernmental actors (Armstrong and Kilpatrick, 2007). But at the other end, it also covers actors that are associated much more closely with the Community method and the core political actors and indeed may be involved in the adoption of legally binding rules. These actors may in turn function as a magnet for broader networks but at the same time they are either part of the Community method or very closely related to it.

One cluster of arenas where the erosion of administrative boundaries occurs is the EU's comitology process (Joerges and Neyer, 1997; Shapiro, 2005; Brandsma, 2010). Comitology committees have in many areas become pivotal gatekeepers of the implementation of EU policies: without their consent, nothing will happen. And, as the example given in Chapter 1 suggests, although their remit may formally be 'technical' – passing judgement on the feasibility and efficacy of proposed programmes and projects – their decisions are hardly small beer in material terms. Yet in terms of good and accountable governance, comitology is notoriously opaque. The committees include experts employed by regional or local governments alongside national civil servants (and used to include representatives of non-governmental research organizations, private enterprises, universities, and the like). They are fed and supported by the Commission, and lobbied intensively by all sorts of organized interests (Van Schendelen and Scully, 2003). Who is running these committees? Who is responsible for them? The questions are more easily asked than answered (see further Brandsma, this volume).

Another area where expert-technocratic input into administrative decision-making reigns is the proliferation of EU-level (quasi-independent) agencies that are increasingly being given regulatory and operational tasks. These include the European Medicines Agency, the European Food Safety Agency, the European Environment Agency, Europol, as well as colourful exemplars such as the European Foundation for the Improvement of Living and Working Conditions and the Community Plant Variety Office. Although the story of the creation of some of these agencies is intensely political (Groenleer, 2009), when settled and operational, most of them embody considerable 'depoliticization' of core decision-making and rule-making processes at the EU level (Curtin, 2005, 2007). And again we can ask: who runs these organizations, who controls them, to whom are they accountable and for what? (See further Groenleer, 2009; Busuioc, 2010 and Chapter 5 in this volume.)

Both committees and agencies are not grounded legally in the Union treaties, but in an array of formal and more informal secondary and tertiary level texts and rules. Both have literally become more 'visible' in recent years thanks to extensive information made available on the Internet (Brandsma, Curtin, and Meijer, 2008). And for both there are concerns regarding their status, the legality of their actions, and their subjection to substantive legal control. Agencies most palpably are not yet subject explicitly to the general and full jurisdiction of the Court of Justice, though this changes with the Lisbon Treaty taking effect. Even in the case of policies where the formal decision-making rules resemble the standard Community method, it can be a struggle to keep the locus of decision-making within the formal rules of the political system. Thus, legislative powers assigned to the Council or Parliament under the treaties are, in the European Parliament's assessment, often being arrogated by comitology committees.

The Problem of EU Legitimacy: Three Cuts

Just as Graham Allison's famous models (1971) did for our understanding of public policy-making, each of the three perspectives on EU governance presented above offers a distinctive analytical 'cut' on the issues of legitimacy and, particularly, accountability that form the key concern of this study. In the next two sections, we briefly outline how each cut conceptualizes these issues, and which normative standards for assessing EU legitimacy and accountability they imply. First, we focus on the respective models' view on legitimacy. Then we show how these views lead each model to both localize and assess accountability for EU governance in a distinctive way.

In terms of Lincoln's famous description of the main elements of democracy, input-oriented legitimacy refers to government *by the people*, whereas output-oriented legitimacy refers to government *for the people*. The levers of legitimacy of these dimensions of democracy are different (Thomassen and Schmidt, 2004). Output legitimacy means that people agree that a particular structure should exist, and even participate in rule-making, because of the benefits (the 'public value': Moore, 1995) it brings.

Social acceptance is thus instrumental and conditional, as well as independent of an affective relation. On the whole, the legitimacy of the EU and its decisions as such has tended to be focused on the output side of the equation (see, in particular, Scharpf, 1999, and Majone, 1996), in particular by those who view the EU as a regulatory regime.

Input legitimacy on the other hand means that social acceptance of the structure in question derives from a belief that *citizens* have a fair chance (however understood) to influence decision-making and scrutinize the results. In short: we accept government X and its policy Y, because we have had a hand in putting X in place, have had the opportunity to influence its choice for Y, and have the possibility of throwing X out in due course when we really do not like Y and/or any of X's other policies and plans.

Hence, political choices are legitimate if and because they reflect the 'will of the people' – if they can be derived from the authentic preferences of the members of a community. The input perspective derives its democratic legitimacy very largely from a pre-existing *collective identity*. As long as a collective identity does not exist at the level of the Union, input-oriented legitimacy is out of reach for the EU for the foreseeable future. On this view, input legitimacy can only be achieved through robust (i.e. consequential, with 'teeth') democratic authorization, representation, and accountability at the level of the national political system. Output legitimacy is, however, available even in the absence of a collective identity provided that effective results are achieved in practice (though arguably it too presumes a set of common values concerning what types of European-level policies are desirable and what key goods/deliverables are expected from EU institutions). Let us now explore further the 'cut' of each of the three perspectives on the level and type of legitimacy that is possible and/or desirable.

Intergovernmentalism: The Primacy of National Legitimation

The model of democracy envisaged by the intergovernmental view of EU governance is inextricably linked to the nation state. It insists that the EU must institutionally ensure that the actors at the EU level are accountable to the member states. The legitimacy of the EU and its institutions is thus indirect, as it is derived from the democratic character of the member states. What matters is that representatives of the member states (in the Council of Ministers, in the European Council, and in intergovernmental negotiations) can and will be held to democratic account at the national level for their actions and inactions. The key levers for this are the national parliaments (see further Van de Steeg, this volume), national elections and, as Europeans have observed with horror or satisfaction in recent years, national referendums (with national constitutional courts increasingly playing a role). So when heads of government prepare for, or return from, European Council meetings about such weighty issues as treaty reform (à la Maastricht, Amsterdam, Nice, and Lisbon), intergovernmentalists want and expect them to be compelled to face their national accountability forums. It is there that they need to explain their positions and actions, to be given a mandate and support, and to be 'grilled' in case of controversy and failure to achieve national objectives.

The presumption in this approach is that only the nation state can foster the type of trust and solidarity required to sustain a democratic polity. At the national level a well-developed collective identity already exists (countries like Belgium and regions like Catalonia and the Basque Country may be partial exceptions). This motivates citizens to participate in opinion-forming processes and hold national governments to account electorally at regular intervals, as well as continuously through public debate. The model presumes that the member states delegate competence to the Union that in principle they can choose to revoke (Pollack, 2003). Although this entails a form of self-binding on the part of the member states, states can impose powerful controls on such delegation in order to ensure that they remain the source of the EU's democratic legitimacy. How? It is the member states that both authorize EU action and confine and delimit the EU's range of operations through the provisions set out in the treaties. It is they who choose to retain or relax European decision-making rules that permit each and every member state to exercise the power of veto.

The intergovernmental model can thus be understood as a way of addressing the democratic problems that complex state interdependence and globalization bring forth. Its preferred mode of doing so is through establishing European institutions that are clearly controlled by and accountable to the national democratic systems (Eriksen, 2009). The assumption of this model is that states are unitary actors interacting with European institutions in a manner that has been specifically authorized at the national level and fitting into national chains of delegation and accountability. It does not address – or even see – problems arising from the so-called disaggregation of states internally (Slaughter, 2004) by the forces of globalization and Europeanization. Nor does it grasp the corollary that component parts of states (e.g. national agencies) may be networking and adopting rules at inter alia the European level of governance beyond the remit or even knowledge of the national governments (Curtin and Egeberg, 2008).

Supranationalism: The Importance of European Legitimation

The supranationalist perspective recognizes the autonomy and discretion of certain core, EU-level, institutions or actors, in particular the Commission and the Court of Justice and also the European Parliament, in conferring legitimacy upon EU governance. The putative 'democratic deficit' arises from the fact that national electoral processes and national representative institutions, while necessary and desirable in their own right, cannot solely hold the entire fabric of EU actors/institutions to democratic account, only at most the (single) national representatives. In other words, there is a fundamental mismatch between the national political level and the European decision-making/policy level (Schmidt, 2006). In order to deal with the reality of autonomous and incremental supranational power, it is necessary to have supplementary institutional arrangements at the level where policies are being crafted and decisions are being taken.

From this perspective, for example, the development of the European Commission into a full-blown politically mandated form of European government led by a prime-minister-style Commission President would be welcomed (Hix, 2008). As will be described in Chapter 4, the early shoots of this type of democratic politicization of the Commission have become visible in recent years. Yet for this to come to fruition would obviously require significant and as yet highly controversial constitutional and electoral reforms at the European level. The same goes for reshaping the EP from a unicameral into a bicameral institution, with an Upper House modelled on that of national federal systems, designed to ensure equal (member) state representation (in contrast with the weighting of state population sizes in the composition of the Lower House). The latter has been part of a reform institutional agenda often put forward by federalists and integrationists – most recently in the Convention process leading to the adoption of the failed European Constitution.

Whichever set of institutional proposals it contemplates, central to this supranational current of thought is that a model of supranational democracy must be constituted at the *European level* (as well as the national level). This would involve the institutional entrenchment at the EU level of essentially state-based forms of legally binding democratic will formation. This requires authoritative institutions at the Union (and member state) level, organized along federal lines and equipped with the final word on those matters that fall under each level's respective jurisdiction (Eriksen, 2009). So when we return to the example of the European Council preparing and deciding upon momentous policy decisions and institutional reforms, the supranationalist expects the EU Presidency of the day as well as the President of the European Commission to be fully accountable to the EP (in addition to its members being held to account by their national parliaments; see further Van de Steeg, this volume).

There is a touch of idealism and hope here. The supranationalist perspective expects that putting such institutions in place will cause European citizens to eventually develop a more inclusive multilevel collective identity. Citizens would start to feel 'European' in addition to feeling, say, French as well as Alsatian. Once this point is reached (arguably way off into the future), the supranationalist ideal of a multilevel, federalist European democracy becomes self-reinforcing. But the supranationalist perspective also harbours a view of democracy that is both postnational and deliberative. The ideal of *postnational* democracy is premised on a separation of the inevitable link between national identity and (a form of) political identity (Cohen and Sabel, 1997; Bohman, 2007). This is at times presented as a political arena that does not replace the national political unit but supplements it (Curtin, 1997). Moreover, some emphasis is given in this postnational model of democracy to a more deliberative conception of democracy, alongside representative democracy (Besson and Martí, 2006). Deliberative democracy emphasizes active dialogic participation rather than the intermittently passive procedural participation (voting) as the key for democratizing decision-making processes, and for contributing over time to the development of a European public sphere. At the same time, it has been used also as a means of testing empirically and evaluating the importance of deliberation in EU-level co-decision in the EP (Stie, 2009). A more extreme version envisages the EU as a type of 'postnational government' subject to the 'cosmopolitan law of the people' (Eriksen, 2009).

Regulatory Regime: Legitimation by Results-oriented Depoliticization

As described above, the third perspective on European governance holds that the EU should be seen as a regulatory regime and that therefore any democratic deficit is not a serious problem (Majone, 1996). In fact, Majone (2005) argues that to speak of a democratic deficit of the current EU is to commit a 'category mistake'. One should not discuss the EU with the same concepts as we use for its component units – as if the Union were a state or a would-be state. This approach is not to deny the existence of a legitimacy problem. Rather it is to say that democratic legitimacy is only one member of a class of normative standards used in assessing governance regimes (Majone, 2005: 619). In a democracy, all non-majoritarian institutions – including constitutional courts, independent central banks, and independent regulatory committees – raise legitimacy concerns (Thatcher and Stone-Sweet, 2002). Yet this does not mean that they suffer from a 'democratic deficit'. The point is that by *design* such institutions are not accountable to the voters or their elective representatives. Rather they acquire their legitimacy by other means: as public institutions, they must prove their 'distinctive competence' (Selznick, 1957; Boin, 2001) by generating and maintaining the belief that they are, of all feasible institutional arrangements, the most appropriate solution for a given range of problems (Majone, 2005).[2]

The regulatory perspective suggests that the Union's overall legitimacy can and must be based on its ability to produce substantive outcomes in line with the principle of Pareto optimality. This dictates that policies are pursued that are to no one's disadvantage (no losers) and that will make at least one party better off (winners), lending (output) legitimacy to international negotiations (Scharpf, 1999: 237). According to Majone (1996, 2005), such a regulatory regime does not need popular legitimation as such. Instead, politically independent institutions, such as executive and regulatory agencies, central banks, judicial review, and the delegation of policy-making powers to independent regulatory commissions, provide the required legitimation of a unit constructed to resolve the perceived problems of the members. If the European Central Bank manages, partly through its very independence from any of the cash-strapped member state governments, to keep the Euro a credible currency during the depths of a financial crisis-cum-recession, the people will notice, remember, and continue to trust it into the future – so the argument goes. Likewise, if European competition law generates strong and independent national watchdog agencies that do not shy away from taking on big corporations when they form cartels or manipulate markets to destroy their main competitors, they are seen to be serving the public interest. That will provide them with legitimacy back home, even though they are implementing essentially European legislation. In extremis, this argument would imply that few would really care whether or not these agencies are controlled by democratically elected parliaments, as long as they provide public accounts to their boards and to the general public of what they do and why.

From the perspective of this more modest, output-oriented form of legitimacy, political choices are legitimate if and because they effectively promote the common welfare of the constituency in question

(Scharpf, 1999) – and, we add, if they are seen to be doing so by being transparent about their actions and their impacts. Government *for* the people derives its legitimacy from its capacity to tackle problems requiring collective solutions. Identifying collective solutions still presupposes the existence of an identifiable constituency, but what is required is no more than the perception of a range of *common interests* that is sufficiently broad and stable to justify institutional arrangements for collective action.

Output legitimacy rests on what March and Olsen (1989) call a logic of consequence: people agree that a particular structure should exist, and even participate in rule-making, because of the benefits it brings. Social acceptance is thus instrumental and conditional, as distinct from institutions that rest on a logic of appropriateness, whose very existence has become 'infused with values beyond the immediate requirements of the task at hand', to use Selznick's classic formulation (1957). Output-oriented legitimacy appeals to citizens, not so much as members of a political community, but as consumers and clients. It is *interest based* rather than *identity based* (Thomassen and Schmidt, 2004). This keeps regulatory institutions on their toes: they need to be seen to keep delivering the goods in order to justify their continued existence (unlike institutions such as the judiciary or the fire service which are among the public sector's strongest brands and are widely seen to be inherently good and indispensable regardless of recent performance).

Contending Legitimacy Claims

The three perspectives on European integration provide us with different accounts of the 'big picture' of legitimacy of EU governance arrangements. They then also allow us to examine how and where accountability fits into that picture. Following Beetham and Lord (1998), we assert that assessing the legitimacy of a governance system involves considering three crucial processes: authorization (how have the basic structures and norms constituting the system come into being, and to what extent do these effectively authorize the basic forms of political leadership being exercised within the system?), representation (to what extent do citizens select and provide mandates to the holders of key public offices within the system?), and accountability (how is the public power exercised by office-holders being checked and balanced by forums that enjoy popular trust?).

Table 2.1 summarizes how each of the three perspectives outlined above would see these three processes ideally being constituted in European governance. The table offers just thumbnail characterizations that may not do justice to the shades and nuances of each of the perspectives, but

Table 2.1 Contending perspectives on democratic legitimacy of EU governance

Legitimacy dimensions	Authorization	Representation	Accountability
EU governance perspectives			
Intergovernmental	Treaty ratification National election/ appointment by the parliament of members of Council/European Council	National governments in European Council/ Council. National allocation of Commissioners and Members of the European Parliament (MEPs)	National parliaments and electorates
Supranational	Constitution/Treaty ratified by all member states (Europe-wide) referendums. Constitution-alization via the European Court of Justice (ECJ)	Politically selected Commission approved by European Parliament. Directly elected EP organized into ideolo-gical groupings	European Parliament European electorate. Other EU accountability forums including ECJ national parliaments and electorates
Regulatory	Delegation via national and European political routes	Non-majoritarian (experts/technocrats)	Procedural: outcome assessment (e.g. via benchmarking)

Source: Adapted from Beetham and Lord (1998).

they will do for our present purposes. Roughly speaking, the intergovern-mental perspective claims to best approximate contemporary institutional realities within the EU system. In contrast, the supranational perspective's vision is by its own admission a long way from realization. And the regulatory perspective is looking largely for something else not rooted in authorization, representation, and accountability – at least not in classical democratic-majoritarian terms. And if it does look for more 'democracy' then it puts its money on negative integration with more input at the national political level (Majone, 2009).

Accountable EU Governance: Perspectives and Actors

As noted earlier, in this study we only tackle one dimension of the broader discussion on the democratic quality of the EU and the alleged 'democratic deficit' that plagues it. Our focus is on *accountability*, and in particular the question whether there is an 'accountability deficit' in European governance. Accountability is a key component of legitimacy, but it can also be concep-tualized and analysed in its own right. As we shall see in more detail in the next chapter, we can discern at least three distinct sets of accountability questions: 'who is accountable?', 'to whom?', and 'for what?' The answers that can or will be given to these very basic questions depend to a large extent on one's perspective on the nature of the EU.

An *intergovernmentalist* will focus on the national actors and accountability forums. Intergovernmentalists regard further EU-level checks and balances at best as supplementary (for a very clear example of this reasoning see the judgment of the German Constitutional Court on the Lisbon Treaty referred to earlier), and more likely as disruptive of what ought to be the main and clear lines of democratic delegation from national electorates through their legislatures, government, and bureaucracies to European institutions. To them, the notion of senior-level national bureaucrats holding their staff who sit on comitology committees in Brussels to account, is both necessary and sufficient in terms of democratic oversight on comitology, since these senior national bureaucrats are in turn firmly embedded in national accountability chains (see Chapter 7). The same goes for European agencies being answerable to so-called management boards composed of representatives from each member state (see Chapter 5). In this way, it remains crystal clear who the ultimate principals of European governance are: member state citizens and their representatives.

A *supranationalist* in turn will focus in addition on the need to hold autonomous EU actors accountable in their own right – and on the desirability of having competent and capable EU-level accountability forums, embedded in European-level delegation chains, to do so effectively. Hence its strong interest in strengthening the institutional capacity of forums such as the European Parliament (EP) and the European Court of Justice (ECJ).

Within the *regulatory regimes* perspective, it is justifiable to remove some areas of governance (as well as accountability processes regarding this governance) from politics for the sake of creating better policies. Its proponents assert that politicians govern pro tempore and that there is a danger of sacrificing long-term benefits for short-term 'scoring'. As a result, in order to ensure credible commitment, the preference in terms of accountability would be for apolitical arrangements so as to avoid undue political influence (e.g. management boards composed of technical experts rather than national representatives overseeing European agencies, peer review committees of experts overseeing comitology committees, or more widespread use of benchmarking and visitation). It should be noted that some key scholars in the regulatory tradition, such as Terry Moe (1987), stress not so much removal from politics but rather the need for a system of checks and balances between principals (in our case accountability forums) to be in place, so that none of the political actors can exercise undue influence on the agent's direction. As Majone (1996), quoting Moe, puts it: 'no one controls the agency, yet the agency is under control'.

In short, when confronted with information about the formal and de facto accountability arrangements around a particular EU institution, proponents of these perspectives will most likely arrive at different assessments of their relevance and appropriateness. This is precisely how we intend to use these perspectives when we revisit them at the end of this study and are able to compare, contrast, and assess our empirical findings regarding accountability of four key EU institutions.

Table 2.2 gives an overview in schematic form of core understandings of the three different perspectives on the nature of the EU with regard to the specific actors of interest to us in the rest of this book: the European Council, the Commission, and the 'lower-level' more technocratic actors: comitology committees and non-majoritarian (executive/regulatory) agencies.

Table 2.2 Contending perspectives on accountable EU governance: who is accountable to whom?

EU actor	European Council	Commission	Comitology	Agencies
EU governance perspectives				
Intergovernmental	To national parliaments and electorates	To member state governments	To national representatives To national hierarchical superiors	To member state governments
Supranational	To European Parliament (collectively) To European Court of Justice (ECJ)	To European Parliament To ECJ	To Commission/ Council To European Parliament To ECJ	To Commission/ Council To EP To ECJ
Regulatory	N.A. (the perspective is focused on role of administrative actors only)	To Court of Audit To sectoral and international expert review/ benchmark bodies	To peer review style audit committees	To management boards composed of technical experts To professional accreditation and benchmark bodies

From Perspectives to Practices: An Empirical Study

This book is not a theoretical study, a normative thesis, or an intervention in a political debate. There are enough of these in the field of EU studies already. This will in fact be the first empirical, comparative, social-scientific study of accountability structures and practices in EU governance. Unlike the many scholars debating the three perspectives, we do not claim to determine what *should* be. We first and foremost describe what *is*. But we will draw upon the perspectives to provide us with bundles of criteria to also assess what is, and to answer the central question we have posed: does the EU suffer from an accountability deficit or not (more precisely: where and where not?). Unlike any other study published on this topic so far, we propose a parsimonious, rigorous analytical framework to accomplish the two tasks we have thus set ourselves.

The three perspectives described above provide the normative foundations for an identification of potential accountability deficits in EU governance. But the conceptual framework for the analysis of accountability to be presented in Chapter 3 provides the tools for systematic description without which any evaluative claim becomes vacuous. At the end of Chapter 3, we shall also describe the methodological choices we have made in carving out particular pieces of the vast terrain of EU governance for systematic scrutiny.

Notes

1. See <http://www.bundesverfassungsgericht.de/entscheidungen/es20090630_2bve000208en.html>
2. Yet as Majone (2005, 2009) himself has started to point out more recently, examples of regulatory failures abound, and the thrust of the regulatory regime is mutating from positive to negative integration (Majone, 2009).

3

Studying the Real World of EU Accountability: Framework and Design

Mark Bovens, Deirdre Curtin, and Paul 't Hart

Accountability and EU Governance: Towards an Assessment Framework

How can we make a more systematic assessment of the various account-abilities regarding the exercise of European governance and establish whether and where accountability deficits do exist? Accountability is used as a synonym for many loosely defined political desiderata, such as good governance, transparency, equity, democracy, efficiency, responsive-ness, responsibility, and integrity (Mulgan, 2000: 555; Behn, 2001: 3–6; Dubnick, 2007). While this has its uses in political rhetoric, White Papers, and media commentary, it has been a strong impediment to systematic, comparative, scholarly analysis. The dearth of such analysis is notable: there are many scholars who *talk* about accountability, but few who study it rigorously.

The aim of this chapter is twofold. First, we develop a parsimonious analytical framework to establish more systematically whether European organizations or officials, exercising public authority, are subject to account-ability at all. This is basically an *empirical* mapping exercise – for example, what are the accountabilities, formal and informal, of a particular European agency, such as Europol, or of a European Union (EU) actor, such as the President of the Commission? To be able to do so, we first need to establish when a certain practice or arrangement qualifies as a form of accountability at all. How do we recognize accountability when we see it? In order to provide texture to our map, we also want to be able to distinguish several, mutually exclusive, types of accountability.

In addition, this chapter aims to develop an *evaluative* framework that can be used to *assess* these accountability maps more systematically. For this purpose, we need perspectives that can help us to evaluate these accountability arrangements: are the arrangements to hold the agency accountable adequate or not, sufficient or insufficient, effective or ineffective?

This chapter is therefore organized around three key questions which provide the building blocks for the analysis of accountability and European governance. The first is conceptual: what exactly do we mean when we talk about accountability? The second is analytical: what types of accountability are involved? The third then tackles the evaluative question: how should we assess these accountability relations, arrangements, and regimes?

Demarcating Accountability: Conceptual Choices

Anyone studying accountability will soon discover that it can mean many different things to many different people (Mulgan, 2000: 555; Behn, 2001: 3–6; Pollitt, 2003: 89; Dubnick, 2005). It is increasingly used in political discourse and policy documents because it conveys an image of transparency and trustworthiness. 'Accountability' often serves as a conceptual umbrella that covers various other, often highly contested, concepts. For example, in its *White Paper on Governance* and in several consecutive documents, the European Commission (2001, 2003*a*) uses 'accountability' rather loosely. It serves not only as a synonym for 'clarity', 'transparency', and 'responsibility', but it is also equated with much broader concepts such as 'involvement, 'deliberation', and 'participation'.

One of the reasons for this conceptual ambiguity and multiplicity is the fact that 'accountability' is an Anglo-Norman concept (Dubnick, 2007), which has no semantic equivalents on the European continent. Other languages, such as Dutch, French, German, Portuguese, or Spanish, have no exact equivalent and do not (yet) distinguish semantically between 'responsibility' and 'accountability' (Mulgan, 2000; Harlow, 2002: 14–15; Dubnick, 2007).[1] Part of the ambiguity and contestation is caused by the very fact that for most European politicians, lawyers, and constitutional scholars, for whom English is a secondary language, accountability is a germane concept to begin with. Continental European constitutions may have provisions for responsibility, such as in the doctrine of ministerial responsibility, or for *Rechenschaft und Verantwortung*, but they have no explicit norms regarding 'accountability'.

Secondly, within contemporary Anglo-American political and scholarly discourse, 'accountability' seems to be an ever-expanding concept (Mulgan, 2000). The term, to quote Mulgan (2003: 8), 'has come to stand as a general term for any mechanism that makes powerful institutions responsive to their particular publics'. Much of the academic literature on accountability is rather disconnected, as many authors set out to produce their own specific definition of accountability. Every newly edited volume on accountability – and even worse, each of the individual chapters within these edited volumes – uses its own concepts, conceptualizations, and frames for studying accountability (Dowdle, 2006; Ebrahim and Weisband, 2007; Boström and Garsten, 2008; Gustavsson, Karlsson, and Persson, 2009). Some use the concept very loosely, others produce a more narrow definition, but few of these definitions are fully compatible, which makes it very hard to produce cumulative knowledge. Also, few papers move beyond conceptual and theoretical analyses and engage in systematic, comparative empirical research, with the exception of areas such as social psychology where laboratory experiments have yielded insight into some of the fundamental processes and preconditions of accountability (Adelberg and Batson, 1978; Tetlock, 1983, 1985; Tetlock, Skitka, and Boettger, 1989; Kroon, 1992; Frink and Ferris, 1998; Lerner and Tetlock, 1999; Green, Visser, and Tetlock, 2000; Markman and Tetlock, 2000; Seidenfeld, 2001; Roch and McNall, 2007).

However, there is a pattern in the expansion. Particularly, but certainly not exclusively, in American academic and political discourse, accountability is often used as a normative concept, as a set of standards for the evaluation of the behaviour of public actors. Accountability, or, more precisely, 'being accountable', is seen as a *virtue*, as a positive quality of organizations or officials. Hence, accountability studies often focus on normative issues, on the assessment of the actual and active behaviour of public agents (Dubnick, 2002; Koppell, 2005). Accountability in this very broad sense is used to positively qualify a state of affairs or the performance of an actor. It comes close to 'responsiveness' and 'a sense of responsibility', a willingness to act in a transparent, fair, and equitable way. Accountability in this broad sense of virtue is an essentially contested and contestable concept (Gallie, 1962: 121) because there is no general consensus about the standards for accountable behaviour. Furthermore, standards differ from role to role, time to time, place to place, and from speaker to speaker.[2]

On the other side of the Atlantic, in British and continental European (and also Australian) scholarly debates, accountability often is used in a narrower, more descriptive sense. Accountability is seen as a social *mechanism*, an institutional relation or arrangement in which an actor can be held to account by a forum (Day and Klein, 1987; Scott, 2000; Mulgan, 2003; Pollitt, 2003; Bovens, 't Hart, and Schillemans, 2008; Schillemans, 2008; Meijer and Schillemans, 2009). Here, the locus of accountability studies is not the behaviour of public agents, but the way in which these institutional arrangements operate. And the focus of accountability studies is not whether the agents have acted in an accountable way, but whether they are or can be held accountable ex post facto by accountability forums.

Both concepts, the broader one, in which accountability is seen as a personal or organizational virtue, and the narrow one, in which account-ability is defined as a social mechanism, are very useful for the study of, and the debate about, European governance. However, they should be distinguished as they address different sorts of issues and lead to different research agendas and different types of studies.

Accountability studies that, often implicitly, use accountability in the active sense of virtue, focus on the actual performance of officials and agents. They, implicitly or explicitly, formulate a set of substantive standards for good governance and assess whether officials or organizations comply with these standards (Considine, 2002; Koppell, 2005; O'Connell, 2005). The main items on the research agenda are the evaluation of the *conduct of actors* and an analysis of the factors that induce accountable behaviour. Accountability studies that see accountability as a virtue are basically studies about good – public or corporate – governance and about how to achieve this. In this line of research, accountability is the *dependent* variable, the outcome of a series of interactions between various factors, actors, and variables. In these studies, accountability deficits manifest themselves as inappropriate behaviour, or 'bad' governance – unresponsive, opaque, irresponsible, ineffective, or even deviant.

Studies that conceive of accountability as a mechanism, on the other hand, focus on the relationship between agents and forums. Some of these studies are basically descriptive; they chart the intricate webs of accountability arrangements surrounding modern public actors (Scott, 2000). Others assess how these arrangements operate and the effects they produce (Day and Klein, 1987; Schillemans, 2007). The main items on their research agenda are the evaluation of *mechanisms* and the positive or negative effects these mechanisms may have. These are basically studies about political or social control. In these studies accountability is the *independent* variable, a factor which may or may not have an effect on the behaviour of actors.

Observing Accountability: Mechanisms, Arrangements, and Regimes

This book employs the narrow concept of accountability as a mechanism. We leave the broader, deontological discussions about accountability and EU governance to others (Schmitter, 2000; Arnull and Wincott, 2002; Harlow, 2002; Lord, 2004; Bogdanor, 2007). We stay close to its etymological and historical roots – accountability comes from accounting – and we define accountability as a specific social relation.[3]

Our definition of accountability has at its core the obligation to explain and justify conduct, implying a relationship between an actor, the accountor, and a forum, the account-holder, or accountee (Pollitt, 2003: 85). We thus define accountability as *a relationship between an actor and a forum, in which the actor has an obligation to explain and to justify his or her conduct, the forum can pose questions and pass judgement, and the actor may face consequences*. This narrow definition of accountability contains a number of elements that need further explanation. The *actor* can be either an individual, in our case an official, or a civil servant, or an organization, such as a public institution or an agency. The significant other, the *accountability forum*, can be a specific person, such as a superior, a minister, or a journalist, or it can be an agency, such as parliament, a court, or the audit office.

The relationship between the forum and the actor can have the character of a principal–agent relation: the forum being the principal (e.g. parliament) which has delegated authority to the agent (e.g. a minister), who is held to account for his performance in office. This is often the case with political forms of accountability (Strøm, 2000: 261–89; 2003: 55–106). However, in many accountability relations, the forums are not principals of the actors, for example courts in the case of legal accountability or professional associations in the case of professional accountability.

The *obligation* that lies upon the actor can be formal or informal. Public officials will often be under a formal obligation to render account on a regular basis to specific forums, such as supervisory agencies, courts, or auditors. Public officials can be forced to appear in administrative or penal courts or to testify before parliamentary committees when those forums have reason to believe these officials are involved in (or hold end responsibility for) wrongdoings, mismanagement, policy failures, and other negative events. An example is former European commissioner Edith Cresson, who was brought before a Belgian penal court and the European Court of Justice after allegations of nepotism and corruption were made against her. But the obligation can also be informal, as in the case of press conferences and informal briefings, or even self-imposed, as in the case of voluntary audits.

The relationship between the actor and the forum, the actual account giving, usually consists of at least three elements or stages. First of all, it is crucial that the actor is obliged to *inform the forum about his or her conduct*, by providing various sorts of data about the performance of tasks, about outcomes, or about procedures. Often, and particularly in the case of failures or incidents, this also involves the provision of explanations and justifications (Bovens et al., 1999; Hearit, 2005; Hood et al., 2007). Account-giving is more than mere propaganda or the provision of information or instructions to the general public. The conduct that is to be explained and justified can vary enormously, from budgetary scrutiny in the case of financial accountability to administrative fairness in the case of legal accountability, or even sexual propriety when it comes to the political accountability of Anglo-American public officials.

The second stage is *debate*. There needs to be a possibility for the forum to interrogate the actor and to question the adequacy of the information or the legitimacy of the conduct – hence, the close semantic connection between 'accountability' and 'answerability'.

Thirdly, the forum may *pass judgement* on the conduct of the actor. It may approve an annual account, denounce a policy, or publicly condemn the behaviour of an official or an agency. In passing a negative judgement, or following it, the forum may impose sanctions of some kind on the actor.

It has been a point of discussion whether the possibility of sanctions is a constitutive element of accountability (Mulgan, 2003: 9–11). Some would argue that a judgement by the forum, or even only the stages of reporting, justifying, and debating, would be enough to qualify a relation as an ac-countability relation. We concur with Mulgan (2003: 9) and Strøm (2003: 62) that the possibility of sanctions of some kind is a constitutive element of narrow accountability and that it should be included in the definition. The *possibility* of sanctions – not the actual imposition of sanctions – makes the difference between non-committal provision of information and being held to account.

However, 'sanction' has a rather formal and legal connotation. It would exclude accountability forums, such as ombudsmen, who in many coun-tries do not have the authority to formally sanction but can nevertheless be very effective in securing redress or reparation via 'public shaming' (cf. Braithwaite, 1989; Braithwaite and Drahos, 2002). Also, the term sanction would bias towards negative forms of scrutiny. Many accountability arrangements are not focused on finding fault with actors – forums will often judge positively about the conduct of actors and will even reward them. We therefore use a somewhat more neutral expression: *the actor may face consequences.*

These consequences can be highly formalized, such as fines, disciplinary measures, civil remedies, or even penal sanctions, but they can also be based on unwritten rules, as in the case of the political accountability of a minister to parliament, where the consequence can consist in calling for the minister's resignation. Sometimes the negative consequences will only be implicit or informal, such as the very fact of having to render account in front of television cameras. Or, as was the case with Edith Cresson and to a large extent also the President of the Commission in which she served, Jacques Santer, the disintegration of public image and career as a result of the negative publicity generated by the process (March and Olsen, 1995: 167). The consequences can also consist in the use of veto powers by the forum, which can block or amend decisions made by the actor (Strøm, 2003: 62).

It should be noted that the consequences faced by the actor are not necessarily brought upon it by the forum itself. Ombudsmen and many chambers of audit, for example, can scrutinize agencies, expose waste or mismanagement, and suggest improvements, but leave it to parliaments to put pressure (backed up by its power to inflict political costs) on the minister or the commissioner, who in turn can put pressure on the heads of the agencies involved.

What Accountability Is and Is Not

In sum, we identify seven constitutive elements of accountability as a mechanism (Box 3.1).

To qualify a social relation as a practice of accountability for the purpose of this book, there should be an actor who provides information about his

---

Box 3.1 THE BUILDING BLOCKS OF ACCOUNTABILITY

1. There is a relationship between an actor and a forum
2. in which the actor is obliged
3. to explain and justify
4. his conduct
5. the forum can pose questions
6. pass judgement; and
7. the actor may face consequences.

---

conduct to some forum; there should also be explanation and justification of conduct – and not propaganda, or the provision of information or instructions to the general public. The explanation should be directed at a specific forum – and not be given at random. The actor must feel obliged to come forward – instead of being at liberty to provide any account whatsoever. There must be a possibility for debate and judgement by the forum, and an optional imposition of (informal) sanctions or rewards – and not a monologue without engagement.

It follows that transparency, which is often used as a synonym for accountability, is not enough to constitute accountability as defined here. Open government and freedom of information are very important prerequisites for accountability in the context of European governance, because they may provide accountability forums with the necessary information. However, transparency as such is not enough to qualify as a genuine form of accountability (Fisher, 2004: 504), because transparency does not necessarily involve scrutiny by a specific forum.

Accountability should also be distinguished from responsiveness and participation (Mulgan, 2003: 21). The European Commission, in its *White Paper on European Governance* and some of the documents following it, sometimes tends to blur accountability with issues of representative deliberation (Harlow, 2002: 185). It calls for more openness and a better involvement and more participation of a broad range of stakeholders in the EU policy process in order to enhance the EU's accountability (European Commission, 2003*a*: 35–8). However, accountability as defined here is fundamentally retrospective. Actors are to account to a forum after the fact. Responsiveness to the needs and preferences of a broad range of stakeholders and new forms of consultation and participation while decision-making is ongoing may be very important to enhance the political legitimacy of the EU, but they do not constitute accountability. They provide proactive inputs into the policy process and should be classified and studied separately for what they are: forms of consultation, participation, and deliberation (Eriksen and Fossum, 2000; Bohman, 2007). They lack the element of justification, judgement, and consequences.

Admittedly, the line between retrospective accounting and proactive policy-making can be thin in practice. It is perfectly sensible to hold actors accountable for their participation in decision-making procedures: members of parliament may scrutinize ministers for their role in the Council of Ministers; lobby and interest groups may have to account to their members or constituencies for their stand in deliberative processes. Moreover, accountability is not only about ex post scrutiny, it is also about prevention and anticipation. Norms are (re)produced, internalized, and, where necessary, adjusted through accountability. The minister who is held to account by parliament for his conduct in the Council of Ministers may feel obliged to adjust his policy, or parliament can decide to amend his mandate. Many actors will anticipate the negative evaluations of forums and adjust their policies accordingly. Thus, ex post facto accountability can be an important input for ex ante policy-making. Finally, actors, such as ministers before Council meetings, may be obliged to explain and justify their stance, for example to parliamentary commissions, before going to Brussels and may be forced to adjust them if their account is not convincing.[4] However, for analytical purposes, policy-making and accountability should be treated as distinct concepts.

Similarly, there is a fine line between accountability and control. Some would equate accountability with controllability (Lord, 2004: 136–59). Lupia (2003: 35), for example, adopts a control definition of accountability: 'An agent is accountable to a principal if the principal can exercise control over the agent.' Accountability mechanisms are indeed important ways of controlling the conduct of public organizations. However, 'control', used in the Anglo-Saxon sense, is broader than accountability and can include both ex ante and ex post mechanisms of directing behaviour (Scott, 2000: 39).[5] Control means 'having power over' and it can involve very proactive means of directing conduct, for example through straight orders, directives, financial incentives, or laws and regulations. But these mechanisms are not mechanisms of accountability per se, because they do not in themselves operate through procedures in which actors are to explain and justify their conduct to forums (Mulgan, 2003: 19). Accountability is a form of control, but not all forms of control are accountability mechanisms (see further Busuioc, 2009).

Webs of Accountability: Relationships, Arrangements, and Regimes

At the most basic level, accountability entails a relationship between an actor and a forum. This can be an occasional, contingent, and informal relationship, for example between a politician and an inquisitive television talk show host, or a blogging politician and her (commenting) readers. In the case of public accountability, these relations have often been institutionalized. They have been laid down in rules; standing practices and fixed routines may be in place, or the accountability process may be laid down in fixed forms, values, and instruments. We call an accountability relationship that has taken on an institutional character an accountability *arrangement.* For example, an occasional, self-initiated one-off external evaluation of an independent agency does not constitute an accountability arrangement; yet a recurring, protocolled national academic research exercise (in which the auditing body or its principal can impose budgetary consequences) certainly does.

An accountability *regime* is one step up from this. We speak of an accountability regime as the sum of a series of interconnected accountability arrangements and relationships regarding a particular actor. An example of this is the political accountability of the members of cabinet in a parliamentary democracy. For example, in the Netherlands, this parliamentary accountability comprises a system of interconnected, standardized forms of accountability (including obligations to inform, interpellations, parliamentary debates, and inquiries) that have been laid down in the Constitution, the Parliamentary Inquiry Act, the rules of procedure for the Houses, and in unwritten constitutional rules.

Mapping the webs of accountability surrounding public institutions may be a complex reconstructive exercise in its own right. One needs not only to grasp if and how particular accountability relations have been institutionalized into arrangements but also to carefully check how various types of arrangements combine into overall accountability regimes. Public institutions such as the European Commission are subject to various accountability regimes, such as a regime of political accountability to the European Parliament (EP) and the Council, legal accountability to the European Court, and administrative accountabilities to the European Anti-Fraud Office (OLAF), the European Ombudsman, and the European Court of Auditors. Each of these regimes may, in turn, consist of various formal relationships and informal practices.

Unpacking Public Accountability: Dimensions and Types of Accountability

Public accountability comes in many guises. Public institutions are frequently required to account for their conduct to various forums in a variety of ways. Figure 3.1 illustrates four key dimensions contained within accountability relationships, arrangements, and regimes.

These dimensions revolve around four essential questions to be asked about accountability. The first question is always: *to whom* is account to be rendered? This will yield a classification based on the type of *forum* to which the actor is required to render account.

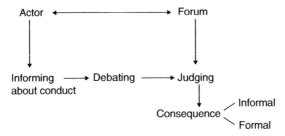

Figure 3.1 Accountability as a social relationship: key dimensions

A second, logical question is: *who* should render account? Who is the *actor* required to appear before the forum? In ordinary social relationships among citizens, it is usually clear who the actor is who will render account. This is a far more complicated question to answer when it comes to public organizations.

The third question is: *about what* is account to be rendered? This concerns the question of the nature of the conduct about which information is to be provided. Is it about the way money is being spent? Is it about the content of policy decisions? Is it about legal compliance? So, accountability relationships may cover, or indeed be constructed around, various types of 'content', for example financial, procedural, or communicative.[6]

The fourth question regards that of *why* the actor feels compelled to render account. This relates largely to the nature of the relationship between the actor and the forum, and in particular to the question of why the actor has an obligation to render account. This will subsequently lead to classifications based on the nature of the *rationale* that underpins the account-giving.

Accounting to Whom? The Problem of Many Eyes

Public organizations and officials operating in a constitutional democracy find themselves confronting at least five different types of forum and hence at least five different kinds of accountability.[7] These forums generally demand different kinds of information and apply different criteria as to what constitutes responsible conduct. They are therefore likely to pass different judgements on the conduct of the public organization or the public official. Hence public institutions are not infrequently faced with the *problem of many eyes*: they are accountable to a plethora of different forums, all of which apply a different set of criteria.

POLITICAL ACCOUNTABILITY: REPRESENTATIVES, PARTIES, VOTERS, AND THE MEDIA

Political accountability is an extremely important type of accountability within democracies. Here, accountability is exercised along the chain of principal–agent relationships (Strøm, 2000). Voters delegate their sovereignty to popular representatives, who in turn, at least in parliamentary democracies, delegate the majority of their authorities to a cabinet of ministers. The ministers subsequently delegate many of their authorities to their civil servants or to various, more or less independent, administrative bodies. The mechanism of political accountability operates precisely in the opposite direction to that of delegation. In parliamentary systems with ministerial accountability, such as the United Kingdom, the Netherlands, and Germany, public servants and their organizations are accountable to their minister, who must render political account to parliament (Flinders, 2001; Strøm, Müller, and Bergman, 2003). In some sense, the people's representatives render account to the voters at election time. Thus viewed, each of the links in the chain is, in turn, not only principal and agent, but also forum and actor. It is only the two ends of the chain – the voters and the executive public servants – who do not exchange roles. In nations characterized by political cabinets and political appointments, such as the United States, France, and Belgium, political parties and party barons often also function as important, informal political forums. In the context of EU governance, the political forum could be a national parliament and in particular its standing committee on European affairs, the EP and its subcommittees and commissions, or voters in parliamentary elections or with referendums. In many countries, the media are fast gaining power as informal forums for political accountability (Elchardus, 2002; RMO, 2003).

LEGAL ACCOUNTABILITY: COURTS

In most Western countries, legal accountability is of increasing importance to public institutions as a result of the growing formalization of social relations (Friedman, 1985; Behn, 2001: 56–8), or because of the greater trust which is placed in courts than in parliaments (Harlow, 2002: 18). These can be the 'ordinary' civil courts, as in Britain, or also specialized administrative courts, as in France, Belgium, and the Netherlands (Harlow, 2002: 16–18). In some spectacular cases of administrative deviance, such as *l'affaire du sang contaminé* (the HIV-contaminated blood products) in France or the Tangentopoli prosecutions in Italy, public officials have even been summoned before penal courts. For European public institutions and EU member states, the Court of First Instance and the European Court of Justice are additional and increasingly important legal forums (Harlow, 2002: 147–59). Legal accountability will usually be based on specific responsibilities, formally or legally conferred upon authorities. Therefore, legal accountability is the most unambiguous type of accountability, as the legal scrutiny will be based on detailed legal standards, prescribed by civil, penal, or administrative statutes, or precedent.

ADMINISTRATIVE ACCOUNTABILITY: AUDITORS, INSPECTORS, AND CONTROLLERS

Besides the courts, a wide range of quasi-legal forums exercising independent and external administrative and financial supervision and control has been established in the past decades – some even speak of an 'audit explosion' (Power, 1994). These new administrative forums vary from European, national, or local ombudsmen and audit offices, to independent supervisory authorities, inspector generals, anti-fraud offices, and chartered accountants. Also, the mandates of several national auditing offices have been broadened to secure not only the probity and legality of public spending, but also its efficiency and effectiveness (Pollitt and Summa, 1997: 313–36). These administrative forums exercise regular financial and administrative scrutiny, often on the basis of specific statutes and prescribed norms. Examples of these forums are the European Ombudsman, OLAF, and the Court of Auditors.[8] This type of accountability arrangement can be very important for regulatory and executive public agencies.

PROFESSIONAL ACCOUNTABILITY: PEERS

Many public managers are, apart from being general managers, professionals in a more technical sense. They have been trained as engineers, doctors, veterinarians, teachers, or police officers (Abbott, 1988; Freidson, 2001). This may imply accountability relationships with professional associations and disciplinary tribunals. Professional bodies lay down codes with standards of acceptable practice that are binding on all members. These standards are monitored and enforced by professional supervisory bodies on the basis of peer review. This type of accountability relation will be particularly relevant for public managers who work in professional public organizations, such as hospitals, schools, psychiatric clinics, research institutes, police departments, fire brigades, or for some of the experts in the EU comitology committees.

SOCIAL ACCOUNTABILITY: INTEREST GROUPS, CHARITIES, AND OTHER STAKEHOLDERS

In reaction to a perceived lack of trust in government, there is an urge in many Western democracies for more direct and explicit accountability relations between public agencies on the one hand and clients, citizens, and civil society on the other hand (McCandless, 2001; Malena, Forster, and Singh, 2004). Influenced by the debate on corporate social responsibility and corporate governance in business, more attention is being paid to the role of non-governmental organizations (NGOs), interest groups, and customers or clients as relevant 'stakeholders' not only in determining policy, but also in rendering account (European Commission, 2001). Agencies or individual public managers should feel obliged to account for their performance to the public at large or, at least, to civil interest groups, charities, and associations of clients. A first step in this direction has been the institution of public reporting and the establishment of public panels. The rise of the Internet has given a new dimension to this form of accountability. Increasingly, the results of inspections, assessments, and benchmarks are put on the Internet (Pollitt, 2003: 41–5; Meijer and Schillemans, 2009).

To what extent these groups and panels already qualify as fully fledged accountability mechanisms remains an empirical question. In many of them, the forum lacks the possibility of judgement and sanctioning. In fact, not all of these arrangements involve clearly demarcated, coherent, and authoritative forums that the actor reports to and could debate with.

Who is to Account? The Problem of Many Hands

Accountability forums, like actors, often face problems of who to engage with, but their problems are of the reverse kind: they can have a hard time nailing down which actors to hold to account. For outsiders, it is often particularly difficult to unravel who has contributed in what way to the conduct of an agency or to the implementation of a policy and who, and to what degree, can be brought to account for it. This is the *problem of many hands* (Thompson, 1980; Bovens, 1998). Policy proposals and implementation plans pass through many hands before they are actually put into effect. Ideas bounce between policy-makers, officials, and staffers before they harden up. Decrees and decisions are often made in committees and other collective, collegial settings. Individual members of committees, of administrative bodies, and of departments, conform to the traditions, rules, and existing practices (or their understandings of them) of these groups and organizations.

Sometimes they contribute ideas and rules of their own. However, they often leave before those ideas and rules can be put into practice.

Who, then, should be singled out for accountability, credits and rewards, or blame and punishment? In legal procedures, it is often the institution as a corporate entity or the organization as a whole, which is held accountable. This can be called *corporate* or *organizational* accountability. An example is the accountability of member states towards the Court of Justice in cases of violations of the treaty (Article 258 TFEU).

In most instances of political accountability, it is only the top of the organization that is called to account externally. The rank and file do not appear before external forums but hide behind the broad shoulders of the minister, the commissioner, or the director of the agency, who, at least in dealings with the outside world, assumes complete responsibility and takes all the blame. In recent decades, CEOs and the senior echelons of public agencies have been subject to performance contracts, in which the terms of their expected achievements over a period of time are specified, and which provide a prime vehicle by which principals (e.g. ministers, boards, or superiors within the organization) can ascertain the behaviour of adminis-trative actors, discuss it with them, and attach direct personal conse-quences to the outcomes of these discussions. These consequences can be positive: bonuses, promotion, or autonomy; or negative: withholding of bonuses, lack of promotion, more intense scrutiny, or even demotion or resignation. In turn, lower echelons can be addressed by their superiors regarding questions of internal accountability. This is *hierarchical* account-ability. In the case of hierarchical schemes, processes of calling to account thus take place along the lines of the 'chain of command'. Senior and middle managers are, in turn, both actor and forum in such 'chains' of accountability. Hierarchical accountability is often the core mode of ac-countability within most public organizations, and with regard to most types of accountability relationships, with the exception of professional accountability. It is also dominant in political accountability relations, for example in the Westminster system of ministerial responsibility.

Within the EU system, accountability within the Commission and its agencies by and large operates along these hierarchical lines. But at the very top of the hierarchy, at the interface of administrative and political accountability, it is still being debated whether individual European com-missioners are accountable for civil servants working in the Commission. So far, there is at least a *collective* accountability of the Commission as a whole to the EP (Van Gerven, 2005: 83). In a similar vein, individual heads of state share a collective accountability for the decisions of the European Council, but cannot be held individually responsible at the European level – their own national parliaments may, however, wish to hold them so as part of their overall political responsibility for all of their governments' stances and actions, although to date this happens infrequently (see further Van de Steeg, this volume).

During the judgement phase, which can involve the imposition of sanctions, hierarchical and collective accountability strategies often run up against moral objections, as a proportional relation between contribution and blame is by no means always evident. *Individual* accountability, in which each individual official or minister can be called to account on the basis of his actual contribution, instead of on the basis of his formal position, is then a far more adequate strategy (Kroon, 1992). This approach is characteristic of professional accountability. In the case of medical errors, individual physicians are called to account by the disciplinary tribunal, which attempts to establish precisely the extent to which the physician's individual performance satisfied professional standards. Although individual accountability has proven to be a far more effective tool for principals in modifying the behaviour of agents, it has important downsides too. Behn (2001: 69) notes that it may induce 'scapegoat hunting'. The symbolic urge to identify individual, tangible scapegoats may be stronger than the forensic rationality suggesting that the undesirable outcomes were in fact a product of many hands. As Behn (2001: 69) puts it colourfully, in the face of outrage, desire for catharsis and retribution may take over among the forum: 'Something has gone wrong. Somebody should be held accountable. Someone – damnit – should be punished.'

What to Account for? Aspects of 'Conduct'

In accountability relationships, the actor is obliged to explain and provide justification for his conduct. There are many aspects to this conduct, making it possible to distinguish a number of accountability relationships on the basis of the aspect that is most dominant (Day and Klein, 1987: 26; Sinclair, 1996; Behn, 2001: 6–10). This will often concur with the classification made according to type of forum. In the case of legal accountability, the legality of the actor's conduct will obviously be the dominant aspect, while professional accountability will be centred on the professionalism of the conduct. Political and administrative accountability frequently involve several aspects. An audit by the Chamber of Audit, for example, may be classified as financial accountability if the focus is on the financial propriety of the audit, as legal accountability if the legality of the conduct is at issue, or as administrative if the central concern is the efficiency of the policy of the organization. Another distinction found in the literature is that between accountability for the procedure or process and accountability for the product or content (Day and Klein, 1987: 27).

Why Account? Rationales for Accountability

Why would an actor render account to a forum? Very generally speaking, there are two possibilities: in the first place, because she is being forced to, or could be forced to, and second, because she voluntarily does so. In the former instance, the rationale for accountability resides in obligation, in the latter in choice. *Vertical* accountability obligations exist when the forum formally wields power over the actor, perhaps due to the hierarchical relationship between actor and forum. A case in point is the public agency being accountable to the minister or (over the head of the minister) to parliament. The majority of political accountability arrangements, which are based on the delegation from principal to agent (Lupia, 2003: 34–5), contain this vertical accountability logic. In most cases of legal accountability too, the forum has the formal authority to compel the actor to give account, although this is not based on a principal–agent relationship, but on laws and regulations. The same goes for disciplinary committees in the case of professional accountability.

At the opposite end of the spectrum is social accountability. Here, a hierarchical relationship is generally lacking between actor and forum, as are any formal obligations to render account. Giving account to various stakeholders in society occurs basically on a voluntary basis with no intervention on the part of a principal. Such accountability could be termed *horizontal* accountability (Schillemans, 2008).[9]

In these cases, the rationale for agencies to account for themselves to the general public may be rooted in moral convictions about their duty to 'taxpayers', 'citizens', 'clients', and the like. This is certainly how many of these arrangements are being presented (rationalized) by agency leaders. But there is often also a strategic component at play. We live in an age of 'responsive government' and 'citizen empowerment', and thus agencies 'look good', 'lead the way', and 'fit the fashion' if they are seen to initiate and institutionalize non-compulsory forms of horizontal accountability. A cynic might say that the boundaries between genuine horizontal accountability and clever impression management are sometimes so thin as to be non-existent, but the emerging empirical evidence is genuinely mixed about the balance between moral and strategic rationales at play (Schillemans, 2008).

Administrative accountability relations are usually an intermediary form. Most ombudsmen, audit offices, inspectorates, supervisory authorities, and accountants stand in no direct hierarchical relationship to public organizations and have few powers to enforce their compliance. However, the majority of these administrative forums ultimately report to the minister or to parliament and thus derive the requisite informal power from this. This indirect, two-step relation with a forum could be described as a *diagonal* accountability, or accountability in the shadow of hierarchy (Schillemans and Bovens, 2004; Schillemans, 2008).

Mapping Accountability Regimes

In mapping the accountability regimes of various EU actors, as we shall do in Chapters 4–7, the first question is whether a social relation or practice is an accountability relationship at all. This is a dichotomous exercise that follows the logic of either–or (Sartori, 1970: 1039). The main question is: do the phenomena singled out for study qualify as full accountability or are they something else, such as participation, responsiveness, or transparency? Next comes the question: what types of accountabilities are present? Boxes 3.2–3.5 summarize the various dimensions of accountability that can be distinguished on the basis of the narrow definition of accountability that is used in this book. These are distinctive, unrelated classification dimensions.

Box 3.2 TO WHOM? TYPES OF ACCOUNTABILITY ACCORDING TO THE NATURE OF THE FORUM

- Political accountability
- Legal accountability
- Administrative accountability
- Professional accountability
- Social accountability

Box 3.3 WHO? TYPES OF ACCOUNTABILITY ACCORDING TO THE NATURE OF THE ACTOR

- Corporate accountability
- Hierarchical accountability
- Collective accountability
- Individual accountability

Box 3.4 WHAT FOR? TYPES OF ACCOUNTABILITY ACCORDING
TO THE NATURE OF THE CONDUCT

- Financial accountability
- Procedural accountability
- Product accountability

Box 3.5 WHY? TYPES OF ACCOUNTABILITY ACCORDING
TO THE NATURE OF THE OBLIGATION

- Vertical accountability
- Diagonal accountability
- Horizontal accountability

Each accountability relation can be classified on each of the four dimensions separately. For example, one could classify the accountability of the President of the European Commission to the EP as political accountability because the EP is a political forum; as hierarchical accountability because the President gives an account on behalf of the Commission as a whole and has been given more extensive powers in the Nice Treaty to guide and control the other commissioners (Van Gerven, 2005: 83–8); as financial or procedural accountability when the propriety of financial management by the Commission is at stake; and as vertical accountability because the EP acts as a political principal and has the power to make its agent (the Commission) resign if the motion is carried by two-thirds of the votes cast, representing the majority of the members of the EP.[10]

Assessing Accountability: From Mapping to Evaluation

Assessing the adequacy of a particular accountability relationship, arrangement, or regime, to which a particular agency or sector is subject, requires more than just empirical mapping. It presupposes applying some normative yardstick to evaluate the observed accountability rules and practices. The key question is obviously what the actual effects are of the various types of accountability and how to judge these effects. At this level, inadequacies can take the form either of accountability deficits: a lack of accountability arrangements; or of accountability excesses: a dysfunctional accumulation of a range of accountability mechanisms. Scholars often claim the former inadequacy afflicts many dimensions of European governance (Arnull and Wincott, 2002; Harlow, 2002; Fisher, 2004), while the latter is increasingly reported by executive agencies and public managers on the national level (Anechiarico and Jacobs, 1996; Power, 1997; Behn, 2001; Halachmi, 2002). The question remains however: how do we establish whether these different sorts of inadequacies do exist?

For an institutionalized ideal that is so broadly supported and applied, there are very few references to be found in the literature that could lead to such an evaluation being performed, let alone any reports on systematic comparative research conducted in this area.[11] So why is accountability important? What is the purpose of its various forms distinguished in this chapter? Three answers to this question recur, albeit implicitly, time and again in academic and practical discourse on the subject. First, accountability is important to provide a democratic means for citizens and their representatives to monitor and control government conduct. Second, it is important for preventing the development of dangerous concentrations of executive power. Third, it is a pivotal tool for making government deliver better public value. Each of these three answers yields a separate theoretical perspective on the rationale behind accountability, and consequently a separate perspective for the assessment of accountability relations.

The Democratic Perspective: Popular Control

Public accountability is extremely important from a democratic perspective, as it helps citizens to control those holding public office (March and Olsen, 1995: 141–81; Mulgan, 2003). This is an approach that reaches back to the tenets of Rousseau and Weber, and has been theoretically defined using the principal–agent model. We saw that the modern representative democracy could be described as a concatenation of principal–agent relationships (Strøm, 2000, 2003; Lupia, 2003). For example, in parliamentary democracies, the people, who are the primary principals, have transferred their sovereignty to popular representatives, who, in turn, have often transferred the actual drafting of laws and policy, and certainly their implementation, to the government. The ministers subsequently entrust the execution of their tasks to the many thousands of public servants at the ministries, or even to more or less independent bodies and institutions. In due course, the public organizations and the executive public servants at the end of the chain have the task of spending billions in taxpayers' money, using their discretionary powers to furnish licences and subsidies, impose fines, and for jailing people.

Each principal in the chain of delegation seeks to monitor the execution of the delegated public tasks by calling the agent to account. At the end of the accountability chain are the citizens, who pass judgement on the conduct of the government and who indicate their displeasure by voting for other popular representatives. Hence public accountability is an essential condition for the democratic process, as it provides the people's representation and the voters with the information needed for judging the propriety and effectiveness of the conduct of the government (Przeworski, Stokes, and Manin, 1999).

Looking back at the three perspectives on European governance presented in Chapter 2, it will be clear that the democratic perspective on accountability is most closely associated with the supranationalist account of the EU. Supranationalists are concerned that in the emerging European polity, the transfer of all sorts of far-reaching decision-making powers from the national capitals to Brussels has not been matched by an equally powerful transfer of accountability powers and provisions to, for example, Strasbourg and Luxembourg. This is vital, because supranationalists wish to be assured that the European electorate, through its elected representatives (at both the national as well as EU level), possesses sufficient means to induce EU actors to observe its preferences.

The Constitutional Perspective: Prevention of Corruption and Abuse of Power

The main concern underlying this perspective is that of preventing the tyranny of absolute rulers, overly presumptuous, elected leaders, or of an expansive and 'privatized' executive power. This perspective reaches back to the liberal tradition of Locke, Montesquieu, and the American Federalists, to name but a few (O'Donnell, 1999). The remedy against an overbearing, improper, or corrupt government is the organization of 'checks and balances' – of institutional countervailing powers. Other public institutions, such as an independent judicial power or a Chamber of Audit, are put in place next to the voter, parliament, and political officials, and given the power to request that account be rendered for particular aspects. Good governance arises from a dynamic equilibrium between the various powers of the state (Witteveen, 1991; Fisher, 2004).

In terms of the perspectives on European governance described in Chapter 2, the constitutional perspective will be the dominant normative lens with which intergovernmentalists will judge EU accountability rules and practices. They will want to know whether the Union does not exceed the limitations and constraints that have been set for it by the member states that have created it, and that ought to be able to keep its behaviour in check. But it is also an important perspective for those supranationalists who advocate the intensification of various checks and balances on over-weening EU-level executive power.

The Learning Perspective: Maximizing Public Value

In the third, learning perspective the chief purpose of accountability is entirely different again. Accountability is seen as a tool to make and keep governments, agencies, and individual officials smarter in delivering on their promises. The purpose of public accountability is to induce the executive branch to learn to deliver better public value (Moore, 1995; Aucoin and Heintzman, 2000). The possibility of sanctions from clients and other stakeholders in their environment in the event of errors and shortcomings motivates them to search for more intelligent ways of organizing their business. Moreover, the public nature of the accountability process teaches others in similar positions what is expected of them, what works and what does not. Public performance reviews, for example, can induce many more administrators than those under scrutiny to rethink and adjust their policies. Accountability mechanisms induce openness and reflexivity in political and administrative systems that might otherwise be primarily inward-looking. There is a long-standing tradition in political science and related fields with which this idea neatly fits (Deutsch, 1963; Easton, 1965; Luhman, 1966). In this context, Lindblom (1965) referred to the 'intelligence of democracy': the superiority of pluralist democracy to that of other political systems lies in the greater number of incentives it contains to encourage intelligence and learning in the process of policy-making. Accountability is a crucial link in this approach, as it offers a regular mechanism to confront administrators with information about their own functioning and forces them to reflect on the successes and failures of their past policy.

The learning perspective for assessing accountability regimes fits quite well within the vision of the EU as a regulatory regime presented in Chapter 2. The EU as a regulatory endeavour, and in particular its reliance on a variety of 'non-majoritarian' institutions and arrangements, is to be legitimized by stakeholders and public satisfaction with its outcomes. Accountability mechanisms that provide incentives to achieve better 'bottom-line' outcomes are therefore to be welcomed; those that constrain the autonomy or effectiveness of EU institutions will be seen as problematic.

Systemic Impacts of Accountability

Behind these three perspectives lurks a far bigger, more indirect logic of assessing accountability practices. Accountability is not just a matter of coming to terms with a particular policy or actor at hand. It also has a wider systemic impact. As we saw in Chapter 1, accountability is one of the three elements that constitute the legitimacy of EU governance. When accountability is seen to work properly, it can help to ensure that the legitimacy of governance remains intact or is increased (see Box 3.6). When it is seen to fail, it detracts from the overall legitimacy of the system.

This is not a purely academic issue. Twenty-first century media, interest groups, and citizens have all been adopting an increasingly critical attitude towards the government and the political system. Respect for authority is fast dwindling and the confidence in public institutions is under pressure in a number of Western countries (Dalton, 2004). Processes of accountability in which administrators are given the opportunity to explain and justify their intentions, and in which citizens and interest groups can pose questions and offer their opinion, can promote acceptance of government authority and the citizens' confidence in the government's administration (Aucoin and Heintzman, 2000: 49–52). But if they are judged to descend into hollow rituals or politicized blame games, they may well end up being counterproductive.

In the incidental case of tragedies, fiascos, and failures, processes of public account-giving may also have an important ritual, purifying function – they can help to provide public *catharsis*. Public account-giving can help to bring a tragic period to an end because it can offer a platform for the victims to voice their grievances, and for the real or reputed perpetrators to account for themselves and to justify or excuse their conduct. This can be an important secondary effect of parliamentary inquiries, official investigations, or public

---

Box 3.6 EVALUATING ACCOUNTABILITY: MULTIPLE PERSPECTIVES

Direct-Substantive

Democratic control
Countervailing powers
Improvement/learning

Indirect-Systemic

Legitimacy
Catharsis

---

hearings in the case of natural disasters, plane crashes, or railway accidents (Tilly, 2007). The South African 'truth commissions', and various war crime tribunals, starting with the Tokyo and Nuremberg trials, the Eichmann trial, up to the Tribunal for the former Yugoslavia, are at least partly meant to fulfil this function (Dubnick, 2007). Public processes of calling to account create the opportunity for penitence, reparation, and forgiveness and can thus provide social or political closure (Harlow, 2002: 9).

Evaluation Criteria

The three perspectives outlined above offer more or less coherent criteria sets to evaluate the effects of specific accountability arrangements. (The two other, indirect rationales for accountability will not be further discussed, as these concern meta-effects that are difficult to evaluate or that play a role in special cases only.)

The question central to the *democratic perspective* is whether the accountability arrangement adds to the possibilities open to voter, parliament, or other representative bodies to control the executive power (see Box 3.7). The major issue in assessing accountability arrangements from this perspective is whether they help to overcome agency problems, such as moral hazard (Strøm, 2003): do these accountability arrangements help to provide political principals with sufficient information about the behaviour of their agents and do they offer enough incentives for agents to commit themselves to the agendas of their democratically elected principals?

From a *constitutional perspective*, the key question is whether the arrangement offers enough incentives for officials and agencies to refrain from abuse of authority (Box 3.8). This requires that public accountability forums be visible, tangible, and powerful, in order to be able to withstand

---

Box 3.7 DEMOCRATIC PERSPECTIVE: ACCOUNTABILITY AND POPULAR CONTROL

Central Idea

Accountability controls and legitimizes government actions by linking them effectively to the 'democratic chain of delegation'.

Central Evaluation Criterion

The degree to which an accountability arrangement or regime enables democratically legitimized bodies to monitor and evaluate executive behaviour and to induce executive actors to modify that behaviour in accordance with their preferences.

Box 3.8 CONSTITUTIONAL PERSPECTIVE: ACCOUNTABILITY AND
EQUILIBRIUM OF POWER

Central Idea

Accountability is essential in order to withstand the ever-present tendency towards power concentration and abuse of powers in the executive power.

Central Evaluation Criterion

The extent to which an accountability arrangement curtails the abuse of executive power and privilege.

---

both the inherent tendency of those in public office to dexterously evade control and the autonomous expansion of power of the all-encompassing bureaucracy. Does the accountability forum have enough inquisitive powers to reveal corruption or mismanagement, are the available sanctions strong enough to have preventive effects?

The *learning perspective* obviously focuses on the question of whether the arrangement enhances the learning capacity and effectiveness of the public administration (Box 3.9). The crucial questions from this perspective are whether the accountability arrangements offer not only sufficient feedback, but also the right incentives, to officials and agencies to induce them to reflect upon their policies and procedures and to improve upon them.

The existence of these various perspectives makes the evaluation of accountability arrangements a somewhat equivocal exercise. First of all, accountability arrangements may score well from one perspective, but not from others. For example, it has been argued that the accountability maps that are emerging around the various non-majoritarian EU agencies are largely sufficient from a constitutional perspective, but much less so from the democratic perspective. Increasingly, the Court of Justice monitors the activities of these agencies and they have become subject to

---

Box 3.9 LEARNING PERSPECTIVE: INCREASING PUBLIC VALUE

Central Idea

Accountability provides public office-holders and agencies with feedback-based inducements to increase their effectiveness and efficiency.

Central Evaluation Criterion

The degree to which an accountability arrangement stimulates public executives and bodies to focus consistently on achieving desirable societal outcomes in the smartest possible fashion.

---

scrutiny from the European Ombudsman and OLAF (Curtin, 2005). However, the link with forums that are democratically legitimized remains more indirect.

Moreover, these perspectives need not always point in the same direction. For example, judicial review of laws and regulations may be considered an adequate form of accountability from a constitutional perspective, and at the same time inappropriate from a democratic perspective, because it suffers from what Bickel (1962) has called 'the counter-majoritarian difficulty': it limits the exercise of popular sovereignty through the legislative branch. Similarly, overly rigorous democratic control may squeeze the entrepreneurship and creativity out of public managers and may turn agencies into rule-obsessed bureaucracies (Behn, 2001). Too much emphasis on administrative integrity and corruption control, which would be considered beneficial from a constitutional perspective, could lead to a proceduralism that seriously hampers the reflexivity, and hence also the efficiency and effectiveness, of public organizations (Anechiarico and Jacobs, 1996).

Assessing Accountability in European Governance: From Theory to Practice

This chapter has tried to get to grips with the appealing but elusive concept of accountability by asking three different questions, thus providing three different building blocks for the analysis and assessment of accountability deficits in European governance. The first question was a conceptual one: what exactly is meant by accountability? Accountability is often used in a very broad sense, as a synonym for a variety of evaluative, but essentially contested, concepts, such as responsiveness, responsibility, and effectiveness. In this book, the concept of accountability will be used in a more narrow sense: as a relationship between an actor and a forum, in which the actor has an obligation to explain and to justify his or her conduct, the forum can pose questions and pass judgement, and the actor may face consequences. This implies that the emphasis is more on ex post facto processes in governance than on ex ante inputs. Most of the ex ante inputs in governance, however important for the legitimacy of the EU, should be studied separately for what they are: forms of deliberation, participation, and control.

The second question was analytical: what types of accountability are involved? Various dimensions of accountability have been distinguished that can be used to classify accountability arrangements in a variety of ways. Taken together, these two building blocks provide a descriptive framework for more systematic mapping exercises: are the various institutions of the EU subject to accountability relations at all, and, if so, how can we classify these accountability relations?

The third question was evaluative: how should we assess these accountability relations, arrangements, and regimes? Three perspectives have been provided for the assessment of accountability relations, each of which may produce different types of accountability deficits.

These building blocks cannot in themselves provide us with definite answers to the question whether accountability deficits in European governance exist. Ultimately, the evaluation of accountability arrangements in the EU, to cite Fisher (2004: 511), 'cannot be disentangled from discussion about what is and should be the role and nature of European institutions'. Behind each assessment lies a theory, often implicit, about what constitutes sufficient democratic control, or adequate checks and balances, or satisfactory reflexivity in the context of European governance (and taking into account its special features and developing status). What, for example, is a sufficient level of democratic control of European agencies? What should be the yardstick: the level of control of independent agencies within the average member state? (And what qualifies as the average member state for these purposes?) Or should we, alternatively, develop a self-consciously European-level yardstick?

This is why, as implied in Chapter 2, the assessment of EU accountability cannot be separated from one's vision of adequate democratic governance in the context of European integration – should we judge the EU as a polity, albeit a supranational one, as an intergovernmental system, or as a regulatory state? These contending visions ultimately determine whether one judges the glass of European accountability to be half full or half empty. We will return to these questions in Chapter 8, but first we conclude this chapter by explaining how we have approached the task of applying the assessment framework presented above to the case of EU governance methodologically.

Some Methodological Considerations

The EU is a vast and complex web of interlocking institutions and both established and emerging practices. How to get a firm picture of the state of accountability within it? Given the realities of limited resources, aspiring for a complete picture of all relevant formal rules and observable practices regarding accountability in every nook and cranny of EU governance is simply impossible. We, like other students of the subject (e.g. Harlow, 2002; also Curtin, 2009) have had to delimit both our object of study and the ways in which we analyse it. The key choices we have made are as follows.

First, we have selected four arenas of European governance as the key actors whose accountability relationships, arrangements, and/or regimes we subjected to in-depth empirical study and systematic evaluation. Two are pivotal and highly visible political executive actors in the EU: the European Council and the Commission. In addition, we have selected two much less seen but perhaps no less important loci of EU administrative executive power: comitology committees and EU agencies. Taken together, these four represent a varied mix of EU executive type institutions. Two were designed on supranational (Commission; agencies) and two on intergovernmental (Council; comitology) principles. Between them, they cover both the front and back ends of European policy processes: agenda-setting and decision-making in the Commission and Council, and implementation design, delivery, and enforcement in comitology, the Commission, and agencies. Of all of these actors, we document and assess both the formal (legal frameworks) and the de facto (observable practices) components of accountability.

Second, we have limited the scope of study in some of the selected cases. Each of these actors has its own, multifaceted accountability regimes. To document such regimes in both their formal and de facto guises in full might well require four separate monographs (see e.g. Brandsma, 2010; Busuioc, 2010). In the present study, different researchers have made different choices. One has tried to cover most components of the regime as a whole (e.g. in Chapter 4). Others have concentrated on particular accountability types and arrangements within it. For example, the study of the European Council naturally looks at political accountability, yet studies two types of arrangements: that between the (rotating) Presidency of the Council (on behalf of the European Council, only after Lisbon a formal institution of the EU) and the EP, as well as that between members of the European Council (heads of government) and their national parliaments (specifically the Dutch Prime Minister and the Dutch Parliament). Likewise, the comitology study focuses on the hierarchical accountability relationship between national public servants who attend comitology committees and their immediate superiors in their home departments (i.e. in Denmark and the Netherlands) – an under-studied dimension in the existing literature. Finally, the chapter on EU agencies concentrates on the political and managerial accountability of agencies both internally to the agency management boards and externally to parliaments and other political actors.

While each of the chapters therefore paints a picture that is more or less incomplete in terms of its coverage of the full accountability regime regarding the actor in question, in combination they yield a significant cross-section of accountability types along the various dimensions discerned in Boxes 3.2–3.5. Moreover, the studies cover not just four different actors but also a wide range of forums at both the national and the European level.

Choosing particular types of accountability arrangements also implies a selection of assessment perspectives. For example, in the context of the hierarchical, administrative accountability arrangement between comitology members and their departmental superiors, it makes little sense to apply evaluation criteria derived from the constitutional perspective. The same goes for assessment of the accountability of EU agencies to their management boards.

All of these choices not only reduce the comprehensiveness of the coverage that this study provides (though, we surmise, not at the price of reducing its relevance), but also limit the comparability of the four assessment exercises that will be presented. Ours is therefore not a comparative study in the classical sense. Rather, it constitutes a series of studies that are comparable to the extent that (*a*) all employ the same definition of accountability, (*b*) all draw on parts of the same analytical framework, and (*c*) all pass judgement on the adequacy of the observed accountability arrangements drawing criteria from the same set of core normative perspectives presented above. While this is certainly not ideal for the purposes of holistic judgement, and explaining observed similarities and variations, we are confident that it is a lot better than any other study on the subject that we are aware of.

Note, however, that we have explicitly proposed it as a framework, not a theory. Frameworks offer a menu for choice, not a one-size-fits-all set of hypotheses and criteria. In applying our framework to the four arenas of EU governance selected for in-depth study, we have had to make choices concerning the scope and locus of observation and the selection of assessment criteria. These choices were driven in part by the specific characteristics of the four arenas under study, but were also the result of the usual methodological constraints and resource trade-offs faced by academic researchers. Although we strove for maximum comparability across case studies, these choices produced a few important differences in their scope and design. It is important to understand these differences when comparing and interpreting the case study findings.

Table 3.1 Case study designs compared

	Case 1	Case 2	Case 3	Case 4
Who?	European Commission President and members, civil servants	EU agencies' director and management board, European and national civil servants	European Council President and members	Comitology participants national civil servants
	Collective and individual (Commissioners and Directors-General)	Collective and individual (agency heads)	Individual	Hierarchical, individual
To whom?	Financial, legal, administrative, and political accountability of EU commissioners and officials to a range of EU forums	Political accountability to Council and EP; managerial accountability to Boards	Political (specifically parliamentary) accountability of EU Council President to EP and heads of government to national parliament(s)	Accountability of national comitology participants to line superiors within their national departments and agencies
About what?	Finances, procedure and content	Finances, procedure and content	Procedure and content	Procedure and content
Nature of obligation	Vertical/diagonal	Vertical/diagonal	Vertical	Vertical
Assessment perspective(s) used	Democratic, constitutional, learning	Constitutional, learning	Democratic	Democratic

Table 3.1 highlights these choices. It notes the principal design features of the four case studies, in terms of the three classic questions about accountability: *who* (actor) is responsible to *whom* (forum) for *what* (content)? Our choices have begun with identifying four 'actors' among a wider range of possibilities: the European Council, the Commission, comitology committees, and agencies. Next, each study has been scoped in terms of covering a particular accountability arrangement (i.e. one actor–forum relationship covering a particular sphere within the actor's roles and competences, for example the financial accountability of European agencies vis-à-vis the European Court of Auditors); a particular accountability regime (i.e. all existing financial accountability arrangements that European agencies are involved in); or multiple clusters of accountability regimes (i.e. legal, financial, and managerial accountability regimes pertaining to European agencies). In the case of the Commission and the agencies, the study encompassed multiple accountability regimes, whereas in the case of the European Council and the comitology participants, the analysis focused on a single accountability arrangement presumed to be the most salient component within these actor's overall accountability regimes (e.g. political/parliamentary accountability in the case of the European Council, and managerial accountability in the case of the comitology participants).

These choices had analytical implications for the design of the assessment exercise. Since none of the studies covered the total sum of accountability regimes pertaining to each of the four actors, we had to decide on a case-by-case basis which of the three sets of assessment criteria (democratic, constitutional, and learning) presented in Chapters 2 and 3 could and should be applied. Table 3.1 provides an overview of the methodological choices made.

In Chapter 8, we shall reflect on the upshot of the four studies and interpret them using the two sets of analytical perspectives presented in this chapter and in Chapter 2. We will revisit some of the caveats of our approach there, but also demonstrate its potential in providing a salient answer to the question of the EU's alleged accountability deficit.

Notes

1. In Germanic languages, such as Dutch, there is a distinction between *verantwoordelijkheid* and *verantwoording*, which to some extent resembles the contemporary distinction in English between 'responsibility' and 'accountability'. In Germanic languages, the word *rekenschap* (Dutch) or *Rechenschaft* (German) would come closest to the original, auditory meaning of 'accountability'.

2. See Fisher (2004: 510) for similar observations about the use of 'accountability' in the European context.
3. Following, among others, Day and Klein (1987: 5), Romzek and Dubnick (1998: 6); Lerner and Tetlock (1999: 225), Scott (2000: 40), McCandless (2001: 22), Mulgan (2003: 7–14), and Pollitt (2003: 89).
4. Compare the very active Danish parliamentary commission on European Affairs.
5. In French, 'contrôle' has a much more restricted, reactive meaning. See Meijer (2002: 3).
6. Compare Day and Klein (1987: 26), Sinclair (1996), and Behn (2001: 6–10).
7. We deliberately use the words 'at least', as this classification is not a limitative one. For example, one can also think of personal accountability, in which an official is accountable to his or her personal conscience (Sinclair, 1996: 230). For similar taxonomies, see Day and Klein (1987), Romzek (1996), Sinclair (1996), Romzek and Dubnick (1998), Behn (2001: 59), Pollitt (2003: 93), and Mulgan (2003).
8. For the rise of administrative accountability in the EU, see Harlow (2002: 108–43), Laffan (2003), Magnette (2003), and Pujas (2003).
9. Another form of horizontal accountability, which is mentioned in the literature, is mutual accountability between bodies standing on equal footing (O'Donnell, 1999).
10. Article 234, second paragraph TFEU.
11. Authors such as Van Twist (2000), Behn (2001), Halachmi (2002), and Mulgan (2003) offer discussions of the many dilemmas and design problems in the structure of accountability arrangements, but the underlying normative questions (what is the purpose of public accountability in a constitutional democratic state and what are the evaluation principles for accountability arrangements ensuing from this?) tend to be glossed over in these contributions.

4

The European Commission's Accountability Paradox

Anchrit Wille

Accountability on the March in Brussels

'It is difficult to find anyone who has even the slightest sense of responsibility' (CIE, 1999: 144). This was one of the sweeping conclusions from the Committee of Independent Experts (CIE) in a report to the European Parliament (EP) probing malpractices in the EU Commission. The publication of the report – following the allegations of mismanagement, irregularities, fraud, and neglect – precipitated the resignation of the complete Commission under the Presidency of Jacques Santer in March 1999.

Accountability was placed squarely on the political agenda of the new Commission (Harlow, 2002: 53). Fundamental reform of the Commission's accountability – along with its efficiency, effectiveness, and transparency – became one of the top priorities of the Commission presided over by Romano Prodi, who was appointed on the basis of a mandate to reform the institution and restore confidence in its organization. The proposals for change initiated by the new Commission had one major objective: instituting accountability in the EU Commission to guarantee that similar scandals would not occur in the future.

In this chapter, I analyse the current architecture of accountability in the EU Commission. Has the thrust to strengthen the accountability arrangements for this institution affected the operation of its power wielders – commissioners and their senior officials alike – and the way they fulfil (or fail to fulfil) their official duties? Do the new accountability arrangements really matter? To what extent have they improved democratic delegation and protected against abuses of power? Did they improve the quality of the

Commission's performance? Drawing on documentary evidence of politics during the Prodi (1999–2004) and Barroso (2004–9) years and interviews held with top officials in the Commission during the Barroso incumbency, this chapter's focus is to evaluate the accountability of the EU Commission, or more precisely, whether accountability mechanisms are doing their work in the projected way in this international institution.

An institution in Crisis: Commission Accountability as Problem and Solution

The EU Commission can be perceived as the Union's 'core executive' (Hix, 2005). The Commission is responsible for the initiation and formulation of policies, has an important monitoring role to play in the implementation of European policies, usually in the form of legislative, budgetary, or programme proposals, and acts as 'the guardian of the treaties' – having an obligation to ensure that member states and other actors implement EU policies. The Commission performs an external representation role that is increasingly important and has a mediating role among the EU institutions and the member states (Egeberg, 2003; Edwards, 2006).

From its very beginnings, running the Commission entailed 'a balancing act between autonomy and dependence on the member states' (Egeberg, 2006: 35), in other words, between an institutional logic shaped by inter-governmentalism and supranationalism. The Commission was meant to act independently from the member states since one of its core tasks was to take care of the common EU interest. But a Commission with a potential to become an independent supranational actor and entrepreneur would not be allowed by the member states. Although they would naturally be drawn towards an autonomy-enhancing supranationalist interpretation of the Commission's mandate, the inescapability of this tension has preoccupied each successive college of commissioners and produced a developmental pattern of 'two steps forward' (towards greater autonomy and scope) and 'one step back' (being 'cut down to size' by the member states).

Accountability had little priority in the European Commission from the 1950s until the early 1990s. Jean Monnet's template for the European Coal and Steel Community (ECSC), today's EC, gave a high authority of appointed expert administrators responsibility for both determining and implementing the policies of the ECSC (Stevens and Stevens, 2001: 220). The Commission was designed as a technocratic body to propose solutions to policy problems, broker deals, provide the impetus for integration, and be the guardian of the common European interest. Its origins lie in an era when the European Economic Community (EEC) was the creature of a technocratic elite; elite governance was central to the conception of European integration (Harlow, 2002: 57; Judge and Earnshaw, 2008).

The structure of the Commission was therefore not designed with political accountability in mind (Harlow, 2002: 57). The Commission, established at the time before a representative parliament existed, looked more like a quasi-autonomous executive agency. These circumstances allowed the Commission to become a special kind of bureaucracy that was characterized by a strong degree of expertise operating under the system of *professional* and *legal* accountability.

The European consensus about the European integration at that time had a significant impact on the development and management of the Commission in its early years (Christiansen, 1997; Harlow, 2002; Judge and Earnshaw, 2008). Technocratic leadership was purposefully insulated from effective parliamentary scrutiny. The ethos was one of consensual decision-making by elites, with the role of the parliament being confined to that of ratifying these decisions. This method worked reasonably well in the early years of the European Community, but it appeared increasingly outdated in the modern world of participatory and 'monitory' democracy (Keane, 2009).

With the gradual erosion of the legitimacy of the EU – which started in the early 1990s – the EU integration process and also the EU institutions came under fire. One storyline was that of an independent, unaccountable, too powerful elite in the Commission (Tsakatika, 2005: 200–4). In order for a sense of democratic legitimacy to exist, scholars and politicians argued that there must be a basic system of accountability with a match between the level at which decisions are taken and the level to which the electorate can in the final analysis hold the decision-makers to account.

Partly in response to this growing chorus of criticism, the central goal of the member states was to make Europe more effective and more democratic and to bring the institutional forms into line with the democratic forces. As a result, there have been a series of hotly debated treaty reforms since the early 1990s, aiming to streamline the internal workings of the EU and meet the call for more democratic decision-making and democratic accountability. This has transformed the legal and political framework governing the appointment, tasks, and duties of the Commission.

At the same time, others argued that the real problem with European governance was not the Commission's traditionally weak democratic credentials but its diminishing problem-solving efficiency. Over the

1990s, as the pace of the European integration picked up, the size of the Union increased, and its range of policies expanded, the Commission suffered the consequences of success: it was assigned an ever-increasing and more unwieldy range of tasks and responsibilities (Christiansen, 2001: 758), diluting its core commitments and competences (Majone, 2002: 389). Predictably, the Commission's organization came under attack in the mid-1990s for the way it carried out its responsibilities. The organization was a 'politicized bureaucracy' (Christiansen, 1997) and had, as Peterson (2006) calls it, 'plumbing problems': it tended to leak money and work inefficiently.

Trying to stem the tide, the Santer Commission launched several reform initiatives designed to improve executive performance (Nugent, 2001: 177). These were largely unsuccessful, as the Commission proved not particularly receptive to new management ideas (Cini, 2000; Stevens and Stevens, 2006), resulting not only in a weakening of the organization but also in a loss of its political capital among its key stakeholders. Weak leadership and ineffective management also eroded its standing vis-à-vis other EU institutions. Dissatisfaction with the way the Commission functioned, especially among the largest and more powerful EU member governments, meant that none of the big players were prepared to spend political capital defending the Commission (Peterson, 2004: 15). Lack of support in major capitals contributed to a political marginalization of the Commission.

Fraud allegations and corruption scandals further tarnished the Commission's reputation. The series of scandals that surrounded the Commission at the end of the 1990s left their mark. The resignation of the Santer Commission in March 1999 following accusations of mismanagement, irregularities, and fraud, pushed the issues of control and accountability to the top of the political agenda.

It was against the background of this institutional crisis that political leaders of the institutions of the EU and the member states were faced with a decline in the Commission's power, legitimacy, and credibility. They then engaged in attempts to put its 'house' in order (Cram, 2002: 310) and to ensure that the expertise and authority available in the Commission bureaucracy were more effectively wielded and more firmly embedded in a system of accountability to democratically legitimate forums.

Santer's successor as Commission President, Romano Prodi, was given a mandate to reform the Commission and to restore public confidence in its organization. In July 2001, the Commission issued a *White Paper on European Governance*, which announced a range of reform proposals that would transform the design of the institution and its executive responsibilities. The intended reform of the Commission was framed in terms of 'principles of good governance' identified in the White Paper as openness, participation, accountability, effectiveness, and coherence. The implementation of the internal reform measures, following from this *White Paper*, in combination with the Treaty revisions since the 1990s, has resulted in the most radical modernization since the Commission was established fifty years ago.

A New Architecture of Commission Accountability

Over the past decade, the accountability mechanisms of the Commission have changed immensely. New structures and rules with a range of ex ante constraints and ex post incentives combine to provide a system of enhanced control and accountability within and vis-à-vis the Commission. An overwhelming proportion of the measures have been swiftly implemented, ranging from measures focused on priority-setting, allocation and efficient use of resources, measures to adjust its human resources policy, and measures to fight fraud and corruption inside the institutions, a state-of-the-art accounting system, a new internal audit culture, a disciplinary office, and whistle-blower provisions (Christiansen and Gray, 2004; Kassim, 2004; Bauer, 2007).

In many respects, accountability has been strengthened considerably. In some matters, the Commission has taken the lead (e.g. the appointment of Neil Kinnock as reform commissioner, and his subsequent administrative reform package); in others, reform has been initiated by political dynamics or independent forces. In any event, there are now more accountability mechanisms than ever before. Political and administrative reforms have contributed to a more rigorous accountability regime for the Commission. Important is that the changes have not exclusively focused on the accountability of the commissioners or that of the public services, but that both levels in the institution have been addressed. Looking at the de jure situation, all the main dimensions of accountability have been strengthened.

Political Accountability

Strengthening the political accountability of the Commission was realized by an enhancement of the EP's capacity to hold commissioners and their officials to account. Since the rise of the deficit narrative at the beginning of the 1990s, the EP in particular has gained considerable powers and influence in the EU policy-making process. First, the term of office of the commissioners has been extended from four years to five, so as to bring it into close alignment with the term of the EP. This means that the appointment of the new college takes place after the EP elections to allow Members of the European Parliament (MEPs) to have a say on the matter. Not only is the EP consulted on the choice of President, but it also has the right to approve his or her appointment. Moreover, steps have also been taken to render the Commission more directly accountable to the Parliament, as illustrated by the fact that the EP committees now scrutinize commissioners, and are even able to dismiss the entire college by taking a vote of no confidence. This enhanced political accountability requires that commissioners report regularly to the EP, appear in parliamentary committees, and are obliged to answer questions.

There has also been a strengthening of political control within the Commission. The President's position has moved away from the 'first among equals' position of the pre-Prodi era. The Amsterdam Treaty increased the ex ante and ex post controls of the President over his fellow commissioners by giving him portfolio (re)allocation powers, and even enabling him to request an individual commissioner to resign. This hierarchization of the Commission aimed to make the commissioners more *accountable* for their portfolios and responsible in overseeing their services. Should they fail to perform, they can be held accountable – and be sanctioned as a result – by the President.

Managerial Accountability

The strengthening of political accountability was complemented by measures to improve the management of the services: that is, by the increased use of result-based reporting and the larger use of reviews and audits, copying the international trends of the era. Performance reporting essentially made top civil servants accountable for the implementation of the Commission's programme. One of the cornerstones of the Commission's reform strategy was the Strategic Planning and Programming (SPP) cycle. The cycle begins every year with the adoption by the commissioners of an Annual Policy Strategy (APS) in which policy priorities and corresponding resources are identified. Each year every Directorate-General must translate this APS into an Annual Management Plan (AMP). Each department has to generate an Annual Activity Report (AAR) for the previous year.

The new requirement for every Directorate-General to publish an AAR has powerfully reinforced the direct internal accountability of directors-general for expenditures authorized by them and by their staff. The report not only states how their services have contributed to the achievement of the Commission's strategic objectives, but also includes a signed declaration vouching that all of its work has been done correctly in the past year and that all the budgetary resources for which the service has been responsible has been used properly.

The introduction of performance-based management and the strategic policy process in the EU Commission was a means not only to rationalize the policy process but also to create new standards of behaviour and performance. Together with the introduction of new incentives for the 'professionalization' of senior management in the Commission, these new standards encouraged more managerial behaviour and a set of accountability expectations against which senior officials were evaluated.

Financial Accountability

To reinforce responsibility and accountability in the services, the so-called Kinnock reforms brought about the complete modernization of the system of financial management and control (Kassim, 2008). Setting up a proper internal audit service, better fraud-proofing structures, and decentralizing the financial controls to individual Directorates-General were part of the reform plans. Directors-general were given direct responsibility for making sure that proper control is carried out within their own departments and that managers are responsible for the financial decisions they take. Auditing is to be carried out at three levels: internally within each Directorate-General or service, centrally by a powerful Internal Audit Service (IAS), and externally by the Court of Auditors.

Audits, monitoring, and control are important mechanism to focus on the misuse and abuse of power or poor performance. They provide an independent and professional assessment to those who must hold others to account and are a necessary part of an effective accountability regime (Aucoin and Jarvis, 2005: 89). To this end, the IAS was established in 2001 tasked with issuing independent audit opinions on the quality of management and internal control systems and to present recommendations aimed at ensuring the efficient and effective achievement of the Commission's objectives. The IAS undertakes audits in individual departments of the Commission, as well as horizontal and thematic audits.

Financial monitoring is further performed by independent external bodies. The European Court of Auditors is the 'financial conscience' of the Union and makes sure that the revenues and expenditures of the EU institutions are legally and financially correct. It reports every year on the management of the EU budget. Stakeholders, who lack the means for holding an institution to account, can request the Audit Office (along with, for example, the Ombudsman) to use its discretionary powers of investigation. In order to strengthen the means of fraud prevention, the Commission established the European Anti-Fraud Office (OLAF) in 1999. The Office has a responsibility for conducting administrative anti-fraud investigations and has a special independent status.

Public Accountability

Increased openness and accessibility are essential prerequisites for effective scrutiny of public institutions (Hood and Heald, 2006; Fung, Graham, and Weil, 2008). Transparency may not be an end in itself, but it is a critical tool to evaluate organizational accountability. The Commission honed transparency into a refined instrument of governance by launching the European Transparency Initiative (ETI) in November 2005. The ETI consisted of a package of four main components: increasing the transparency of interest representatives seeking to influence EU decision-making and upholding minimum standards of consultation; increasing transparency about the use of EU funds; sharpening and polishing ethical rules and standards for public officials; and enlarging the public access to documents and information from the EU institutions. With the introduction of the ETI, the Commission has tried to effectuate its public accountability.

Efforts to broaden the practices of holding the EU Commission to account have, thus, resulted in an expanded set of accountability arrangements that is built in and around the institution. Table 4.1 gives an overview of the mechanisms that are effective in the EU Commission accountability architecture. As the arrangements in Table 4.1 show, a considerable development has been made in the accountability in what once was a technocratic-oriented international organization. What are the consequences of this development for the way power wielders at the helm of the EU Commission can be held accountable?

Evolving Executive Accountability: Towards a New Regime

In the new accountability architecture, European institutions and actors have gained an increasing role in ensuring the Commission's accountability. A major expansion to the mandate of the EP, in the capacity of

Table 4.1 Overview of the EU Commission's accountability architecture

Accountability type	Accountability arrangement	Main features
Political	Elections for European Parliament (EP) since 1979	An electoral process that secures competition between political parties and that enables a change of those who hold the positions or offices through election defeat or dismissal
	EP exercises democratic oversight over other EU institutions, particularly the European Commission	Parliamentary scrutiny. Parties extract accounts from the executive. Parliamentary process requires the executive to prepare performance reports for scrutiny by parliamentary committees. Parliament has the tools to discipline or sanction those found responsible for wrongdoings or shortcomings
	Responsibility of commissioners for what happens in their departments. In College: principle of collegiality	Political executives with the political incentive to take their responsibility seriously and to hold their departments (and agencies) to account in a governance structure of superior–subordinate relationships (hierarchy). Subordinates report to superiors on their use of authority in the discharge of their responsibilities
Managerial	Strategic Planning and Programming (SPP) with Annual Policy Strategy (APS), Annual Management Plan (AMP), Annual Activity Report (AAR), and Synthesis Report	Activity-Based Management (ABM) with performance-oriented reviews and reports
	Career Development Review (CDR) for senior officials in Commission	Internal performance appraisal of staff by their superiors
Financial	Decentralization of controls. Separation of financial control from internal auditing	Financial rules/regulation
	Internal Audit Office European Court of Auditors	External audits and performance reviews of the administration of public services; independent evaluations of policies and programmes; Internal audit, monitoring, and control capacities
	Codes of Conduct, Declarations of Interests, Code of Good Administrative Behaviour (2001)	Protocols that explicitly or implicitly address the mutual obligation of all those involved in the accountability relationship
Administrative	European Ombudsman (1992) OLAF: EU's Anti-Fraud Office (1999)	Checks, controls, and fire alarms
Judicial	European Courts	Judicial review of administrative decisions
Public	European Transparency Initiative (2005) Whistleblowers Charter (2002)	Public access to government information. Protection for officials who release information as a response to a undisclosed wrongdoing

organizing audits, reviews, and the institutionalization of offices (ombudsman, audit, and anti-fraud) that function as forums for intense scrutiny, has meant that the Commission's accountability holders are increasingly situated at the supranational level.

The overall thrust of the reforms was to make the Commission more accountable to politicians and to EU citizens. Whereas in the early years the EU founders had sought to insulate the Commission from politics, insulation is, since the 1990s, perceived as the problem to be solved. The reforms have emphasized political and bureaucratic sources of control over pure legal and professional approaches.

Coupled Accountability Arrangements: A Chain of Delegated Authority

The strengthening of accountability mechanisms is intended to improve executive leadership and to integrate authority and accountability within the executive more tightly. But simply multiplying and strengthening accountability arrangements is not enough if the basic building blocks of accountability either are not in place or are not effectively coupled (Aucoin and Jarvis, 2005).

One of the significant features of the new accountability architecture is that several of these arrangements have placed the accountee (actor) and the accountor (forum) in a clearer 'hierarchical', 'vertical', relationship. Parliamentarization of the EU (since the Amsterdam Treaty, 1999) has created a chain of delegated authority in which the Commission, as political executive, has become involved in a principal–agent-like relationship with the EP (Judge and Earnshaw, 2008: 16). An important feature of this parliamentarization is that the political executives 'are responsible to the legislatures in the sense that they are dependent on the legislature's confidence and that they can be dismissed from offices by a legislative vote of no confidence or censure' (Lijphart, 1984: 68). Parliament as a superior places restrictions and checks on the use of authority in the Commission, and has the power to discipline or sanction those found responsible for shortcomings or wrongdoings.

This 'verticalization' of accountability relationships is mirrored inside the Commission. In the accountability system of the Commission, 'the chain of delegated authority and accountability' has become more closely tied as an 'organizational' structure of assigned responsibilities. The Commission President has achieved a stronger control over the Commission – helped by a stronger Secretariat General. Moreover, responsibilities of commissioners have been clarified and they are expected to control the use of authority in the departments that they are responsible for (Van Gerven, 2007). Consequently, directors-general have become more clearly subordinate to the direction of their commissioner. The element of hierarchy is reinforced precisely to ensure that democratic control over the institution is not lost or compromised (Aucoin and Jarvis, 2005: 36; Schillemans, 2007).

A New World of Political and Managerial Accountability

Treaty and administrative reforms have broadened mechanisms of political and administrative accountability and this has also brought new behavioural expectations of political and managerial accountability in the EU Commission. The enlarged array of accountability mechanisms has provided an increased number of opportunities for holding Commission officials answerable for their use of authority and for their performance.

The considerable shifts in the accountability expectations of commissioners and their senior officials have increased a demarcation of responsibilities. It is possible to discern different dimensions of political and managerial accountability for the commissioners and their top officials.

In Figure 4.1, the lines are drawn to indicate demarcations of accountability. The lines in fan-shaped formation mark approximate 'zones of responsibility' of commissioners and their top officials (cf. Barberis, 1998: 466). The top part of the diagram lies mostly within the political accountability system. A commissioner can, for example, be asked to give an account to parliamentary committees. The bottom part of the diagram contains accountabilities that lie mostly within the managerial accountability system.

The figure depicts overlap in the areas of responsibility of the commissioners and their directors-general. The responsibility of commissioners is more of an open-ended or residual type that embraces most of the 'zones of responsibility' of the directors-general. Managerial accountability is thus embedded in political accountability. But it was also recognized – as the figure illustrates – that senior officials rather than commissioners have a direct, first line responsibility for certain limited areas. The enhanced transparency and disclosure that have resulted from adopting performance management and reporting regimes for managing outputs and outcomes have strengthened not only managerial but also, indirectly, political accountability mechanisms (cf. Aucoin and Heintzman, 2000: 84).

New accountability arrangements have, thus, resulted in the establishment of a revised accountability regime. On paper, that is. The question to

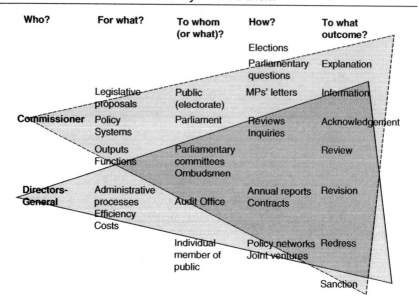

Figure 4.1 Dimensions of political and administrative accountability
Source: Adapted from Barberis (1998)

be asked now is, of course, whether this new regime has actually made the Commission more accountable.

Assessing the Commission's New Accountability Regime

How can we determine whether these accountability arrangements are doing their job? To gauge whether the various accountability arrangements in and surrounding the EU Commission are doing their job, I have followed this volume's three-part assessment framework, employing a democratic, a constitutional, and a learning perspective to the empirical evidence gathered from documents and interviews. As pointed out in Chapter 3, a fully fledged accountability relationship presupposes: *information* – so that facts and files on a matter for which an account must be rendered are provided to and digested by the relevant forum(s); *debate* – so that office-holders can be questioned and challenged by the forum(s); and *sanctions* – a forum's ability to assign positive or negative consequences to the actor. I shall evaluate the basic workings of the new accountability regime by focusing on these three conditions for effective accountability, looked at through the three evaluative lenses as provided by the normative perspectives presented in

Chapter 3. The assessment is based on an analysis of documentary material from the Commission and the EP on the practices and experiences with the Commission's accountability arrangements. In addition, I have conducted in the period 2006–8 a set of qualitative in-depth interviews with over fifty senior executive officials (commissioners, heads and members of cabinets, and directors-general). These officials work at the top of the Commission in an environment in which accountability may be a salient concern and who have been confronted first-hand with the impact of the multiple initiatives and efforts to improve the Commission's accountability.

Democratic Perspective

Have the new accountability mechanisms enhanced the democratic control of the Commission? The new powers of the EP require that the Commission regularly submits reports to Parliament. Through its scrutiny of these reports, Parliament is able to exercise oversight. By means of the tabling of written and oral questions, it is able to extract additional information and accounts from individual commissioners, and it appears to do that quiet vigorously (Judge and Earnshaw, 2008: 217–28). As one Commission official indicated:

> On many matters where treaties have given the EC the initiative on legislation, the Commission is quite autonomous in spending its budget. However, the Parliament has a *droit de regard*, and MEPs mostly do not refrain from asking a lot of questions. On our side we are required to give an answer to every single request (even the stupidest) fast. This is what I call democracy and accountability. It surely happens at the national level in some countries, but rest assured that we are controlled by a democratic body.

Strengthening of parliamentary accountability has had important consequences for the answerability of commissioners to MEPs. Being held accountable by MEPs, today's commissioners are required to defend and justify the decisions and actions falling within their sphere of competence.

The lines between ex post accountability and ex ante control have, in fact, become blurred as a result of this. For example, in their relation with the EP, many commissioners are obliged (as a result of the introduction of co-decision brought about by the Maastricht Treaty) to include MEPs in their negotiating strategies. And this can be useful for the Commission, as a director-general explained: 'We need them and it works extremely well. It is an extra source of power for the Commission. It gives our proposal more strength. If we bring a proposal to the Council, we can say we have negotiated this with the European Parliament and they are behind it as well. It is not just our crap, it is crap supported by parliament. That is a good tool.' Apart from more clout it also legitimates the work of the Commission, as a director-general made clear: 'What we do here in the Commission has become more democratic, and has an increased legitimization attached to it now that it is debated in parliament.'

This does not imply that the relationship with Parliament is always appreciated, or that each Commission official values the new form of oversight:

> We feel the existence of the European Parliament, mostly, not all the time but most of the time, through its negative effect. Every time we have to go there, I wonder what is the added value? It is democratically correct, but it has no contribution to the substance. In our field MEPs do not ask the right questions; and the end result is a complete fragmentation of our policy; they make our policies worse. It is contra productive. A parliament is there to control, not to do micro politics.

Other Commission officials are more circumspect in interpreting the influence of the EP: 'Although there are sometimes large differences, our view is that parliament is our natural ally. Not on all points but in general. But they are giving us a hard time, by putting the Commission on the edge.' The empowerment of the EP has thus introduced a new dynamic into the work of commissioners (and no doubt by extension for their public servants). In the words of a Commission official: 'I actually welcome this scrutiny, because it just reminds us that policy isn't just a theoretical exercise. It might be harder to work through the politics of the Parliament, but it is much healthier.'

As the intensity and scope of accountability of the Commission to the EP has increased, this has also had negative consequences for the effective workings of these accountability arrangements. In order to ensure continued 'output' and remain efficient in the face of increasing powers and complexity, the EP has had to streamline its working procedures, moving more decisions to parliamentary committees, and cutting down time for debate (De Clerck-Sachsse and Kaczyński, 2009). Measures to increase the efficiency have led to a bureaucratization of procedures (reduced speaking time in plenary). Decisions are increasingly taken at the level of EP committees and after only one reading in the Parliament, leaving little time for debate and scrutiny. Pressures to increase efficiency have run the risk of undermining the EP's role as a forum of debate.

Though the EP's means of democratic supervision of the Commission may have grown, its means to sanction it are still restricted. There is no treaty provision that gives the EP the power to sack individual commissioners. The only sanction is to dismiss the full body of commissioners as a whole – hardly a form of precision punishment, and therefore by definition bound to be used only in extreme cases. That said, some strengthening of the EP's clout in influencing the careers of commissioners has taken place – but more ex ante (control) than ex post (accountability). MEPs can now hold hearings of individual commissioner candidates. When members of a new Commission are nominated by the national governments, the EP interviews each candidate individually – including the prospective Commission President – and then votes on whether to approve the Commission in its entirety. A new Commission cannot be appointed without EP approval. And if the EP votes by majority to withdraw confidence in an individual commissioner, the President will either ask that member to resign or will justify before the EP their refusal to do so. A further acceleration of the (informal) process of parliamentarization of the Commission can be expected in the appointment of the Commission (especially by the hearings) and in the role that the EP plays in different dossiers.

As the EP has acquired more powers, it has started to take on the characteristics of a 'normal' national parliament as regards its workings, procedures, party cohesion, and coalition formation (De Clerck-Sachsse and Kaczyński, 2009; Hix and Noury, 2009); and accordingly, the Commission has been pushed to become more like a 'normal' core executive. But this normalization does not appear to spill over to the relationship of the EU institutions with the European voters, who seem lost in the EU's labyrinth of accountability. EU elections appear to hold little political relevance next to national electoral cycles. Participation in the EU elections has been constantly decreasing from 62 per cent in 1979 (in an EU of 9) to 43 per cent in 2009 (in an EU of 27) (Malkopoulou, 2009). In the seven direct elections to the EP so far, turnout has fallen by an average of 3 per cent each time, the largest drop occurring in the 1999 elections (7 per cent). These low turnout levels diminish the legitimacy of the electoral process and of the EU as a whole; in any case, they testify to the limited impact of the post-Santer reforms on the ultimate democratic principal, the European electorate.

Information to the electorate, the opportunity for political debate, and the opportunity to attribute salient electoral consequences to the EU institution's performance, all remain underdeveloped when it comes to the relationship of voter to the EU Commission. To start with, lack of information and the common perception that 'Brussels is far away' illustrates the voters' sense of detachment from the EU. Recent figures indicate a general lack of knowledge among Europeans about the EU's institutional structure, which appears too complicated and inaccessible. In the 2009 Eurobarometer (EB71), almost one in two Europeans declared that they do not know how the EU works (48 per cent); and only a little over one-third of the Europeans (38 per cent) think that their voice counts in the EU.[1]

Moreover, the absence of a politicized European debate reduces the ability to capture public attention and can be clearly detrimental to the EP's capacity to present itself as a relevant political actor (Mair, 2008). This is evident in the EP's agenda, which features very technical issues (most often referred to as the curve of cucumbers or the size of strawberries) that seem to have little connection with the issues that are foremost on the minds of EU citizens. The increasing focus on streamlining procedures in the EP and the focus on technical detail outlined above only exacerbate these problems. They may produce 'good governance', but they may at the same time hinder rather than strengthen popular interest and involvement in that governance.

Lastly, the fact that the EP elections are not linked to the appointment of a government also plays a role in making European elections less salient than national ones. At national level, elections not only allow electors to choose a government and to help determine the direction of public policy; they also provide a recognizable human face for government in the form of a political leader – a president or prime minister (Bogdanor, 2007). The voting public of the EU has, however, no direct input into who serves on the Commission. The appointment procedures through which the Commission is (s)elected are far from transparent. Beyond its obligations to the member states and the EP, the Commission is not in any way directly accountable to European citizens (Cruz, 2007). 'Governments are "accountable" if voters can discern whether governments are acting in their interest and sanction them appropriately', write Manin, Przeworski, and Stokes (1999: 40). The complicated system of (s)election and accountability governing the Commission appears not have offered citizens the confidence that the 'people who run Europe' are actually accountable to them (Page, 1997; Bogdanor, 2007; Malkopoulou, 2009). This poses a considerable problem for the legitimacy of the EU. If an enhanced accountability architecture is matched with continually falling turnout, the logic of strengthening the accountability as a means of democratizing EU governance is undermined.

The new democratic accountability arrangements in the EU have turned accountability inwards (to the other EU institutions) rather than outwards (to the EU citizens). Direct accountability of the Commission to European citizens through the EP is an obvious potential answer to this tendency and to some of the problems of the 'insulation' of the EU-level politics.

The Constitutional Perspective

How to assess the accountability mechanisms and practices in the EU Commission from a constitutional perspective? Can they be seen as a safeguard against abuses of power? The complex division of power in the EU system means that the EU Commission will seldom play a simple role alone. The functioning of the EU is split into intergovernmental and supranational spheres which provide for a system of checks and balances, limiting the Commission influence. Without the EP and the Council, the EU Commission is not able to exercise its executive function. The institutions are accountable to one another for the discharge of their respective responsibilities.

A considerable part of the new accountability arrangements in and around the Commission was intended to address misuses of authority. In the past, the Commission was criticized for its lack of vigour in spotting and dealing with misconduct. New financial rules and regulations were designed to constrain the behaviour of public officials, limit their discretion, and prevent them from abusing power. By establishing audits, whistle-blowing provisions, the OLAF agency, codes of good administrative behaviour as well as its new-found concern with transparency, the Commission has focused not only on efforts to tighten the rules and regulations to prevent wrongdoings, but also on designing accountability arrangements that purport to act as a deterrent on the abuse of power.

To learn if actions of executive actors conform the laws and norms, the provision of accurate, timely, and useful information is key. An accountability holder can only hold officials accountable in so far as they have reliable records about their behaviour. In and around the Commission, the investigative powers and information-processing capacity to evaluate the Commission's behaviour have been enhanced and strengthened. Setting up a proper IAS and better 'fraud-proofing' structures and decentralizing the financial controls to individual Directorates-General were part of Kinnock's reform plans. Moreover, a revision of the codes of conduct (governing the relationships between commissioners and their services) included a specific procedure that commissioners had to be informed twice a year of the result of all audits – whether carried out by the Directorate's own auditors, the central IAS, OLAF, or the Court of Auditors. Furthermore, they had to be informed about all questions arising from management, especially financial management, which could call into question their responsibility.

Not only is the provision of information relevant to make accountability arrangements effective from a constitutional perspective: clarifying responsibilities can be a solution to 'the problem of many hands' (Bovens, 2006) in which it is unclear who is to be blamed for an organization's outcome. Decentralization in the Commission of financial responsibilities, audit, and ex post control activities at department level (Schön-Quinlivan, 2007) is supposed to give heads of unit and directors-general more autonomy and flexibility in their work and also more responsibility. The direct accountability of directors-general for expenditures authorized by them and their staff has been powerfully reinforced by a new requirement for every Directorate-General to publish an AAR that includes a signed declaration vouching that all of its work have been done correctly in the past year and that all the budgetary resources for which the service has been responsible have been used properly. This practice attaches culpability to the provision of information. This *responsibilization* of the directors-general, means a shift of collective accountability for some functions in the Commission's performance towards individual accountability of specific senior officials, in which they could be held liable for their actions, punished for malfeasance, and rewarded for success. Senior officials interviewed for this study underlined the importance of the new checks and controls, and they emphasized that these new standards have increased the reliability of the organization. But they also expressed their concern with this displacement of responsibility onto senior officials; overly detailed definitions of responsibility limit flexibility and result in risk-avoiding behaviour. As one official observed: 'The introduction of personal responsibility has made that a lot of people here do not have the guts any more to take a decision, let alone, to take any risk. This has resulted in putting off and delaying of decisions, asking more advice, an endless culture of signing off and signatures, and a cover-up culture. Nobody wants to be associated with errors or mistakes any more.'

Almost all senior officials expressed their dissatisfaction with the extra bureaucratic red tape resulting from the new internal and external regulations and complained about the new system as being very costly in terms of time and energy and that well-intentioned reform measures have produced a heavy burden of requirements upon them (cf. Behn, 2001; Bovens, Schillemans, and 't Hart, 2008; Ban, 2008). A majority of interviewees felt that the balance has been lost: there are now, they claim, too many legalistic procedures, too much reporting, and too heavy supervision.[2] One director-general describes his concern as follows: 'There is an enormous cramp in the organization after the Santer resignation which has led to overregulation and containers full of auditors and controllers within the organization. Everything has become strictly regulated, nothing can be done spontaneously.

We are controlled by DG legal and budget, and it is nearly impossible to change this.'

Apart from a risk-averse culture and stifled creativity produced by the new accountability arrangement, the EP (2007a: 4) has also raised doubts about the quality of the information in some of these accountability documents:

> The director general will, without any doubt, do his utmost in order to describe the 'reality' as objectively as possible. But any 'assessment' is also about 'what shall be mentioned' and 'what shall not be mentioned'. Can we be sure that information which from an 'integrity of information' point of view should be mentioned also will be mentioned in the annual activity report if the public access to this bit of information would or could have a negative influence on the reputation and power of the director general? In the process leading up to the Commission's 'giving account' there is no one besides the managing director general who is empowered to give an independent check of the reality as described by the director general.

Finally, the Commission's attempts to improve public access to information and expand transparency remain modest. As part of the ETI, the EU Commission opened in 2009 a register in which non-governmental organizations (NGOs), private companies, law firms, and trade unions that are in daily contact with staff at the European institutions can sign. This new lobbyist register is intended to shed light on the estimated thousands of lobbyists working in Brussels and influencing EU policy-making. One of the problems of this effort to increase transparency is, however, that registration remains voluntary and that the register gives no detail on the areas that are lobbied on, or potential conflicts of interests. One of the transparency pressure groups described the register, therefore, as being 'as useful as a phonebook without any numbers'.[3]

Lack of transparency in the Commission has been the object of much criticism. The European Ombudsman (2009) reports that most inquiries opened in 2008 concerned the Commission (66 per cent). As the Commission is the main EU institution that makes decisions having a direct impact on citizens, it is normal that it should also be the principal object of citizens' complaints. But by far the most common allegation that the European Ombudsman examined was lack of transparency in the EU administration. This allegation arose in 36 per cent of all inquiries and included refusal of information or documents. It is perhaps hardly surprising that the Commission in popular images is pictured as a secretive organization. A true revolution in transparency would require more candour on the part of the Commission.

The Learning Perspective: Enhancing Performance

The design of the Commission's accountability architecture is in many respects focused on enhancing democratic controllability and on preventing the misuse of power. But by providing feedback-based inducements to improve institutional performance, accountability can also enhance institutional learning capacities. So, the third perspective asks whether the new accountability mechanisms and practices in the EU Commission have made the EU Commission more effective in delivering its policies.

For many years, the EU system of management and budgeting was based on a very centralized and 'input-based' approach, in which neither the subsequent results nor the overall resources needed to achieve them were clear to anyone. The Strategic Planning and Programming (SPP) system, Activity-Based Management (ABM), and Activity-Based Budgeting (ABB) all sought to resolve this situation by fundamentally changing the way the various policies are identified, prioritized, and evaluated within the EU Commission. Moreover, since 2005, there has been a rule that Impact Assessment, a form of ex ante evaluation that is part of the Commission's Better Regulation Programme, should be applied to all items included in the Commission's APS and Legislative and Work Programme (CLWP) (Hardacre, 2008; Robertson, 2008).

All these arrangements provide for an institutional infrastructure for organizational learning. SPP is a crucial part of a larger effort that seeks to improve management through results-based reporting, but also seeks to improve accountability not only to parliament, but also to the college and to the public. New arrangements of all types, including evaluation, monitoring, review, and impact assessment, offer potentially useful feedback on what works and what does not, and the reasons for success or failure. Ideally, the use of these new arrangements allows the executive, the legislature, and all stakeholders to reflect on their work, revisit their understanding of the project's goals and activities, assess their effectiveness, and use the evaluation findings to improve the policies. The new knowledge, the experiences, and the lessons learnt from these arrangements subsequently provide a basis for better project planning and implementation.

The officials interviewed were decidedly mixed in their reactions to the impact of these new systems on the learning capacity of the Commission. Some indicated that the entire reform process, and SPP in particular, has contributed positively to a change of culture, turning the focus on the actual results of EU policies. The implementation of these arrangements was said to have made management more effective, results-oriented, and transparent. As an official pointed out: 'The reforms have caused a lot of moaning and groaning; and things take incredibly longer. That is true. But the quality of the output is better, there are new systems of planning introduced and people have become aware that we have to perform on time. The discipline in the organization has been improved immensely.'

The majority of the interviewees highlighted, however, the unintended consequences of these new accountability arrangements. The problem of *bureaucratization* – or 'fundamentalistic bureaucratisme' as one official named it – looms large in their accounts. The proliferation of arduous and demanding rules and cumbersome procedures and the heavy reporting burdens induced a sense of compliance and frustration among the staff and not a real learning culture. In the words of an official: 'we are chasing around paper in huge amounts in this organization.' The perception of ABM/ABB as an 'administrative burden', rather than as a tool for success, is of crucial importance for an effective use of these procedures. A second recurrent complaint was that in most issue areas there was *a lack of* 'ownership' in the Commission. The absence of clearly defined roles and responsibilities following from these programmes was an obstruction for the application of lessons learnt from these arrangements. Finally, the abundance of reports, the vast array of stand-alone studies, and evaluations carried out by the Commission made the integrated use of the output of all these tools, procedures, and instruments nearly impossible, in the view of Commission officials.[4]

The fundamental ambivalence about the learning potential of 'new' accountability procedures conveyed by the interviews corresponds with Ban's conclusion (2009: 8) based on her own interviews with commission officials that SPP 'has devolved in a bureaucratic process, overly time consuming, generating a great deal of paper that is in fact rarely used'.

The provision of performance information from these new arrangements not only might be relevant for the executive but can also increase the transparency of the Commission's operation to the EP, enabling the possibility of better parliamentary scrutiny. Yet, a report of the EP Committee on Budgets (2009) on the use of SPP made it clear that Parliament is not using this information very systematically and indicated how the Parliament should reconsider the use of information from the SPP/ABM reports to strengthen its dialogue with the Commission. Instead of the extensive scrutiny with regard to controls and legality, the EP should give more attention to the actual results achieved in EU programmes when evaluating the overall annual performance of the Commission.

Ultimately, the capacity of both organizations (EP and Commission) to learn through the use of accountability arrangements clearly demands a balanced and sophisticated use of performance data and evaluations. To assume that new routines of information collection are automatically followed by routines of information use, reflective debate, and sensible improvement initiatives simply neglects the precariousness of the conditions that encourage learning, and the prevalence of those that block it (cf. Moynihan, 2005: 205).

The Commission's Accountability Paradox

Executive accountability in the Commission has undergone a considerable change in the past decade. The evolution of political control and accountability in the Commission highlights the transformation of the Commission from an 'international organization' into a European-level 'core executive'. In the international organization perspective, democracy and accountability were assured through the national political process, supplemented by some weaker forms of politicization at the European level. The deepening and widening of European integration have not only expanded the duties of the Commission but also changed their character from rule-making and market regulation to advising on foreign affairs, justice, immigration, and international issues (Harlow, 2002: 63). An increasingly demanding and changing political environment, in which the Commission finds itself entrenched, imposed political requirements on the organization of the Commission in terms of responsiveness, responsibility, effectiveness, and transparency.

Creation of new arrangements in the last decade, especially at the supranational level, has allowed for the stronger accountability of the EU Commission from a democratic, constitutional, and learning perspective. The broadening of the system has advanced the instruments with regard to five elements of the accountability equation: the agent (clearly assigned collective, but also individual, accountability by means of 'responsibilization' of Commission officials), the forums (new powers and institutions: EP and European Audit Office), the provision of information (reports and audits), standards for assessing executive action, and the repertoire of sanctions at the disposal of forums.

Some even consider the Commission to be the most controlled executive in the world, subject as it to an extraordinary range of checks and balances (Lord, 2004). But though the Commission's accountability system may well have gained considerable 'bite' internally, the problems of rendering account externally – to the public at large – seem undiminished. This chapter too suggests that new accountability arrangements may meet the standards of good governance at the international level, but that this does not automatically imply high levels of legitimacy for the Commission. In fact, in the eyes of the public, the Commission remains a remote and secretive entity made up of unaccountable public servants that deserve closer public scrutiny.

Part of the problem may be the continued invisibility of the Commission in the public mind. 'Brussels bureaucrats', invisible as they are to the public gaze, still *appear* to be unaccountable. The large emphasis on technical and procedural dimensions of accountability under the Kinnock reforms, while vital to increasing performance measurement, transparency, and accountability, risks missing the 'big picture' in terms of contributing to wider public trust and acceptance.

New political and administrative arrangements have turned accountability practices 'inwards': by and large the Commission is now highly accountable towards the other EU institutions, while 'outward' accountability has remained rather underdeveloped. And herein lies the *accountability paradox* referred to in the title of this chapter: the demands of the Commission's internal accountability regime will probably continue to rise, whereas in the eyes of the public, the EU and the Commission have not nearly become accountable enough. The Commission may find itself in the uncomfortable situation of facing simultaneous accountability overload and deficit. To escape from this potentially debilitating paradox, the Commission and its principal accountability forums will need to get the balance right. They need to reduce bureaucratization of existing internal accountability arrangements without being accused of emasculating them. Yet at the same time, the Commission needs to be bolder, braver, and more creative than it has so far been in bringing about more meaningful and appealing accountability conversations with the EU's citizens.

Improving the Commission's accountability outwards can only be a part of an ambition of the EU to become a democratic polity and of a broader process of citizen control. A central feature of representative democracy is that the voters elect and remove those who govern. In EU elections, it should, therefore, become possible to substantially determine and influence the composition and colour not only of the EP, but also of the Commission. Simplifying the complex EU system of accountability may contribute to a better understanding and knowledge of the role, the working procedures, and the decisions of the Commission and the EP. But this means that both institutions have to invest in the capacity to present themselves as relevant and independent political actors; and that more efforts should be made to politicize the debate in the EU and to structure it around the most politically salient questions (cf. De Clerck-Sachsse and Kaczyński, 2009). The 2009 Eurobarometer (see note 1) shows that support for making policy at the European level was relatively high for several relevant policy areas. Moreover, a personalization of politics, that is presenting 'faces' that the public can recognize and relate to, may make EU politics more relevant to the public (Malkopoulou, 2009). Linking the nomination of the Commission directly to the result of the European elections – and this should apply not only to the nomination of the Commission President, but to the Commission as a whole – could encourage the development of a Commission that is accountable to a broader public as well.

Notes

1. Does this mean that governance at EU level is irrelevant for most Europeans? An absolute majority of respondents in the 2009 Eurobarometer (EB71) believed that more decisions in a number of areas should be taken at the European level. This support is greatest in the case of the fight against terrorism and the promotion of democracy and peace in the world (81 per cent), fighting organized crime (78 per cent), protecting the environment (77 per cent), securing energy supply (76 per cent), managing major health issues and the equal treatment of men and women (72 per cent), ensuring food safety, and ensuring economic growth (70 per cent). Support for taking more decisions at European level was relatively high and has risen over the years and in all the areas discussed.
2. Discontent among top officials about the growing body of rules and regulations which is thought to be burdensome, frustrating, and demotivating, emerges also from other studies. Schön-Quinlivan's (2007) and Ellinas and Suleiman's (2008) findings indicate dissatisfaction among officials in the Commission about the tendency towards the bureaucratization brought about by the reforms, especially with regard to financial rules; and that the reform had overhit the mark and significantly increased the level of red tape in the institution.
3. The transparency pressure group is Corporate Europe Observatory (*Source*: *EUObserver*, 22 June 2009).
4. The Commission services annually produced in 2007 around 120 retrospective evaluations (interim and ex post), mostly carried out through external evaluators and it produces a slightly lower number of ex ante 'impact assessments'. This number does not include the large number of evaluations that are carried out by national or regional authorities.

5

European Agencies: Pockets of Accountability

Madalina Busuioc

Agencies and Executive Power in the EU

The EU is no longer primarily a legislative player, as it has become capable of exercising executive power in its own right. The European *agencification* process is part and parcel of this highly relevant ongoing development: the emerging, composite European executive (Egeberg, 2006; Curtin, 2009). The European Commission, the Council, or even the member states have delegated a whole range of powers to a new breed of executive creations, meant to operate at an arm's length from political control: European agencies. European agencies have been set up in a multitude of relevant and sensitive fields such as medicines, food safety, chemicals, border control, police cooperation, telecommunications, energy, disease prevention, to name just a few areas. The EU's appetite for doing so has been described as 'limitless' (Geradin and Petit, 2004: 4). In fact, 'one could even get the impression that for each and every new threat that the European Union is faced with . . . the first reaction is to set up yet another Agency' (van Ooik, 2005: 127). At present, approximately thirty agencies exist, with more than half created in the past decade alone.

The institutional configuration of such bodies includes traces of all three models of EU governance identified in Chapter 2. Agencies, it has been argued, have emerged as a strategic compromise between the main inter-institutional actors at the EU level (Keleman, 2002). On the one hand, member states saw the setting up of agencies steered and monitored by management boards composed largely of member states' representatives, as an institutional solution allowing them to maintain greater control (Keleman,

2002). In other words, rather than delegating such powers to the European Commission, member states opted for the creation of European agencies as an opportunity 'to wield more influence and exert more control on EU law making and implementation' (Groenleer, 2006: 163). This is in line with an intergovernmental view of EU governance.

On the other hand, simultaneously, the creation of agencies was perceived (by the Commission) as an opportunity to further expand EU capacity to pool powers at the EU level, especially as some of these powers were not previously 'Europeanized' (Dehousse, 2002; Curtin, 2009). Thus, they can be perceived as supranational elements of EU governance. After all, agencies are (quasi-)autonomous bodies in their own right, operating and exercising a broad array of powers at the European level.

Finally, agencies can be viewed as perfect specimens of the regulatory perspective. The delegation of far-reaching powers to independent European agencies has been described as a solution to the credibility crisis affecting the Community (Majone, 2000). The agency model is expected to bring about more efficient and legitimate decisions based on technical rather than political considerations, leading to credible commitment.

Regardless of which perspective one adheres to, the fact is that these bodies have real power and their opinions and decisions can have a direct impact on individuals, regulators, and member states. This raises inevitable questions: To what extent are these 'micro institutions of macro impact' (European Parliament, 2008: 4) accountable for their behaviour? Can they be held in check so as to prevent misbehaviour and abuse of powers? Are they held in check in practice?

Scholars have pointed at the risk of placing too much power in the hands of such agencies operating at arm's length (Everson, 1995; Shapiro, 1997; Vos, 2000; Flinders, 2004; Curtin, 2005; Williams, 2005; Dehousse, 2008). In this chapter, I investigate this matter empirically by zooming in on two major forms of agency accountability: managerial accountability and political accountability. This entails looking at and assessing agency relationships with three different accountability forums at the formal (i.e. de jure) level as well as in terms of their operation in practice (i.e. de facto level). Throughout the analysis, I use the key components of the analytical framework described in Chapter 3. The analysis demonstrates that while there are accountability arrangements in operation and there has even been an expansion of agencies' accountability obligations, the existing fabric of accountability has significant imperfections that need to be addressed in the future.

Investigating EU Agency Accountability

Agencies are enveloped in a complex web of accountability relations to multiple forums. A mapping exercise of the various accountability arrangements in place reveals four main forms of agency accountability: managerial, political, financial, and (quasi-)legal accountability (Busuioc, 2010). Table 5.1 provides an overview of the various forms of accountability to which agencies are subject and the main forums involved.

This chapter focuses on managerial and political accountability (see further Busuioc, 2010). Management boards represent the main and most immediate confines on the grant of authority to agencies and their directors. Political accountability forums are high-profile, outside checks on agency behaviour. Both are crucial to preventing agency misbehaviour by taking a broad view of and monitoring agency behaviour and performance at large (as opposed to only 'specific' and/or technical aspects).

However, despite their key role in holding agencies in check, both represent greyish zones of agency accountability as they are more ad hoc in nature and less explicitly formalized in terms of their operation. Rules and practices of (quasi-)legal and financial accountability are documented in case law (of the European Courts and the European Ombudsman) and, respectively, in detailed financial reports which are part of a broad reporting cycle (i.e. discharge) and are largely publicly available. In contrast, managerial and political accountability arrangements are not. At the de jure level, these arrangements have been defined in a cursory fashion. The legal provisions give little guidance how they are to be implemented in practice. Empirical research therefore becomes indispensable to investigate how these arrangements have been fleshed out in practice and assess how they operate, whether they operate appropriately, and where failures (deficits or otherwise) occur.

Table 5.1 Types of accountability of EU agencies

Accountability types	Accountability forums
Managerial	Management boards
Political	European Parliament (EP); Council
Financial	Internal Audit Capacity, Internal Audit Service of the European Commission, European Court of Auditors, EP, Council
(Quasi-)legal	Court of Justice of the European Communities; European Ombudsman

Based on such research, this chapter casts light on EU agency accountability practices. It investigates the political and managerial accountability of five agencies: the European Aviation Safety Agency (EASA), the European Medicines Agency (EMEA), Europol, Eurojust, and the Office for Harmonization in the Internal Market (OHIM). This case selection provides for variation in terms of pillar structure that was relevant before the Treaty of Lisbon entered into force. Thus, both Community agencies (i.e. agencies belonging to the Community pillar) as well as EU agencies (i.e. agencies belonging to the intergovernmental pillars) are included in the sample. Thus for the purpose of investigating practices, it is the pre-Lisbon situation that is of relevance and will be discussed. This pre-Lisbon criterion is relevant given the fact that agencies that belonged to the Community pillar display different accountability practices from those in the intergovernmental sphere. This is particularly relevant for political accountability, as intergovernmental agenices were primarily accountable to the Council, whereas for those operating in the Community sphere, a stronger role was reserved to the European Parliament (EP). Furthermore, as accountability issues are most pertinent for the most powerful agencies, the selection focuses on the more powerful agencies possessing decision-making, (quasi-)regulatory, and operational cooperation tasks (Busuioc, 2010). The five agencies selected are instances of these three categories, that is, OHIM (decision-making), EASA and EMEA (decision-making and quasi-regulatory), and Europol and Eurojust (operational cooperation) (see Table 5.2).

This analysis draws on two main sources of data: (legal and policy) documents and interview material. The main source of data for accountability practices is constituted by forty-seven expert interviews (see Busuioc, 2010).[1]

Table 5.2 Investigating EU agency accountability: case selection

	Seat	Tasks	Pillar	Financing scheme	Staff[a]
EASA	Cologne	Decision-making and quasi-regulatory	Community pillar	EU budget (and partially self-financed)	362
OHIM	Alicante	Decision-making	Community pillar	Fully self-financed	708
EMEA	London	Decision-making and quasi-regulatory	Community pillar	EU budget (and partially self-financed)	518
Eurojust	The Hague	Operational cooperation	Union pillars (third pillar)	EU budget	179
Europol	The Hague	Operational cooperation	Union pillars (third pillar)	Member state financed[b]	433

[a] For EASA, OHIM, EMEA, and Eurojust, see the latest special annual reports of the European Court of Auditors from 2008 for the financial year 2007, OJ C 311, 05.12.2008. For Europol, see <http://register.consilium.europa.eu/pdf/en/08/st07802.en08.pdf>, the number of staff was for the 2008 budget.
[b] This changes with the Europol Council Decision, the Europol budget becomes communitarized.

Respondent selection was focused on creating a balanced variety of roles, perspectives, and experiences, encompassing senior agency officials as well as representatives of the three accountability forums (management boards, EP, and Council structures).

Promises and Pitfalls of Managerial Accountability

Boards are referred to by different names across agencies. Several terms are used to refer to what is by and large the same type of body: management board (i.e. the most commonly used, which we will adopt hereafter), administrative board, budget committee (i.e. OHIM), College (i.e. Eurojust), etc.[2] Also, in the case of agency heads, different terms are used for this function across agencies: executive director (most commonly) and president (e.g. OHIM, Eurojust). Management boards carry out two basic functions: they steer the organization and they exercise oversight over the functioning of the agency by monitoring the work of the director. It is this monitoring role of the board vis-à-vis the agency and the director that is of relevance for the present study.

By virtue of their hybrid role, boards carry out a broad array of functions ranging from supervisory roles in terms of budgetary and planning matters, monitoring the work of the director and the agencies' performance as well as tasks in terms of setting the strategic direction of the agency, approving the work programme, adopting legally binding implementing rules, etc. Moreover, although rules on this vary, most basic regulations reserve a role for the board in the appointment and the removal of the director. For example, in terms of appointment, some management boards appoint the director on a proposal by the Commission. In some other cases, the board draws a shortlist of applicants from which the Council or the Commission makes the final selection and appointment.

Rules regarding the composition of the management boards vary but, in general, boards tend to be very large, comprising a representative from each member state as well as depending on agency representatives from the Commission and, in some cases, the EP and/or relevant stakeholders.[3] Given their composition, management boards not only are an instance of managerial accountability, but in fact can also be seen as a lower tier of political accountability. This is then supplemented, as we shall see later on in this chapter, by other upper echelons of political accountability in the form of political accountability to the EP and the Council.

Formal lines of accountability to the board tend to be defined very broadly: 'the director shall be accountable to the Management Board in respect of the performance of his duties', 'the Management Board shall exercise disciplinary authority over the Executive Director and over the Directors', etc.[4] Such provisions give little guidance as to how this accountability arrangement is (to be) implemented in the real world. For what is the director accountable to the board? How does it take place? And to what extent? Is it a fully fledged process of accountability informing, debating, and sanctioning, or is it more truncated?

Information: Provided, but Processed?

We consider two key aspects of informing: whether information is supplied by the actor, and whether this information results in the forum being 'informed'. Below we will see that whereas the first element is generally satisfied, failures intervene in terms of the forum actually processing the information received from the actor.

The manner and content of information provision by the agency vary in practice from one agency to the next depending on, among others, the frequency of board meetings, agreed rules of procedure, established practices, and internal dynamics of the executive–board relationship. All of the agencies are legally required to provide the board with the annual report and with information regarding the execution of the budget. These documents are part of a bigger reporting cycle. After the board has seen them, they are also submitted to several European institutions. They are also publicly accessible. These most basic of reporting obligations are complied with in all the agencies studied.

Moreover, according to the framework Financial Regulation, all European agency directors, in their authorizing officer capacity, are expected to submit an annual activity report to the board.[5] Additionally, by virtue of the same regulation, agencies are required to regularly undertake evaluations of their programmes and activities, which are to be submitted to the management boards.[6] The basic regulations of some agencies also provide for an initial evaluation after three or five years of operation, which is to be followed by subsequent evaluations at regular intervals. In its 2008 special audit report, the Court of Auditors concluded that all the agencies had submitted activity reports to their boards as well as complied with their evaluation requirements, with reports being produced within the time limits (European Court of Auditors, 2008a: 24–5).

Informal informing practices have also emerged. For example, the EMEA director gives a verbal 'highlights' presentation during each board meeting, describing the work of the agency for the previous three months as well as planning for the following three months. The Europol director gives a brief written and oral report at every management board meeting. Moreover, once a year, in addition to the annual report, he submits an internal evaluation report to the board on the performance of Europol.

Generally, management board representatives felt that they were sufficiently and adequately informed by the agency. Not all boards were satisfied, however. In the case of Europol for instance, respondents found it difficult to give an overall assessment of the information received from the agency and pointed out that 'it's difficult to judge whether we are getting enough information, the right information' (Respondent #16). One of the main problems was deemed to be the fragmentation of information provided by Europol to various Europol structures: the management board meetings, the Heads of National Unit meetings, and the liaison officers meetings.

There is also a certain amount of confusion over what exactly the accountability of the director to the board amounts to: what are his precise obligations and what precisely is the division of responsibilities? Various accounts (e.g. multiple interviews and board minutes; Europol Management Board, 2006: 28) refer to recurrent tensions over reports to be drafted, being sent back, redrafted, and rejected yet again. As observed by the Europol director at the time, 'if you look at the management board meetings, we have now had 64–65 meetings of the management board, you will see that very often the core of the debate was what are the rights of the director what are the rights of the management board'.

Furthermore, in the case of Europol there is a second tier of reporting, vis-à-vis the Council. The accountability lines become entangled and distorted, with the two forums pointing in different directions and the board occasionally taking a different stance from the Council. This complicates the director's life from time to time:

> when I present to the management board what was discussed with the Council, I sometimes get as a reaction from the board and this happened last week, 'we do not fully share the view of the Council'. Interesting to me, how can a board not fully share the view of the Council. I was raised as a civil servant in Germany and being a civil servant in Germany, there's a clear law that political will is guiding the system and the civil servants have to support the political system unless it's contrary to the law, of course.

Such dynamics are not coincidental. They reproduce tensions inherent in the creation of Europol, and in fact of the EU in general, as a top-down, political project. In the case of Europol, this seems to have engendered resistance and mistrust at the lower levels with a clear dissonance between the higher political-level will and the more street level of the management board.

The quality of *being informed* not only depends on being provided with sufficient information. The forum should also be able to prepare for the meetings, digest the information provided, and have the expertise to assess the information provided. These conditions are not always met. Firstly, a significant number of delegations tend to be ill-prepared for meetings. This constitutes a significant cross-agency concern. One of the EASA directors observed, 'I think that the vast majority of the members of the board do not have time enough to go in detail and to be sufficiently informed about the agency. They know of course the agency but not sufficiently in detail and maybe they don't read sufficiently all the documents we send to them and it doesn't appear that they make a reflection on those documents'.

Similar observations were made in connection with some of the members of the EMEA management board. Respondents generally believed that not all EMEA board members prepared the documents provided for the board meetings. Its director gave a very telling example: 'Some years ago, we made a mistake. We sent a mailing to the board in paper format, now we send it electronically and we forgot to copy, we had double copies . . . there was one page missing, not for all the members but for half of the members of the board. And before the meeting we didn't hear anything. Nobody noticed. They didn't read the document before they came to the meeting'.

Secondly, a recurring issue across agencies pertains to underlying knowledge deficits of board members on financial, administrative, and strategic matters. This compromises their ability to process the information received and to assess the actor's performance in these matters. While generally experts in the core substantive subject matter of the agency's work, most delegations are not equipped with managerial knowledge. In the words of one agency director, 'the quality of the members of the delegation is not high. These are not really good people . . . I think they are so much in their specialized world that they forgot normal management and normal policy making issues'.

Again, this ought not to surprise anyone. Foundational discussions on board composition have tended to be fairly politicized and frequently entailed avid debate between the Commission, member states, and even the EP on issues of representation and voting rights of the various parties concerned. How to safeguard their competence and commitment as members of an accountability forum was not much of a consideration.

The discussion is ongoing, with the Commission trying to obtain more votes in the management boards (Commission of the European Communities, 2008).

Debate: Imperfect Interaction

Information submitted by the director to the board is largely discussed during the meetings of the management board, whose meeting frequencies vary. The management board of Europol meets six times a year, those of EASA and EMEA four times, OHIM's only twice. A more special case is Eurojust, where the management board representatives (i.e. the College members) are also the drivers of the operational work, and so they meet twice a week. All board respondents felt that there were satisfactory possibilities for discussions with the director. They did, however, mention various impediments to quality deliberation: board size, board focus, board conflicts of interest, and inadequate participation from board delegations.

Firstly, boards are generally outright plethoric in their composition, which seriously restricts their capacity to enact their roles. In some agencies, the size of the board (when including the presence of alternates, observers as well as other members of member state delegations, e.g., in some cases advisers and experts) actually eclipses the size of the overall staff of the agency. For example, the European Agency for Health and Safety at Work (EU-OSHA) is listed in the latest audit report of the agency by the Court of Auditors as having a total staff of sixty-three employees (European Court of Auditors, 2008*b*: 52). Its management board, however, has a grand total of eighty-four management board members without even counting in alternates. Similarly, the European Police College (CEPOL) has a staff of twenty-one employees (European Court of Auditors, 2008*c*: 139) and a governing board composed of one representative from each member state, so twenty-seven board members. And, wider research shows that EU-OSHA and CEPOL are by no means alone in this predicament (Busuioc, 2010).

Though not so utterly excessive, board *size* in the five sampled agencies is nevertheless unwieldy. Member state delegations have not only one representative but an alternate as well, and in some cases delegations are composed of three or four persons. The Europol board thus counts well above one hundred participants, for example. The sheer size of such boards allows very little time for interventions, let alone for debate going into any depth on specific topics. In this connection, one agency director remarked, 'when you have large boards like this they are not operational, they can't be an inspiring partner to you, so the board and the construction of this kind of board does not help an executive director and does not help the agency in a professional way to steer the organization'.

Secondly, respondents felt that the board's *focus* was unhelpful. Two problems stood out: overemphasizing micromanagement details at the expense of strategic discussion, and focusing on issues affecting national interests to the detriment of scrutiny of overall agency performance. The bias towards micromanagement seems to be particularly problematic in the case of Europol. The board gets almost completely sidetracked into administrative and technical details as opposed to considering the status of analytical work files (AWFs) or the agency's strategy. In the words of one respondent, 'the agenda of the management board is in my opinion too much buried in details. I think there is at the moment a lack of discussion on substance' (Respondent #26). This is further corroborated by Peter Storr, the UK representative in the Article 36 Committee, who in his evidence before the House of Lords stated that the management board of Europol was becoming 'a little bit bogged down in the sort of day-to-day detail which in a police force within this country you would expect the chief officer of police to undertake without reference . . . ' (House of Lords, 2008: 42).

The strategy deficit in the case of Europol was perceived to be so significant that remedial measures were undertaken. The new Council Decision that is to replace the Europol Convention as of 1 January 2010 specifically mentions that the board is 'to adopt a strategy for Europol' and that it is the responsibility of the chairman of the board to ensure 'a specific focus on strategic issues' on the part of the board.[7]

Board focus on micromanagement at the expense of strategic discussion is not restricted to the sampled agencies. The 2003 meta-evaluation refers to an overemphasis of boards' activities on administrative details to the detriment of strategic issues in the case of several other agencies, that is, CEDEFOP, ETF, EEA, EMCDDA (European Commission, 2003*b*: 53). This ties in with the previous observations concerning board recruitment and the fact that board composition is not fully tailored to the needs of the agency and the subsequent tasks that board members are expected to fulfil. In this connection, studies at the national level observe that 'the selection of board members for their management expertise and experience contributed to the board's strategic contribution and its capacity to influence strategic decisions' (Edwards and Cornforth, 2003: 91). It is not surprising that the boards of agencies fall short on this aspect given that expertise does not feature among the criteria for board selection and the dominant consideration remains representation.

In some cases, respondents noted board tendencies to be preoccupied by national interest issues rather than overall agency performance. This situation was most pronounced in case of OHIM, where, reportedly, aspects pertaining to the agency's performance did not raise much interest in the board. The board is composed of the heads of national patent and trademarks offices, which exist in parallel with OHIM. So board members are heads of corresponding national agencies and they also head, steer, and monitor a European agency that is in direct competition with their national offices. Not surprisingly, board delegations show little concern for the performance of the European agency. As observed by one board representative, 'I personally appreciated very much what Mr. de Boer [the president of OHIM] has done, I support him as much as I can but there are people who have shown so far a limited interest. They think it is interesting that he has raised efficiency but if he had not then that could go by' (Respondent #19). The same situation is also reported by the president, who feels that the performance of the agency is of minimal concern among board members. In his own words,

> the agenda of the board would be that in a meeting of a day and half we would spend perhaps one hour at most on what happens in the Office: performance, developments, plans and the rest is about themselves. I remember one delegate saying, at the beginning of one meeting as I was about to set out on my half an hour reporting of what happened in the last months, 'can we not speed this up?'

There are clear indications that OHIM's board behaviour is shaped in no small part by *conflicts of interest*. Keen to protect their national offices, not only do board members not take an interest in the performance of the European office, but according to the president, they effectively seek to halt it. In his own words, 'when they come to Alicante, they talk about the "worries of their offices". They don't say it in that way but they try to stop development from our side. That's what it is. And that is a very strange role for an administrator: they don't want us to get better'. Given the multilevel nature of EU governance, struggles for competing, legitimate interests between the EU level and the national level are to some extent part and parcel of the system. However, in this case, the board members (by virtue of their double-hattedness) have a vested interest running contrary to their acting as a proper accountability forum at the European level.

A final constraint on the quality of debate in some boards is that a large number of *delegations do not participate*. Some delegations systematically abstain from raising questions or making comments. In the case of EASA, a management board representative observed that 'there are at least half the people, to be honest, who virtually say nothing, which is slightly strange'. Similarly, one EMEA board member observed that 'there's a substantial part of the board that doesn't speak during the meetings. Mostly there are some people that you are absolutely sure that they will say something. I can give you 5 or 6 names that will speak up during the meeting next Thursday, maybe even more, but I can also tell you about 10 people that I am dead sure that they won't speak up'. Similar concerns were voiced in the context of Europol.

In both EMEA and EASA, board members' lack of time and resources were at the heart of the problem. By default, board debates are dominated by only a handful of delegations whose constituent organizations do properly facilitate their work. In addition to resource issues, lack of interest in the workings of the agency, lack of preparation, or even language problems have also been put forward as possible explanations for the lack of participation in debates. With the exception of Eurojust, where the members of the management board (i.e. the College) are virtually the drivers of the operational work and are involved in the day-to day work of the organization, the members of the management board of all the other agencies are employed full time in national agencies or ministries. As such, they remain nationally minded bureaucrats, whose local priorities and national outlook dominate their encounters (Geuijen et al., 2008: 86).

Consequences: All or Nothing

Agencies' basic regulations provide for only one direct formal sanction: the dismissal of the director. There are different rules in place over who is the final authority to exercise the ultimate sanction vis-à-vis the director. An overview of these provisions for the five agencies researched is provided in Table 5.3.

Indirectly, the board does possess other sanctions. Agency work programmes and budgets need their approval; withholding it constitutes an important stick that boards can wield. The ultimate sanction of dismissal has never been used in practice in any of the five agencies studied. Strong reluctance to do so was voiced by all the management board respondents. Similarly, directors also observed that dismissal was not a likely sanction to be employed by the board. In the words of one of them, it 'is like the nuclear bomb you know... You don't want to use it because if you do, it destroys everything' (Respondent #53). Several respondents felt that incompetence or inefficiency alone would not result in removal and that it

Table 5.3 Management boards' sanctioning powers vis-à-vis agency directors

EMEA	The management board may dismiss the director based on a proposal from the Commission
EASA	The management board can dismiss the director on a proposal from the Commission
OHIM	The president can be dismissed by the Council acting on a proposal from the administrative board
Eurojust	The administrative director may be removed from office by the College by a two-third majority
Europol	The director can be dismissed by a decision of the Council after obtaining the opinion of the management board

would only be used in cases of criminal activities and fraud. Hence, as Thatcher (2002: 960; 2005: 352) argues for domestic agencies, principals do not use such strong sanctions because they feel that alternative methods are more effective, and that agency losses from not doing so are outweighed by the costs of using controls (see further Busuioc, 2010). To this extent, formal sanctioning is a sort of Damocles' sword, hanging over the directors' heads but rather unlikely to be wielded.

Political Accountability on the Rise

Having examined agencies' accountability towards their boards, let us now turn to the high-level political echelons, that is, the EP and the Council, and observe how they hold agencies as bodies to account politically, at the European level.

Political Accountability (I): The EP

The accountability powers of the EP vis-à-vis agencies pertain primarily to budgets and money, as well as aspects of agency performance. With regard to the latter, the EP has a few instruments at its disposal (e.g. annual report, hearings) that allow it to scrutinize aspects relating to the performance of a particular agency and the execution of its tasks. The locus of this type of monitoring tends to be primarily within specialized, technical committees. Specific agencies are linked to a specialized committee in their area of expertise. In the case of our sampled agencies, those are the Committee on Transport and Tourism (i.e. TRAN) for EASA, the Committee on Environment, Public Health, and Food Safety (i.e. ENVI) for EMEA, the Committee on Legal Affairs (i.e. JURI) for OHIM, and the Committee on

Civil Liberties, Justice, and Home Affairs (i.e. LIBE) for Europol and Eurojust (European Parliament, 2008: 15–17). As far as money and budgets are concerned, the EP is the authority responsible for the budget discharge of agencies funded from the EU budget. In this context, the EP is at the centre of a nexus of forums, including the Commission's internal auditor (i.e. IAS) and the European Court of Auditors, that are involved in the financial accountability of agencies.

The formal accountability obligations of different agencies vis-à-vis the EP vary. Agencies that belonged to the Community pillar, where the EP has long had a strong role as the joint legislative and budgetary authority, have a broader array of accountability obligations vis-à-vis the Parliament.[8] The EP has been able to progressively expand its powers vis-à-vis these agencies particularly in the third wave of agency creation. This is most likely a by-product of the growing legislative influence of the EP (Groenleer, 2006: 164). The Parliament used its co-decision powers to insert new procedures of parliamentary accountability in the basic regulations of agencies thus increasing parliamentary power vis-à-vis agencies. Consequently, hearings of the director prior to appointment and/or regular hearings on the carrying-out of his/her tasks by the competent committee of the EP were provided for in the case of more recent agencies (e.g. EASA, European Railway Agency, European Chemicals Agency, etc.). This was also the case for already established agencies whose legal basis was revised and the new basic act was adopted on the basis of co-decision (e.g. EMEA).

In the more intergovernmental second and third pillars, the EP's almost non-existent role in practice in agency oversight is a reflection of the minimal powers reserved to the EP in these areas pre-Lisbon. The EP was not involved in the setting up of the three agencies belonging to the second pillar (i.e. the European Institute for Security Studies, the European Defence Agency and the European Union Satellite Centre). Similarly, it was not even consulted in the negotiation and drafting of the Europol Convention (den Boer, 2002: 283; Curtin, 2005: 100; Peers, 2005). As a result, procedures of parliamentary accountability are largely lacking in the case of all four agencies and instruments of accountability remain in the hands of intergovernmental actors such as the Council and the management boards.

Moreover, these bodies are funded not from the EU budget but directly by member state contributions. They are thus not subject to the discharge procedure by the EP. Exceptions to this rule are the European Police College (CEPOL) and Eurojust which, although third-pillar agencies like Europol, have been 'communitarized' in terms of their budget. As such, the EP has a stronger position as the budgetary authority and, implicitly, the budget discharge authority. Further improvement in the status of the EP vis-à-vis Europol will come about with the application of the new Europol Council Decision.[9] By virtue of the Decision, Europol's budget becomes 'communitarized', and thus the EP becomes the budget discharge authority. Below we will focus on the role of the EP in holding agencies politically accountable by means of its specialized committees without delving into EP's role in supervising agencies on more technical budgetary and financial matters.

INFORMATION: DE JURE AND DE FACTO

All agencies under study submit an annual report as well as, in some cases, work programmes to the EP. Europol and Eurojust, as stipulated in their constituent acts, do not submit their reports directly to the Parliament but instead to the Council, which subsequently forwards it to the Parliament – highlighting the lack of a direct line of accountability between these agencies and the Parliament. There are no legal provisions for dialogue between the EP and the agencies regarding these reports. De jure, the EP is not required to react on the annual report and in practice it has not reacted on any of the agencies' reports, according to directors. This makes it difficult to assess the informative character of the report and the extent to which it is being read and has an impact. The EP Committee on Budgets felt that the attention given to the annual report by the specialized committee was poor (Respondent #13) and in 2007 it introduced as one of the conditions for the release of 10 per cent of agency reserves that 'the specialized committees have to give a positive evaluation of the performance of the agency against its work programme' (European Parliament, 2007b: 5–6). Such a letter of assurance is not a watertight guarantee that the two reports have an actual impact. Yet it is meant to ensure that the reports are considered by the specialized committees. This guarantee, however meagre, does not apply to Europol, or any other agency not funded from the EU budget, since the Committee on Budgets has no powers in this case.

In addition to the annual reports the Parliament also has access to the horizontal evaluations of agencies. As noted above, independent evaluation reports are to be undertaken periodically by virtue of the framework Financial Regulation, as well as the constituent acts of some agencies. Likewise, with the amendments to the Eurojust Decision and the adoption of the new Europol Decision, independent periodic evaluation reports are to be undertaken for these bodies as well, which are to be forwarded to the EP.[10] In September 2003, a meta-evaluation was published by the Commission based on the external evaluations available at the time (European Commission, 2003*b*). A new horizontal evaluation is envisaged to take place and the Commission is to submit the results to the EP and the Council. The EP has already urged the Commission to ensure that the results of the evaluation are submitted before the end of the 2009–10 period (European Parliament, 2008). They are meant to serve as a basis to assess agency performance, revise or in extreme cases even end an agency's mandate. They are also to serve as a source of information for an envisaged inter-institutional working group, which is to draw a common framework for agencies and to define the competences of each EU institution vis-à-vis agencies.

DEBATE: PATCHINESS PREVAILS

In addition to receiving agency information the Parliament can choose to conduct hearings on agency matters. There are three possibilities: (*a*) budget cycle hearings before its two budgetary committees (only agencies funded from the EU budget take part in this type of hearing), (*b*) appointment hearings with candidate directors, and (*c*) performance hearings with incumbent directors. The latter two take place before the specialized 'parent' committee of the agency and they are more common in the case of agencies set up on the basis of co-decision procedure (e.g. EASA and EMEA).[11] Moreover, in addition to appointment hearings, EASA basic regulation also provides that the EP 'may invite the Executive Director to report on the carrying out of his/her tasks'.[12] No similar provisions are contained in the basic regulation of EMEA.

The heads of Europol, Eurojust, and OHIM are not required to appear for hearings before the EP. In the case of Europol, the director may, but need not, appear before the EP. Instead, the Presidency of the Council 'may appear before the European Parliament with a view to discuss general questions relating to Europol', and 'may be assisted by the director' when doing so.[13] In practice, the heads of EASA, EMEA, Eurojust, and Europol do appear for hearings before the relevant technical committees of the EP. Particularly in the case of Europol, much has been made in the literature about the lack of any form of parliamentary accountability. Yet in reality there are regular contacts between MEPs and Europol (i.e. parliamentary visits to Europol, parliamentary requests for information) as well as informal hearings of the

Europol director before the LIBE committee. These hearings become formalized with the application of the Europol Decision.[14] Finally, the director of OHIM is not required to appear for hearings and de facto also has not attended any hearings before the JURI Committee. Thus, based on the overview of de jure provisions and de facto practices, the EP's role vis-à-vis OHIM is most restricted compared with the other sampled agencies as the EP receives only a management report.

I noted earlier that the lack of interest of account-holders (i.e. management board members) impedes meaningful accountability debate. In the case of the EP the results are mixed, with some committees reportedly displaying a high level of interest in their agencies, and others a very low level. Agency respondents from EASA and EMEA report that members of the relevant technical committees are interested in the agency and its work. In the words of the EMEA executive director, 'we always have good relations and they are always interested in what we are doing and they have been happy what we have delivered'. Or according to the EASA administrative director, 'they [TRAN Committee MEPs] are very active and they know us well and they support us as well'.

This constitutes a clear break from the past. At the early stages of the agencification process, the interest and involvement of the EP was close to zero. It was left to agencies to virtually lobby for the attention of the EP. In the words of the first EMEA executive director,

> at the beginning of the EMEA (in 1995), it was difficult to get the attention of the Parliament. In a way, the appointment of two university professors in the board was considered sufficient to represent Parliament's interests. In fact, the EP Committee responsible for Environment and Health did not have regular contacts with their own representatives (no funds available initially for them to meet the Committee). I had to ask to be heard and invited MEPs to visit the EMEA in London. This started a tradition of annual 'hearings' of the EMEA during the Parliament's Environment and Health Committee sessions in Brussels, in the presence of the two EP representatives in the Board.

The improvement in the debate between the EP and agencies is also echoed from within the Parliament itself. According to one of the EP rapporteurs, 'in the past the connection between all the agencies and the European Parliament was not so strong, not so clear but now the communication and the working together has improved a lot' (Respondent #63).

This growth of parliamentary interest in agencies is partially the result of ad hoc accountability practices initiated by some agencies in an effort to gain parliamentary attention. With the passage of time, these procedures have developed into regular practices. One of the possible explanations for the proactive role of agencies in seeking parliamentary accountability could be that voluntary accountability arrangement serve as a strategy to promote agency visibility, credibility, and, paradoxically, to achieve greater autonomy (Schillemans, 2006).

In addition to this, an even more vital element to organizational survival might have played a role: competition for resources. Agencies have to compete with each other for a limited amount of resources and the EP can be a powerful ally in this struggle. They have partly embraced new practices of informing and account-giving in order to raise their profile with the EP as a way to enlist parliamentary support at the budgetary phase. As one director noted: 'The support of the technical committee is indispensable' (Respondent #56). In the words of another director: 'Every year it's a new issue, because every year you need to get money. So you need to interact with them in order to have the right relation with them and give them the right information and justification why we should have all the money and not the other ones' (Respondent #39). This is confirmed by the rapporteur on agencies in the Budget Committee. According to the rapporteur, a strong connection with the specialized committee is crucial: 'some colleagues in the specialized committees are very strong and they know a lot about their agency and the connection is very strong between the specialized committee and the agencies. I think this is the best way to get what you need to get as an agency. To have a strong connection to your parent committee.'

Accountability can thus be 'good for business'. Some agencies have therefore grabbed the opportunity to 'invest' in new accountability relations to the EP. Not all of them have been equally successful in capturing the attention of their 'parent' parliamentary committee. Whereas EMEA and EASA directors reported strong interest from their technical committees, this does not apply to, for instance, the third-pillar agency Eurojust. As explained by the Eurojust president,

> I think what is disappointing is that there are not actually many deputies there [when he presents to LIBE]. We go to the Committee and expect a lot of deputies to be there and sometimes there are seven or eight. And they come in and go during the course of the presentation. Maybe one and two stay and ask questions.

Full participation of only one to two MEPs signals low involvement in the accountability of the agency, given that the LIBE Committee has a total of fifty-five permanent members. The low level of attendance of LIBE

Committee members during agency hearings has been corroborated on the parliamentary side as well. The explanations put forward referred to the busy parliamentary agendas, the different interests of the various committee members as well as the lack of public allegations of misconduct or underperformance involving the agency. Clearly, no news is good news for a 'fire alarm'-type accountability ethos. In fact, one MEP observed that 'if only there were one or two allegations, please be sure that there would be enough colleagues to have a tough discussion' (Respondent #60).

Parliamentary interest is also low in the case of OHIM. As we have seen, there are no formal provisions in place for parliamentary scrutiny. Neither has this been overcome by informal practices as in the case of the other agencies studied. So poor was the level of interest that the president of OHIM remained unaware for a period of two years that OHIM's 'parent' committee had changed from the Committee on Internal Market and Consumer Protection (i.e. IMCO) to the Committee on Legal Affairs. In his own words, 'we seem to belong to the field of the Legal affairs committee. Mark my words, "seem to". I have never appeared before this committee. Never, ever. It took me two years to realize that it had changed from one parliamentary committee that I did not meet to another committee that I did not meet either.'

When the EP committees do debate agency work, what do they focus on? Like other parliamentary bodies, they exercise oversight by 'fire alarm'. In the words of one of the directors, 'EP hearings and "grillings" are impressive but tend to focus on a limited number of sensitive issues, rather than on the overall performance of an agency or its director' (Respondent #56). Highly mediatized and politicized issues gain most attention. This in itself is not surprising, nor is it necessarily problematic. It has been suggested that fire alarm supervision is a more desirable role for the EP than ongoing supervision (i.e. police patrolling), which would be a huge drain on the EP's financial and staffing resources (Hix, 2000: 76–8). Nevertheless, this does mean that parliamentary accountability is a blunt tool for assessing overall agency performance.

To be sure, many of such limitations of EP scrutiny of agencies have been reported in terms of national parliaments and their propensity to interrogate national agencies. In this connection, Mulgan (2003: 61) observes,

> legislative committees continue to disappoint as mechanisms for monitoring the performance of government agencies . . . Key accountability issues relating to the quality or cost of government performance in major areas of public expenditure are often neglected in favour of more politically sensational

inquiries. Topics for investigation tend to be set by political rather than administrative agendas, undermining the expectation, probably unrealistic, that committees of politicians could act as professional and dispassionate scrutinizers of bureaucratic efficiency and effectiveness.

On a similar note, Schillemans points at the inadequacies of parliamentary accountability in ensuring comprehensive and systematic scrutiny. In his words, 'the oversight of ministers and parliament is always focused on a limited number of politically salient issues...The consequence is that demands for accountability from the centre may focus on issues that are peripheral to the tasks of specific agencies and that important or even all aspects of their behaviour remain unaccounted for' (Schillemans, 2009: 10).

While acknowledging that the EP is not alone and that similar failings occur at the national level, this nevertheless remains problematic, as without the supplementation of other forms of accountability, key areas of European agencies' behaviour would remain shaded from scrutiny. Moreover, the patchiness of these accountability processes also translates into a lack of a coherent view on the future of the agency and the impossibility to have discussions on the development of the agency and long-term strategic planning. In the words of an agency director,

> I think that the Parliament should have a clear view on the future of the agency and the strategy of the agency...I feel a bit isolated, I would say, regarding strategy. We are doing our strategy together here with the directors but it is difficult to discuss the strategy of the agency with someone else, be that either the Commission, the management board or even the Parliament. (Respondent #45)

CONSEQUENCES: THE EP EMPOWERED OR 'TOOTHLESS'?

What happens in case of a negative parliamentary assessment resulting from the examination of the annual report and/or following from hearings? Is there any possibility for sanctions? Or is the EP 'toothless' vis-à-vis agencies? As mentioned above, in its attempt to ensure a rapprochement between agencies and their relevant specialized committees, the Committee on Budgets has 'armed' the specialized committees. Should the relevant specialized committees choose to withhold endorsement of the agencies' annual report and work programme, the Committee on Budgets will refuse to release 10 per cent of the respective agencies' budget. This has not yet taken place. The Committee on Budgets declared itself satisfied, pointing out that 'most committees have already sent official letters to the Committee on Budgets giving the green light for releasing the reserves for their agencies' (European Parliament, 2008: 6).

Additionally, the specialized committee can play a role in the budget set-up process and the specialized committee could champion the cause of the agency before the Committee on Budgets. However, in case of dissatisfaction of the committee or poor relations between the agency and the relevant committee, this implicitly contains a negative sanction: the withdrawal of support. These sanctions, however, apply only to those agencies funded from the Community budget. Self-funded (e.g. OHIM) or member-state-funded (e.g. Europol prior to 1 January 2010) agencies are not subject to committee sanctions.

Finally, the EP has the ultimate weapon at its disposal: it can rewrite or even terminate the mandate of its agencies in the event of underperformance. In fact, in expectation of the upcoming horizontal evaluation of European agencies, the Parliament has requested the Commission to devise clear benchmarks for comparing cross-agency results and 'to lay down clear rules for ending the mandate of agencies in the event of poor performance' (European Parliament, 2008: 7). But it is yet to use its 'big stick'. Vis-à-vis Europol, the EP lacked the power to block amendments to the Europol Convention or implementing measures and to exert any type of control over the conclusions of treaties by Europol with third countries or bodies. In an attempt to express its disapproval, the EP has rejected all proposals for implementing measures or protocols to the Europol Convention (Peers, 2005: 259). De facto, this remained a moot exercise in terms of impact, since the refusal of the EP has no binding power. This situation will greatly improve with the new Council Decision, which will result in a veritable empowerment of the Parliament as the budgetary authority.

Political Accountability (II): The Council of Ministers

Both Europol and Eurojust are primarily creatures of the Council. Political accountability of these bodies takes place largely via the Council structures. The Council is also the discharge authority for agencies funded by member states, whereas for agencies funded from the EU budget, the Council only issues a recommendation on discharge to the EP.

INFORMATION AND DEBATE: FLUID PRACTICES

In terms of reporting, both Europol and Eurojust are required to submit reports to the Council. According to the Eurojust Decision, the president is expected to 'report to the Council every year on the activities and management, including budgetary management, of Eurojust'.[15] In addition to this annual report, the Decision provides that the president should submit any report or any information on the operation of Eurojust required by the Council, thus granting unbounded access to information to the Council on issues pertinent to Eurojust's operation. The new amendments to the Eurojust Decision also provide for periodic independent evaluation reports on Eurojust's activities to be commissioned by the College, which are to be forwarded to the Council.[16]

According to the Europol Convention Article 28 (10), the management board of Europol is required to submit to the Council an annual report and a work programme.[17] With the new Decision, as in the case of Eurojust, provisions are made for the undertaking of periodic external evaluations, which will be forwarded to the Council.[18] Moreover, the director is required to report regularly in its annual report on Europol's external relations with third states and non-EU-related bodies.[19]

It should be noted that the Council also exercises *control* as opposed to *accountability* (Busuioc, 2009) over Europol's agreements with third states and non-EU-related bodies. It has several controls at its disposal. First of all, the director can only start negotiations with third states and non-EU bodies that the Council has unanimously agreed upon.[20] The director needs the specific authorization of the Council and this authorization can be conditional. Moreover, the draft agreement negotiated can be concluded only once the Council has given its unanimous approval after receiving a report from the Joint Supervisory Authority on data protection rules. This is an instance of control, as the Council not only retrospectively demands explanations from the actor (i.e. Europol) but in fact, remains in the driving seat during the whole process and the actor is unable to act without the prior consent of the principal (i.e. the Council). This is particularly relevant as this is an area where the EP was powerless. While the supervision as well as the control exercised by the Council are not a substitute for the oversight of a democratic, directly elected EP, this nevertheless entails that the Europol director is by no means a free agent in the adoption of such agreements.

The Council does not hold first-pillar agencies accountable except for provisions for receiving the annual report and the work programme (e.g. for EASA and EMEA). EASA's basic regulation does create the possibility of hearings before the Council (just as in the case of the EP).[21] It also has some role in relation to two fully self-financed agencies, that is, OHIM and the Community Plant Variety Office (CPVO). In the case of OHIM as discussed above, the EP receives only a management report and there are no hearings before the specialized committee, either de jure or de facto. The powers of the Council at the formal level are broader. According to the OHIM constituent act, the Council 'shall exercise disciplinary authority' over the president and the vice-president(s).[22] Furthermore, the Council has a role in the appointment and removal of the president and vice-president(s). The Council appoints the president from a shortlist drawn up by the administrative board and it can dismiss him/her at the administrative board's proposal.[23]

Does the Council actually engage agencies in discussions? Not so for EASA and OHIM. No hearings are undertaken with EASA, and the OHIM president reports never having had to appear before the Council. The texts of the Europol Convention and the Eurojust Decision do not provide for any form of debate on the annual reports or any hearings before the Council or its lower structures. De facto, however, such meetings take place regularly. Both the director of Europol and the president of Eurojust appear before the Council and/or its lower structures at the latter's invitation. This is usually complemented or even replaced by meetings before lower Council structures: lower working groups and the Article 36 Committee particularly, which prepare the meetings and the agenda for the Justice and Home Affairs (JHA) Council.

Thus, accountability practices before the Council are fluid. They depend on patterns of previous hearings, priorities and interests of the Council Secretariat, and the current Presidency, as well as the overall level of satisfaction with agency performance. Even when they do take place, hearings at the full Council level are more like 'ritual dances' given the fact that a significant number of the issues are being decided upon in the lower structures and the ministers simply rubber stamp these decisions (Hayes-Renshaw and Wallace, 1997: 78).

However, in the case of Eurojust, the examination of the annual report does result in direct Council feedback. The Council reacts on the annual report of Eurojust with conclusions which contain both an assessment of its performance during the previous year and of future directions and tasks to be taken up by Eurojust in the following year. The conclusions also invite Eurojust to report on the implementation of the conclusions. In other words, there is a follow-up and Eurojust is expected to give feedback to the Council on the state of implementation.

The picture for Europol is yet again different. The annual report of Europol is submitted to the Council only 'to take note and endorse'.[24] To this extent, the accountability process through the Council structures is more comprehensive and better developed from an institutional learning perspective in the case of Eurojust than it is for Europol. Moreover, respondents from the board reportedly regard the assessment of Europol at the ministerial level as unrealistically positive. Respondents felt that the ministers have a skewed view compared to the reality on the ground. In the words of one respondent:

> the political speech is very much in favour: 'you are so important, you are doing so well' whereas in reality, most member states in the board say 'it's not going well at all', 'this organization is not really effective and we are not really co-operating well'. But yeah, they can't say it because their ministers would not be pleased . . . (Respondent #14)

This was confirmed by one of the management board respondents who had previously been part of the Article 36 Committee and, as such, involved in the Council oversight of Europol. Having been on both sides of the divide, he felt that the Council assessment of Europol was overly positive:

> I was active in the framework of Article 36 Committee, which is the prepara-tory meeting for the JHA Council, so I've been on the other side for almost four years . . . so I can make a comparison between what the Council thinks of Europol and what I see as a member of the management board, and the esteem or the expectations the Council has on what Europol is and what Europol could do are too high.

This relates to earlier observations concerning the dissonance between the high political level (i.e. Council) and the lower level represented by the management board. The Council has generally been very supportive of Europol whereas the board displays a much more distrustful and critical attitude. In this connection, it has been observed that 'there has been a wide gap in support between the political and the bureaucratic and profes-sional level . . .' (Groenleer, 2009: 287–315). This dissonance is further exacerbated by the lack of a direct line of communication between the board as a whole and the Council. The communication is restricted to only a handful of formal moments relating to the appointment of the director, the endorsement of the work plan and the budget, etc.

CONSEQUENCES: POSSIBLE BUT NOT LIKELY

The Council has various potential sticks at its disposal. According to the Europol Convention, the Council appoints the director and the deputy directors of Europol and it can also dismiss them, after obtaining the opinion of the management board.[25] Similarly, in the case of OHIM, the Council appoints the president and the vice-presidents and it can remove them from Office, on the proposal of the administrative board, yet the latter has never happened.[26] The Council lacks such sanctioning powers vis-à-vis the Eurojust president and the administrative director and only has an approval power in terms of the appointment of the president.[27]

Furthermore, an implicit sanctioning instrument of the Council is the possibility to rewrite and amend the basic act of these agencies. In the case of Europol, this was a very difficult process and could only be achieved through the adoption of protocols to the Convention, which had to be ratified by the national parliaments of all member states. With the application of the new Europol Decision, the process becomes much less cumbersome and the Council can make amendments through the adoption of new Council Decisions.

As in the case with other forums, the Council has not resorted to its sanctioning powers. The very act of doing so would likely become a highly public and politicized issue. And so the Council has so far been content to leave the threat lurking in the background, presumably only to be resorted to in extreme situations.

A Balance Sheet: Expanding Possibilities but Weak Practices

Where does this leave us? Is the accountability glass of EU agencies half full or half empty? I tend to say: both. It is half full in that this study reveals that formal procedures of managerial and political accountability are in fact in place for European agencies. Agencies are far from operating in an accountability-free no-man's-land. Accountability requirements are in place and the actors comply with them. Furthermore, a process of expansion of accountability has taken place at the de jure level in some cases or even outside and beyond formal provisions. In the case of managerial accountability, existing procedures are a combination of formal requirements and institutional practices that have been developed by the actors and forums concerned. Political accountability, though still patchy as we have seen, is on the rise, particularly in the case of the EP. It forms part of an evolving process, with the EP gaining formally a larger foothold in agency oversight on a par with the increase in its legislative powers. Additionally, in the case both of the Parliament and of the Council, there has been a supplementation of accountability practices (i.e. particularly in the form of hearings), which have developed informally, as a matter of practice, going above and beyond the stated obligations.

Despite this proliferation and supplementation of accountability, the existing arrangements are however by no means comprehensive, and this is where the glass is half empty. First of all, the empirical investigation reveals that in some cases there is an underuse of accountability mechanisms. Thus, while some EP committees demonstrate interest and are involved with the agencies within their remit, others display a low level of involvement and a very low attendance during hearing meetings. Correspondingly, the Council shows a predisposition towards scrutinizing more intensively its agencies (i.e. Europol and Eurojust), while all but ignoring some first-pillar agencies (i.e. OHIM and EASA), despite formal powers to engage. Particularly in the case of OHIM, this is highly unsatisfactory as the Council is the only political European principal foreseen in its contract design. Currently, there is no one to counteract the strong push for national interests and negative politicization in the OHIM board.

Such failures of practice where de jure powers do exist also apply to management boards in their monitoring roles. Boards suffer generic shortcomings, for example size and composition of the board, and often lack time, resources, or simply interest and involvement. Some boards are dominated by national interests and a mindset which is not aligned with their European roles. As a result, the asymmetries of information inherent in any delegation process are exacerbated through failures of a large number of delegations to the boards to prepare for meetings and participate in discussions. Furthermore, in cases of dissatisfaction with the performance of agency heads, board members are very reluctant to resort to formal sanctions as this can cast a negative reflection on the performance of the boards themselves. Consequently, formal sanctions run the risk of becoming an ineffective and non-credible means of exerting compliance.

The issue of underuse pertains not only to specific arrangements but also to the monitoring of particular aspects of agencies' functioning. Thus, an overwhelming number of board members lack knowledge and expertise in financial, budgetary, and managerial issues, which represent a significant part of their monitoring and steering responsibilities. Political accountability practices tend to be less intensive, incident-driven, focused on a limited number of issues, and guided by political priorities and political saliency. Both boards and political accountability forums often lack a coherent view on the future of the agency and the impossibility to have discussions on the development of the agency.

Furthermore, the manner in which formal procedures are enacted in practice becomes a source of tensions if there is an imperfect alignment of interests between the agency and the forum. As we have seen, management boards at times push for the national interest to the detriment of the agency's interest. Agencies may thus find themselves occasionally in the position of having to fight their own boards. Similarly, in the case of

Europol, tensions arose between the political will and oversight as expressed and enacted on the part of the Council and the management board. Interviews reveal the presence of a disconnect between the political level and the lower management level, with a reluctance and resistance of the latter to Europol as a top-down political project. Thus, the tensions encountered appear to stem not from inherently conflicting aims between two different accountability arrangements but rather from an imperfect alignment of interests and preferences between the agency and (one of) its forums.

The Future of Agency Accountability

This chapter suggests that the core problem in the political and managerial accountability of European agencies is generally not the absence of such arrangements but the manner in which they are enacted and operate in practice. So the road to take in improving agency accountability is generally not one of stacking up more accountability arrangements per se.[28] The emphasis should rather be on fine tuning and nurturing the arrangements already in place. Some of the failures relating to management boards could be addressed. One could create smaller-scale 'bureaus' composed of fewer delegations functioning on a rotating principle. Another option is to explicitly stipulate the formal obligation of the board to monitor strategic aspects. One might also regulate the requirements and qualifications that national delegates to the board should satisfy, which would equip them for their role and tasks on the board. Finally, certain issues, for example, fees and payments, could be removed from the boards' remit. Combined, this would allow for more efficient decision-making and monitoring by the boards while at the same time not alienating the member states since they would not be ousted from the boards altogether.

Some improvements, however, would have to go beyond changes to legal provisions and are more difficult to achieve. One of the main findings of this analysis was that, in some cases, the quantity and quality of the forum's input to the accountability process is substandard. To improve this would require a change in the culture, outlook, and mindset of the forums' members, in line with their new roles at the European level. This is an evolutionary process and will require time. Better involvement of forums, however, could be generated by raising awareness of agencies and their profiles within the EP's committees, the Council, as well as the member states.

At the same time, however, these observations need to be put into perspective. Whereas shortcomings are present, these forums are not alone in holding agencies to account, and political and managerial forums are supplemented by legal, quasi-legal (i.e. the European Ombudsman), and financial forums. Research demonstrates that these forums are actively and in fact proactively (e.g. the European Court of Justice) discharging, and in some cases even expanding, their monitoring roles (Busuioc, 2010).

Furthermore, even occasionally passive high-level political forums should not be quickly dismissed in terms of their (potential) contribution to furthering agency accountability. While reluctant or simply too busy to 'police patrol' agencies, their strength lies in cases of 'fire alarm' where they have the capacity to take sweeping remedial action. Whereas MEPs might lack the incentive to listen to a director's report and engage the latter in a debate, in situations of crisis or where serious problems involving a particular agency come to the public eye, these forums are likely to 'get their groove back' and very eagerly request information, demand answers, and enact consequences.

Notes

1. The total interview sample was sixty-three interviews. However, only forty-seven are relevant for the arrangements dealt with in this chapter.
2. In the case of OHIM, there is a split between the functions of the board, with two bodies carrying out board functions as opposed to one: the administrative board and the budget committee.
3. An exception to this is the European Food Safety Authority.
4. First quote: Article 29 (4) of Council Act of 26 July 1995 drawing up the Convention based on Article K.3 of the Treaty on European Union, on the establishment of a European Police Office (Europol Convention), OJ C 316, 27.11.1995, pp. 2–32. Second quote: Article 33 (2) (h) of Regulation (EC) No 216/2008 of the EP and of the Council of 20 February 2008 on common rules in the field of civil aviation and establishing a European Aviation Safety Agency, and repealing Council Directive 91/670/EEC, Regulation (EC) No 1592/2002 and Directive 2004/36/EC, OJ L 79, 19.03.2008, p. 1.
5. Article 40 (1) of Commission Regulation (EC, Euratom) 2343/2002 of 23 December 2002 on the framework Financial Regulation for the Bodies Referred to in Article 185 of Council Regulation (EC, Euratom) 1605/2002 on the Financial Regulation applicable to the General Budget of the European Communities, OJ L 357, 31.12. 2002, p. 72.
6. Article 25 (4) of Commission Regulation (EC, Euratom) 2343/2002 of 23 December 2002 on the framework Financial Regulation for the Bodies Referred to in Article

185 of Council Regulation (EC, Euratom) 1605/2002 on the Financial Regulation applicable to the General Budget of the European Communities, OJ L 357, 31.12. 2002.

7. First quote: Article 37 (9) (a) of Council Decision of 6 April 2009 establishing the European Police Office (Europol) (2009/371/JHA), OJ L 121, 15.05.2009, p. 37. Second quote: Article 37 (3) of Council Decision of 6 April 2009 establishing the European Police Office (Europol) (2009/371/JHA), OJ L 121, 15.05.2009.

8. With the exception of OHIM, CPVO, and the Translation Centre for the Bodies of the European Union, which are entirely self-financed, Community agencies are fully or at least partially financed from the EU budget and as such the EP acts as the discharge authority.

9. Council Decision of 6 April 2009 establishing the European Police Office (Europol) (2009/371/JHA), OJ L 121, 15.05.2009, p. 37.

10. Article 41 (a) of Council Decision 2009/426/JHA of 16 December 2008 on the strengthening of Eurojust and amending Decision 2002/187/JHA, OJ L 138, 04.06.2009, p. 14; Article 37 (11) of Council Decision of 6 April 2009 establishing the European Police Office (Europol) (2009/371/JHA), OJ L 121, 15.05.2009, p. 37.

11. Article 39 (1) of Regulation (EC) No 216/2008 of the EP and of the Council of 20 February 2008 on common rules in the field of civil aviation and establishing a European Aviation Safety Agency and repealing Council Directive 91/670/EEC, Regulation (EC) No 1592/2002 and Directive 2004/36/EC, OJ L 79, 19.03. 2008, p. 1; Article 64 (1) of Regulation (EC) No 726/2004 of the EP and of the Council of 31 March 2004 laying down Community procedures for the authorization and supervision of medicinal products for human and veterinary use and establishing a European Medicines Agency, OJ L 136, 30.04.2004, p. 1.

12. Article 38 (2) of Regulation (EC) No 216/2008 of the EP and of the Council of 20 February 2008 on common rules in the field of civil aviation and establishing a European Aviation Safety Agency, OJ L 79, 19.03. 2008, p. 1.

13. Article 34 (2) of the Europol Convention, as substituted by Articles 18 of the Danish Protocol, OJ C 002, 06.01.2004, pp. 3–12.

14. Article 48 of the Council Decision of 6 April 2009 establishing the European Police Office (Europol) (2009/371/JHA), OJ L 121, 15.05.2009, p. 37.

15. Art 32 (1) of Council Decision 2002/187/JHA of 28 February 2002 setting up Eurojust with a view to reinforcing the fight against serious crime (Eurojust Decision), OJ L 63, 06.03.2002, p. 1 last amended by Council Decision 2009/426/JHA of 16 December 2008 on the strengthening of Eurojust and amending Decision 2002/187/JHA (the New Eurojust Decision), OJ L 138, 04.06.2009, p. 14.

16. Article 41 (a) of the Eurojust Decision inserted by Council Decision 2009/426/JHA of 16 December 2008 on the strengthening of Eurojust and amending Decision 2002/187/JHA, OJ L 138, 04.06.2009, p. 14.

17. Article 28 (10) of the Europol Convention replaced by the Council Act of 27 November 2003, OJ C 002, 06.01.2004, p. 7.

18. Article 37 (11) of Council Decision of 6 April 2009 establishing the European Police Office (Europol) (2009/371/JHA), OJ L 121, 15.05.2009, p. 37.
19. Article 6 of Council Act of 3 November 1998 laying down rules governing Europol's external relations with third states and non-EU-related bodies (1999/C26/04), OJ C 26, 30.01.1999, p. 19.
20. Article 6 of Council Act of 3 November 1998 laying down rules governing Europol's external relations with third states and non-EU-related bodies (1999/C26/04), OJ C 26, 30.01.1999.
21. Article 38 (2) of Regulation (EC) No 216/2008 of the EP and of the Council of 20 February 2008 on common rules in the field of civil aviation and establishing a European Aviation Safety agency and repealing Council Directive 91/670 EEC, Regulation (EC) No 1592/2002, and Directive 2004/36/EC, OJ L 79, 19.03. 2008, p. 1.
22. Article 125 (4) Council Regulation (EC) No 207/2009 of 26 February 2009 on the Community trademark, OJ L 78, 24.03.2009, p. 1. Similar procedures are in place for the Community Plant Variety Office, with the power to appoint and dismiss the president being lodged with the Council.
23. Article 125 (1) Council Regulation (EC) No 207/2009 of 26 February 2009 on the Community trademark, OJ L 78, 24.03.2009, p. 1.
24. Article 28 (10) of the Europol Convention replaced by the Council Act of 27 November 2003, OJ C 002, 06.01.2004, p. 7.
25. Article 29 (1) and 29 (6) of the Europol Convention, amended by the Council Act of 27 November 2003, OJ C 002, 06.01.2004, p. 0008; According to the new Europol Decision, the Director and Deputy Directors will be appointed by the Council from a list drawn up by the management board (Article 38 (1) and (2)) and may be dismissed by the Council after obtaining the opinion of the management board (Article 38 (7)), OJ L 121, 15.05.2009, p. 37.
26. Article 125 (1) and 125 (3) of Council Regulation No 207/2009 of 26 February 2009 on the Community trademark, OJ L 78, 24.03.2009, p. 1.
27. Article 28 (2) of Council Decision 2002/187/JHA of 28 February 2002 setting up Eurojust with a view to reinforcing the fight against serious crime (Eurojust Decision), OJ L 63, 06.03.2002, p. 1, last amended by Council Decision 2009/426/JHA of 16 December 2008 on the strengthening of Eurojust and amending Decision 2002/187/JHA (the New Eurojust Decision), OJ L 138, 04.06.2009, p. 14.
28. There are exceptions of course; OHIM is one, where a redesign of existing arrangements is needed. Strong conflicts of interests were observed in the boards, with no European institution being in a position to counteract such forces. Although the Council does have a mandate to exercise in the OHIM accountability scheme, it has reportedly never done so and kept itself aloof. Consequently, the legal framework of the agency could be altered to allow for the role of other EU forums such as the EP or the Commission to help offset the strong push for national interests and negative politicization in the board.

6

The European Council's Evolving Political Accountability

Marianne van de Steeg

The European Council's Role in European Integration

A battle for power between Europe's large and small states last night scuppered a deal on key areas of reform in the Amsterdam Treaty negotiations. After 18 months of negotiation, European leaders decided to defer a decision on a fairer distribution of votes among member states, following the failure of the 15 countries to reach a deal. The deadlock on sharing votes meant member states were also unable to finalize a new deal on streamlining the European Commission, which had been another key objective of the Amsterdam talks. One of the key objectives of the latest round of talks, launched to re-write the 1991 Maastricht Treaty, was to re-design European Union institutions in order to prepare for the accession of new EU members from east and central Europe. European heads of government were negotiating the final shape of their new treaty late into the night, as negotiators battled to secure compromises, which they would be able to sell to voters back home.

(Sarah Helm reporting from Amsterdam, *The Independent*, 18 June 1997)

Late in the evening of Tuesday, 17 June 1997, the European Council came to an agreement on the Amsterdam Treaty. The European leaders had been having difficulty coming to an agreement on the objectives they had set themselves. The Amsterdam Summit was an important next step in European integration, preparing the European Union (EU) for doubling its membership. European Council members had to weigh their vision on Europe's future against the EU's immediate needs and their own member state's interests. A deal had to be struck to which all members in the closed rooms of the negotiations could agree and which every member could

117

defend when they faced their national parliament, press corp, and citizens. Years later, the EU was enlarged and much of the criticism that had been aired when the European Council presented its newborn Amsterdam Treaty was forgotten. The Amsterdam Summit of 1997 is now just another reference point among the ranks of the Luxembourg compromise, Maastricht 1991, the Copenhagen criteria, and the Lisbon process. The names of these European Council summits need only to be mentioned to invoke images of complex European decisions, treaties, or policy plans.

The European Council, comprising the heads of state or government of EU member states, is the EU's main political institution. Until the Lisbon Treaty entered into force, the member states that held the Council Presidency prepared the European Council meetings with the assistance of the Council General Secretariat and functioned in practice as the European Council Presidency. Hereafter, the European Council Presidency will be referred to as 'the Presidency'.

The European Council is vested with the ultimate responsibility for all decision-making related to the EU and decides on the EU's development by setting its general political guidelines. Besides being the final decision-making authority on issues unable to be settled by the Council of Ministers, the European Council provides the EU with strategic direction, sets the agenda for further integration, negotiates treaty revisions, and discusses relevant recent developments that require a political response (Dinan, 1999: 251). In other words, the European Council functions as the principal agenda-setter, the ultimate arbiter in decision-making, and the motor behind European integration. Article 15, paragraph 1 of the Treaty on EU captures this as follows: '[t]he European Council shall provide the Union with the necessary impetus for its development and shall define the general political guidelines thereof'.

The intergovernmentalist Moravcsik (2002) called the European Council the EU's dominant institution. Supranationalist Curtin (2009) called the European Council *the alpha and omega of executive power in the EU political system*. The Lisbon Treaty codifies the European Council's present powerful position. With the ratification of the Lisbon Treaty, the European Council has at last formally become an EU institution. Moreover, the provisions in the Lisbon Treaty open up the door for the European Council to continue to grow in power and stature (Curtin, 2009). The decision to appoint a semi-permanent President of the European Council, who will serve in addition to the existing semi-annual Council Presidency, may help to institutionalize the preparation and the follow-up of European Council summits. So far, the civil servants who prepared a European Council summit have changed along with every semi-annual change in Presidency. In the future, the semi-permanent President's staff will work on the summits. This will provide more stability in the bureaucratic support and thus further strengthen the European Council's position.

In view of the impact and scope of the decisions made by the European Council, democratic oversight is warranted. Williams (1990) and Harlow (2002) explicitly raise the issue of the European Council's lack of accountability in relation to the European Parliament (EP). Moreover, the European democratic deficit may extend to the national level, as European integration has widened the gap between the governments of individual member states and their national parliaments (for an overview of this argument, see Williams, 1990; Neunreither, 1994; Lord, 1998; Katz, 2001; Maurer and Wessels, 2001; Decker, 2002; Harlow, 2002).[1] The following question thus needs to be addressed: *Is the European Council held to account at both the European and the national level for its conduct during European summits?*

This chapter takes up this question. It studies whether and how the European Council is publicly held to account by European and national parliamentary representatives for the constitutional development of the EU via treaty changes and for dealing with the policy consequences of crises. The reason for focusing on treaties and crises is that these circumstances hold so much at stake for the EU that we as citizens should be able to expect the European Council to be obliged to explain to a parliamentary body why these decisions are made in our name. Furthermore, the chapter focuses on public accountability. European Council members and parliamentary representatives often meet each other in non-public venues; however, this chapter will deal with the accountability visible to the citizen. Public accountability gives citizens the ability to monitor the manner in which the decision-makers and parliamentarians to whom sovereignty was delegated use the power bestowed on them.

This chapter proceeds as follows. First, I shall frame the European Council's accountability in the perspective of the power delegation chain from the level of citizens to that of the European Council. The question is whether there is a reverse chain of accountability from the European Council to the citizens. European multilevel governance complicates the accountability relations for both the forum and the actor. First, it doubles the forum that holds the European Council to account to the EP and the national parliaments. Second, it doubles the role for which members of the European Council can be held to account, namely giving them an individual responsibility as part of a national delegation as well as a collective responsibility as members of a European institution. Next, I clarify the study's research design, followed by a description of the de jure accountability arrangements at both the European and the national level. Then follow detailed examinations of the de facto accountability relation between the EP and the Presidency and between the Dutch Parliament and the Dutch delegation to the European Council, in the context of parliamentary debates about Council decision-making during European summits. Towards the end of the chapter, I assess whether the European Council has an accountability deficit, extrapolate the findings of this chapter into the future, and propose some ways in which the public accountability of the European Council can be improved.

Who may Hold the European Council to Account?

The guiding principle in the democratic perspective of accountability is that those who are given the power to make decisions on behalf of the citizens are ultimately accountable to those citizens for the manner in which they use that power. This is called the chain of power delegation and accountability. In Figure 6.1, the power delegation chain runs from the citizens via intermediate steps to the European Council.

Most countries in the EU (with the exception of France) have parliamentary governments. In parliamentary systems, citizens delegate power via elections to parliamentary representatives, who in turn delegate power to a national government. In the French presidential system, citizens delegate power directly to the President via elections. The national governments and the French President represent EU citizens at the European level with

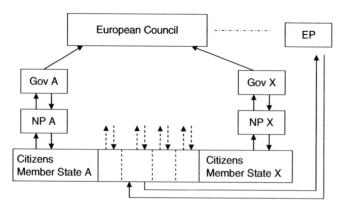

Figure 6.1 The chains of power delegation and accountability: from the citizens to the European Council

the delegated power bestowed on them. The heads of government and state form the European Council. This is the power delegation chain.

Running in the opposite direction should be an accountability chain. Those who have been delegated power are supposed to render account on how they have used this power. As can be seen in Figure 6.1, the accountability chain stops at the national level. We know that the national governments are obliged to be accountable to their national parliaments. Yet does this accountability include the decisions made in the European Council?

Another power delegation and accountability chain runs between EU citizens and the EP. Via direct elections, EU citizens delegate power to the EP. However, the EP, unlike the national parliaments and their governments, does not delegate any power to the European Council. Can the EP hold the European Council to account on behalf of the European citizens in this absence of a power delegation chain? Indeed, is any parliamentary body able to hold the European Council to account for the decisions it makes? There is not a univocal answer to this question, which is a problem from the democratic perspective on accountability.

A democratic deficit looms because the European Council can easily avoid rendering account to any parliamentary body. This is a good example of the democratic problems caused by the multilevel nature of European governance, which causes a doubling of both the actor and the forum in the accountability relation between the European Council and a parliamentary body. The actor doubles because the members as national delegations in the European Council wear two hats. Collectively, the members of the European Council make European politics, which may serve the European interest. Individually, they are the national representatives and are supposed to serve the national interests in the European Council. In other words, a member of the European Council simultaneously wears a European hat as a member of the collective, and a national hat as an individual representative.

The forum for democratic accountability doubles up, too. The parliamentary body that is directly situated in the chain of delegation is the national parliament of each individual member of the European Council. Apart from the French President, all members of the European Council are a head of government and, therefore, formally accountable to their respective national parliament. This is related to the doctrine of ministerial responsibility. Theoretically, there is no reason why a member of the European Council could not render account to his national parliament while wearing both his national and his European hat.

Besides the twenty-seven national parliaments, the EU itself has a parliamentary body, namely the EP. The EP is the only institution at the European level that is directly elected by the European citizens. The EP is not linked by a chain of delegation of power to the European Council but, like the European Council, is a supranational institution. This makes the EP perfectly situated to hold the European Council to account as a collective. The problem is that, formally, the European Council does not have an accountability relationship with the EP. However, in practice, the Presidency of the European Council always appears after the semi-annual summit in the EP to inform it of the progress made. This could provide an occasion for accountability.

In order to find out whether the European Council is accountable to a parliamentary body we need to empirically analyse its relation with both the EP on the European level and the national parliaments on the national level. In this chapter, the EP and the Dutch Parliament (as an example of a national parliament) are studied. The problem for the democratic perspective on accountability is that only the individual accountability of a member of the European Council as a national representative in front of a national parliament fits the chain of delegation and accountability well. This is the lower left box in Table 6.1. If empirical research were to prove that this works well, we would still have an accountability deficit for the European Council as a collective. Individually, the head of government may be held to account and render account solely as a national representative. Only if in all twenty-seven national parliaments the individual members were to render account from the perspective of their European hat and as a member of a collective would the actors' double hats not create an accountability deficit (lower right box in Table 6.1). Another solution for the accountability deficit of the European Council as a collective is

Table 6.1 Accountability in multilevel governance: doubling of the actor and the forum

	National hat: member European Council as an individual national representative	European hat: member European Council as part of a collective
European Parliament (EP)	Theoretically conceivable, empirically irrelevant	The Presidency informs the EP: empirical research needed
National parliament	Chain of delegation: empirical research needed	Chain of delegation: empirical research needed. A single national parliament is only one of twenty-seven national parliaments

indicated in the upper right box in Table 6.1. The regular meetings between the EP and the executive of the European Council after summits could cover the European Council's accountability as a collective.

Case Selection and Operationalization

Case Selection

Three types of choices were made regarding the case selection: the identification of the actor and the forum, the selection of issues, and the selection of public sessions between the actor and the forum on these issues.

IDENTIFICATION OF THE FORUM AND THE ACTOR

On the supranational level, the EP is the forum. On the national level, one national parliament is selected. In the conclusions, the general literature on the functioning of national parliaments will be used to make inferences about the other national parliaments on the basis of this case study. The Dutch Parliament is selected as a most-likely crucial case (George and Bennett, 2004: 253) for detecting whether national parliaments hold their governments to account on European affairs. The Dutch Parliament is namely among the (formally) better-equipped national parliaments in the EU-15 to put its mark on European decision-making. For example, the Dutch European Affairs Committee (EAC) is classified in the better half of the EACs with respect to its information procedure (Maurer, 2002). Maurer and Wessels (2001), Maurer (2002), and Bergman et al. (2003) classify the Dutch Parliament as among the six best-equipped parliaments in the EU-15. Furthermore, the characteristics of Dutch parliamentarism increase the likelihood for ex post public accountability. Even though there is a tendency for coalition parties to coalesce with the government, when it comes to the right of parliament to be correctly informed by the government, the norm that parliament controls government is upheld (Andeweg, 1992). On those occasions, coalition partners can be expected to support a request for information made by a member of the opposition. Coalition partners have even more manoeuvring room to take sides with the opposition and form a parliamentary majority, since European decision-making is usually not included in the elaborate coalition agreements (Holzhacker, 2002). In other words, the Dutch Parliament lacks the formal instruments of champions such as Denmark and Finland but may serve as a most-likely case for specifically ex post public accountability. The results of this case study are valid for parliaments that are similar or tend towards an even more dualistic relation with the government. Parliaments that have a significantly more monistic relation with their government than the Dutch Parliament does will probably encounter more difficulties in holding their national delegation in the European Council to account. In general, monistic national parliaments will find it difficult to hold their government publicly to account on national matters, let alone on European affairs.

This text always refers to parliaments as institutions. Yet a parliament can only act as an institution if a majority is gathered. For the accountability relation between a national parliament and the European Council (member), it is relevant that members of the opposition can sometimes form a majority with the support of some governmental party members, as will be discussed later.

The European Council is the actor in this chapter on the EU and public accountability. The representative of the European Council who stands before the parliaments changes depending on the type of forum. The representative of the European Council in the EP is the member state that holds the semi-annual Council Presidency. With the ratification of the Lisbon Treaty, the semi-annual Presidency is replaced by a permanent President of the European Council, who is to be appointed for two and a half years. However, so far, the European Council is still usually represented in the EP by the head of government and/or the Minister of Foreign Affairs of the member state who holds the Council Presidency. The representative of the European Council in a national parliament is always the national delegation of that member state. In the Dutch Parliament, the Prime Minister appears in the Lower House usually within a week after a summit. The Dutch Upper House is very active in European affairs but does not provide a setting for ex post accountability immediately after European Council summits.

THE ISSUE SELECTION

The issue selection focuses on treaties and crises. From a democratic perspective, it is important that at least for decision-making on these key issues in the life of a polity, parliamentary accountability is present. Four considerations guided the issue selection. First, in order to guarantee both the availability of material in the archives and a certain distribution over time, the cases had to fall between 1990 and 2005. Second, the EU had to be the main international organization involved. Military crises were excluded because in such cases the EU member states cooperate with the United States through North Atlantic Treaty Organization (NATO). Third, in order to increase the chance that the selected case was the main topic of the summit, and thus of the parliamentary sessions, the discussions on a case had to be concentrated in time. New treaties are usually adopted during one or two summits held during one Presidency. However, crises may run for many years and receive attention in a large number of summits dedicated to other issues. Therefore, the crises selected were those that concerned a precise, single moment of sudden emergency for the EU. Only those parliamentary sessions were sampled that were related to that moment of sudden emergency. Fourth, in relation to the idea that public accountability is warranted when something essential to the polity is at stake, cases with great public saliency were preferred. This is the reason why the Constitution for Europe was preferred over the Treaty of Nice. The six issues selected for the EP are:

- the Maastricht Treaty,
- the Amsterdam Treaty,
- the Constitution for Europe (Dublin Treaty),
- the Bovine Spongiform Encephalopathy (BSE) crisis,
- the political crisis of Haider and the sanctions against the Austrian government, and
- the sinking of the *Prestige* off the coast of Galicia (Spain).

The five issues selected for the Dutch Parliament are:[2]

- the Amsterdam Treaty,
- the Constitution for Europe (Dublin Treaty),
- the BSE crisis,
- Haider and the sanctions against the Austrian government, and
- the political crisis of the failure of the Constitutional Referendum in France and the Netherlands.

UNIT OF ANALYSIS

The unit of analysis is a complete public session of one of the selected parliaments on the selected issues. Since the forum (EP and Dutch Parliament) and the actor (European Council) both have their own parts to play in bringing about accountability, any parliamentary session on the selected issues must be considered in its totality. In principle, both parliaments' public sessions and their stenographic records are open to the public. The EP's archives were examined for plenary and committee sessions with the Presidency held after meetings that dealt with, among other things, the selected three treaties and three crises. Regarding the plenary sessions, the EP's archives contain eleven sessions with the Presidency for ex post accountability. All of the relevant committees for public sessions with the Presidency on the six selected issues were also researched. The conclusion from this search is that the EP did not have the opportunity to demand *ex post* accountability in the committees. The same search was done for the Dutch Parliament on the five selected issues. Seven plenary sessions and four committee sessions were found for the Lower House (and none for the Upper House). This brings the total number of public sessions to be analysed for the EP to eleven and for the Dutch Parliament to eleven as well, so the total *N* is 22.

Operationalization

Since the actor and the forum are already known, namely the European Council, and the EP and the Dutch Parliament, respectively, the definition presented in Chapter 3 can be applied as follows:

1. Is the Council representative obliged to appear before the EP or the Dutch Parliament and does it give *information* on its conduct?[3]

2. The EP or the Dutch Parliament asks questions in the *debate*, expresses appreciation, and raises criticisms. Does the Council representative explain and justify its conduct in response to EP queries and critiques?

3. Does the EP or the Dutch Parliament pass *judgements* on the Council's actions? This may hold either positive or negative consequences for the Council. (However, whether this is the case is beyond the scope of this chapter.)

This model will be used in the next section on the de jure accountability arrangement. However, it is still not sufficiently operationalized to measure de facto accountability. In this section, I will indicate how, in general, de facto accountability is operationalized. This chapter combines the results from empirical research on the EP (Van de Steeg, 2009) and the Dutch Parliament (Van de Steeg, 2010). First, every single statement that could be linked to demanding and giving accountability was coded, using an elaborate coding tree (for the coding tree, see Van de Steeg, 2009*a*). For the EP, the coding was done by hand, because for most issues the stenographic records were not easily available in a digital format. For the Dutch Parliament, software for qualitative research, MaxQDA, was used. The coding tree was partly derived from Müller (1994: 104–5) and was partly developed inductively by analysing a plenary session of the EP and of the Dutch Parliament as a pilot.[4]

Second, since the unit of analysis is a complete public session of the EP or the Dutch Parliament, the individual coded statements have been aggregated to this level. The aggregation is based on the tenor of what was being said, not by quantitatively adding the codings together. We want to know whether the EP and the Dutch Parliament demand accountability and come to a judgement, and whether the Council representative was accountable for his past actions. In order to find this out, the information obtained in the detailed coding stage was aggregated by applying a set of questions to the actor and a set of questions to the forum, respectively the EP and the Dutch Parliament. The set of questions relating to the accountability of the Presidency before the EP can be found in Van de Steeg (2009). The set of questions relating to the accountability of the Dutch delegation before the Dutch Parliament can be found in Van de Steeg (2010). The sets of questions used in these two articles are slightly different because they take into account the different formal positions of the two parliaments and the different contexts in which the sessions on ex post accountability take place. For the purpose of this chapter, the specific sets of questions are summarized in order to provide insight into the analysis made for both settings.

The scope of the following boxes for the actor and the forum is to distinguish between the presence of accountability and an absence of accountability. The actions in the box on the forum (Box 6.1) and all actions except for the last one in the box on the actor (Box 6.2) are designed in such a manner that a 'no' for any of them implies the absence of accountability. The actions are formulated as minimal conditions that have to be fulfilled in order to maintain that accountability was present in a particular parliamentary session. Thus, what actions by the forum and the actor qualify for at least a minimal contribution to accountability?

Box 6.1 THE FORUM'S CONTRIBUTION TO ACCOUNTABILITY

The forum, either the EP or the Dutch Parliament, demanded accountability when:

Information

1. The EP or the Dutch Parliament was present to receive information.

Debate

2. There was a focus on demanding accountability.

3. The Members of the European Parliament (MEPs) or Members of Parliament (MPs) indicated what they wanted to know.
4. The MEPs or MPs indicated that they wanted an answer to their comments and questions.

Judgement

5. The EP or the Dutch Parliament made their positive or negative judgement explicit. (The EP usually lays its judgement down in a resolution. The Dutch Parliament almost never adopts resolutions in sessions immediately after European summits. As a proxy, a judgement is considered to be absent when the judgements expressed by parliamentarians from the coalition parties and the opposition are diametrically opposed to each other.)

Box 6.2 THE ACTOR'S CONTRIBUTION TO ACCOUNTABILITY

The actor, either the Presidency or the Dutch delegation, was accountable when:

Information

1. The Presidency or the Dutch delegation was present in Parliament.

Debate

2. The actor mentioned in the reply most of the central issues raised by the EP or the Dutch Parliament. The central issues were those that received most comments (positive or negative) from the forum.

3. The actor provided a somewhat explicit answer to the central issues raised by the EP or the Dutch Parliament.

4. The following action is related to accountability, even though it is not a condition that has to be fulfilled to conclude that accountability is (minimally) present: if applicable, the actor accepted responsibility for failures. This statement is not applicable in cases where the summit went smoothly and the Parliament was generally positive about the work of the European Council. A Presidency accepted responsibility for his or the Council's actions during the previous summit by expressing regret about mistakes that he or the Council had made, by making promises about ways to amend the situation, or by acknowledging his or the Council's shortcomings. By accepting responsibility for failures, the Presidency adopted a vulnerable attitude.

Can the European Council be Held to Account?

The de jure accountability arrangement between the EP and the European Council is much weaker than that between the Dutch Parliament and the Dutch delegation to the European Council. The formal position of the Dutch Parliament is as can be expected of a parliament, but the position of the EP is in line with the *sui generis* nature of the EU. While the relation between the Dutch Parliament and the Dutch government fits the chain of delegation, the EP has never delegated power to any other European institutions. In fact, the directly elected EP as we know it today has only existed since 1979. The EP's relation to other European institutions and its role in the decision-making process are still developing with each successive treaty revision negotiated by the European Council. The difference in the position of the Dutch Parliament and the EP within the Dutch and the European political system, respectively, is reflected in their de jure accountability arrangements.

The de jure accountability arrangement with regard to the Dutch Parliament fully covers all three aspects of the empirical model of Bovens' definition of accountability. The government, that is, the Dutch delegation, is obliged to *inform* the Parliament (Article 68 Constitution). The Rules of Procedure allow the MPs to place interruptions and ask follow-up questions. The MPs can use these instruments to repeat in the *debate* demands for accountability that have not received an explicit answer from the Dutch delegation. The Dutch Parliament may lay down its *judgement* in a motion. A negative judgement may have serious consequences for the Dutch delegation, since either the Parliament or the government could label a motion as a 'motion of censure' (Bovend'Eert and Kummeling, 2004). The Dutch government needs the support of at least half the Parliament to stay in power and pass legislation. In case Parliament does not feel it is being taken seriously by the Dutch delegation in its request for accountability, the Parliament theoretically has many opportunities to make the Dutch delegation bear the consequences. The flip side of this argument is that a Dutch delegation that is sure to have the support of at least half the Lower House – namely all coalition MPs who want their party to stay in power – may feel free to ignore demands for accountability made by opposition MPs. In other words, the strength of the de jure accountability arrangement may become its weakness.

The de jure accountability arrangement for the EP is very limited: only the obligation to *inform* the EP after a summit is formally laid down (Article 4 Treaty on European Union). The *debate* may suffer from the strict format of the plenary sessions (Rules of Procedure) that restrict the possibilities for MEPs to explicate or repeat their demands (see Van de Steeg, 2009 for more details). The EP may lay down its *judgement* in a motion; however, there are no formal consequences attached to this. The European Council does not depend on the EP as a government depends on (the majority of its) parliament. Possible consequences of negative or positive judgements of the EP

Table 6.2 De jure accountability arrangements

	National hat: individual	European hat: collective
EP	N.A.	Weak: only obligation to inform; small risk incurred by the Presidency if accountability is not given; soft sanctions
National parliament	A complete de jure accountability arrangement. The Dutch delegation needs the support of the majority of the Dutch Parliament	

are reputation effects or effects on network ties, labelled by Grant and Keohane (2005) as soft sanctions. Besides soft sanctions, something else that might induce the Presidency to take the EP seriously, even without any formal sanctions, is the fact that the EP is a parliament. Those who hold the Presidency are accustomed to appearing before a parliament. The fact that the venue is a parliament may induce the Presidency to act as if the EP's judgement has consequences.

On the basis of the differences in the de jure accountability arrangements, it can be expected that the Dutch Parliament will receive more consideration in its request for accountability than the EP (see Table 6.2). In other words, in view of the de jure accountability arrangement, it is not to be expected that the Presidency would take any unnecessary political risks by providing explicit answers to painful aspects of an issue brought forward by the EP. Whereas the Dutch Parliament has a strong formal position to guarantee that the session does not turn into a platform for propaganda, the EP has at its disposal only its name and soft sanctions.

Accountability in Practice: The Dutch Parliament

Accountability Associated with the Dutch Delegation's National Hat

In most of the public sessions analysed, both the Dutch Parliament and the Dutch delegation contributed to creating accountability in the debates after European Council summits. Of course, this observation may be different for other national parliaments, since it may depend on the executive–legislative relations in general.

The Dutch delegation always appeared within a few days after a summit in a public session of the Dutch Parliament. The forum was always present to receive the actor's *information*.

The characteristics of *debate*, at the heart of the empirical model for accountability, were detected in most sessions to such an extent that it qualified for accountability. In other words, accountability was usually present in the sessions of the Dutch Parliament. However, the contributions made to accountability by the Dutch Parliament and the Dutch delegation ranged from being barely sufficient for accountability to being perfect examples of putting the concept of accountability into practice. In order to illustrate how accountability is enacted, Box 6.3 first discusses a session in which both forum and actor contributed to accountability and then one in which accountability was absent.

Box 6.3 ACCOUNTABILITY IN THE DUTCH PARLIAMENT

Accountability was present: the session on the Haider crisis, March 2000

Forum: Opposition and majority active in demanding accountability. In March 2000, the Dutch Parliament discussed the Haider crisis with the Dutch delegation. However, this session dealt mostly with other issues related to the previous Lisbon Summit. Therefore, only a small portion of the session was dedicated to the Haider crisis and not all MPs made a statement on this topic. With this in mind, the Parliament contributed reasonably well to accountability. Both the opposition and the majority demanded accountability. Two of the three majority parties and two of the opposition parties made comments on the Haider crisis. The smaller majority party, D66, and the biggest opposition party, CDA, made both positive and negative remarks. In total, five positive remarks were made, one of which was by an opposition MP, and four criticisms, one of which was by a majority MP.

Both opposition and majority MPs expressed in an explicit manner what they wanted to know from the Dutch delegation – first the D66 majority MP and then later, with a similar criticism, the CDA opposition MP. The D66 majority MP:

> The situation in Lisbon was somewhat embarrassing with the [official] photograph, the coincidence of the Mexican guest, and a Chancellor Schüssel who literally and metaphorically operated marginally. . . . [After the European Council meeting, an official photograph of all the European leaders was taken. However, some did not want the Austrian Chancellor to be in the photograph. This produced a fuss. The solution was that since the European Council's guest, the Mexican President, was in the photograph, it was not considered to be an official European Council photo.] I wanted to ask the Prime Minister whether the speech by Foreign Minister, Van Aartsen, for a VVD public in Amsterdam can be understood as follows: the Foreign Minister confirmed the measures taken by the 14, but only made a comment regarding the treatment of people from Austria.

The CDA opposition MP:

> For a change, I think Minister Van Aartsen was right. He said that the sanctions were fine and had to be observed, but that we should stop avoiding Austria in

---

131

official EU meetings. Did Minister Van Aartsen question all the sanctions last Monday? What is the opinion of the Prime Minister on the sanctions? . . . Did the Prime Minister undertake any actions to stop the joke regarding the official photograph? Has the dinner of the European Council made anything clear or led to new insights?

Actor: After some follow-up questions, the actor provided accountability on all issues raised by the MPs. The delegation's first reply to the questions raised on a statement made by Foreign Minister Van Aartsen [VVD], and on how Austrian politicians were and will be treated, dealt with the issue but initially glossed over the essence of the matter. Prime Minister Kok [PvdA]:

> Furthermore, there was enormous excitement on what should happen with the photograph, with dining and talking, and that kind of things. Two things happened: The Portuguese Presidency decided – they just took up their own responsibility – to make a group photograph in combination with the presence of the Mexican President. . . . The excitement about whether or not the photograph should be taken – who is on it and who is not – was ten times bigger outside than within the realm of participants. . . . We are not making any unnecessary show out of it, but as long as the ÖVP/FPÖ-government exists, these measures will remain in force. In this manner you may understand the words of the Minister of Foreign Affairs [Minister Van Aartsen]. . . . [Continuing as if this were part of the issue raised by the opposition MP, the Prime Minister added of his own accord that] Measures against the Austrian population were never considered, nor were they foreseen.

After this reply, both the opposition and majority MP asked follow-up questions. Their questions on what was decided regarding the policy towards the Austrian government had received only a partial reply. At first, the Prime Minister explained what had happened during this European Council meeting but glossed over what would happen at any subsequent European meeting. However, the Prime Minister's final statement did indeed contain an explicit reply, but not the answer the MPs had hoped for: 'The relationship between the Austrian representatives and us . . . was icy, but held respect for each other's contributions during the Summit. As far as I am concerned, not much will change in the icy relationship, as long as the situation remains the same.'

All issues brought forward by the MPs ultimately received a reply. However, follow-up questions were necessary. Three replies were factual, one of which even contained a highly detailed explanation; only one reply was shallow. Overall, the conclusion on this session is that both the Parliament and the Dutch delegation contributed to accountability. Accountability was present in this session, even though the Dutch delegation could have been more forthcoming.

Accountability was absent: the session on the BSE crisis, April 1996

Forum: Opposition lacked the support from the majority MPs in holding the Dutch delegation to account. In April 1996, the spokespersons of majority and opposition parties were present to receive the information from the Minister of Agriculture [VVD] who had just had a crisis meeting in Brussels on BSE. In its demand for accountability, Parliament was split between a majority and an opposition. The three majority MPs made twenty-two positive remarks and only one of criticism.

The picture of the opposition MPs was the exact reverse: three positive remarks and forty-five criticisms. The opposition MPs mostly raised criticisms, asked follow-up questions, and criticized the Minister for refraining from replying to their questions. On the other hand, the majority MPs mostly praised the conduct of their government and did not ask any follow-up question to sharpen the explanations offered by the Dutch delegation. What is more, the Minister was thanked for his contribution. VVD majority MP: 'I thank the Minister for his extensive reply, and then I refer to both content and procedure. More answers were given than questions asked.' The appreciative and supportive attitude of the majority MPs signalled to the Minister that he could count on the majority's support. In this way, the majority MPs signalled that it was not necessary for the Minister to provide an adequate answer to the issues raised by the opposition.

Actor: The Dutch delegation avoided explaining and justifying his conduct. Various issues raised by the opposition parties did not receive any reply, not even after follow-up questions. The proportion of factual answers provided by the Minister of Agriculture was almost equal to the number of shallow answers or answers unrelated to the question asked, namely 12 to 10. Several replies touched upon an issue raised by the opposition but missed the essence. For example, a GroenLinks opposition asked whether the destruction of 64,000 calves younger than six months in the Netherlands was, in view of the decisions made later in Brussels, the right signal to give to consumers in the Netherlands and elsewhere, because 'the consumer is signalled that it is not a good idea to eat this type of meat. The consumer will run risks and cannot trust veal meat from other countries.' The Minister replied that 'immediately a public warning had been issued' on the dangers related to meat from the United Kingdom. 'Regarding that matter, the Dutch government has immediately given adequate information.' The Minister did not provide a reply to the MP's question on the distorted message the Dutch measures may have given to consumers. The self-appraisal on having adequately warned Dutch consumers missed the essence of the issue raised by the MP.

Actor: The Dutch delegation treated the opposition with contempt. On several occasions, the Minister of Agriculture provided a summary of the issue that was the contrary of what the MP wanted to say. For example, after many criticisms by the CDA opposition MP, the Minister stated: 'Furthermore, I deduce from the resolutions tabled by Mr Van der Linden that he in principle respects the decision made by the Dutch government.' The MP objected to this reading and asked the Minister to make a modification. The opposition MP:

> I am sorry, but I had not expected this remark from the Minister. . . . I indicated the consequences of the perspective chosen by the Minister. That has led us to tabling these motions. I do not think it is correct that the Minister has made this link. I would appreciate it if he would restate that.

> The Minister: I do not see any reason for that.

Forum: Parliament is de facto weak when the opposition is alone in its request for public accountability. In the session on BSE, the opposition parties were alone in demanding accountability, and their efforts were to no avail. The government needed the support from the majority parties and was aware that this support was secured. This can be noted from the following exchange between an opposition MP and the Minister of Agriculture. The CDA opposition MP tabled two resolutions criticizing a decision already made by the Minister before the Brussels meeting. The Minister advised against it, but at one point in the discussion said: 'I will wait and see what the proportions in the votes are regarding the resolutions.' With these words, the Minister signalled that he was not worried about the resolutions, because the majority of the Parliament would not adopt them. The opposition MP's reaction confirmed this reading: 'It has become clear to me that before this debate the support of the coalition partners was sought in favour of the view presented by the Minister.' The MPs from the majority coalition denied this allegation, but the Minister was correct in expecting that none of them would vote in favour of the resolutions.

In the same manner as the sessions on the Haider crisis in March 2000 and the BSE crisis in April 1996, all eleven sessions were analysed for *debate* and *judgement*. In seven out of the eleven plenary and committee sessions analysed, accountability emerged out of the interaction between the forum and the actor. However, in four sessions, the contribution of the forum and/ or the actor in the *debate* was judged to be problematic. For the Dutch Parliament, in the sessions on BSE in April and June 1996, as well as the session on a Constitution for Europe in June 2004, accountability was not demanded by the Parliament as an institution. The problem in all three sessions was that the opposition was alone in demanding accountability. On the other hand, the Dutch delegation was not accountable in the session on BSE in April 1996 and the session on the political crisis after the failure of the Constitutional Referendum in June 2005. Only for the session on BSE in April 1996 was there a correspondence between the lack of demand for accountability by the Dutch Parliament and the absence of rendering account by the Dutch delegation. Nevertheless, in most (i.e. eight out of eleven) sessions, the Dutch Parliament demanded that the Dutch delegation explain and justify the decisions and actions made at the previous summit. In these sessions, both opposition and majority MPs were sufficiently explicit in what they wanted to know. Likewise, the Dutch delegation provided at least a somewhat explicit answer to all or almost all of the central issues raised by the MPs in most (i.e. nine out of eleven) sessions.

The last dimension of the accountability model, the *judgement*, was present in all but one session (the same one as also featured a lack of debate). Apart from one motion, the Parliament's judgement was never laid down in a motion. It is common for motions not to receive a majority. The opposition often files motions and the government advises against them. As long as the majority MPs do not vote in favour of a motion, a motion is not

Table 6.3 Contribution to accountability by the Dutch Parliament and the Dutch delegation

Session	Dutch Parliament	Dutch delegation
BSE crisis April 1996	Absent ('no' on debate and 'no' on judgement)	Absent ('no' on debate)
BSE crisis June 1996	Absent ('no' on debate)	Present
Amsterdam Treaty March 1997	Present	Present
Amsterdam Treaty May 1997	Present	Present
Amsterdam Treaty June 1997	Present	Present
Haider crisis February 2000 (plenary)	Present	Present
Haider crisis February 2000 (committee)	Present	Present
Haider crisis March 2000	Present	Present
Constitutional Treaty March 2004	Present	Present
Constitutional Treaty June 2004	Absent ('no' on debate)	Present
Referendum crisis 2005	Present	Absent ('no' on debate)

Note: Accountability was coded as being present or absent. For those sessions in which accountability was absent, it is indicated between brackets on which part of the accountability definition the actions of the Dutch Parliament or the Dutch delegation received a 'no'.

passed. It was uncommon that the motion filed after the session on the Treaty of Amsterdam in 1997 could count on the support of one of the majority parties. For this reason, it is more worthwhile to investigate the judgement expressed by Parliament during the session itself. The judgements about the Dutch delegation's conduct made in the statements by the opposition and majority MPs did not differ much. Only in the session on BSE in April 1996 did opposition MPs criticize the Dutch delegation heavily, whereas the majority MPs praised the delegation or stayed silent. In all other sessions, both opposition and majority MPs had a critical or reasonably positive attitude towards the actions undertaken by the Dutch delegation.

Taking *information*, *debate*, and *judgement* together, the Dutch Parliament and the Dutch delegation created accountability via their statements in public parliamentary sessions. As can be seen in Table 6.3, accountability was rarely absent. The de jure accountability arrangement coincided with a de facto accountability relation between the Dutch Parliament and the Dutch delegation. Of course, there is always room for improvement. Accountability was considered present even when Parliament needed to ask several follow-up questions in order to induce the Dutch delegation to provide an answer. In other words, in some sessions accountability was rather minimal, in other sessions much more extensive. Occasionally, majority MPs were as active in holding the Dutch delegation to account as opposition MPs. Once, in the June 1997 session on the Amsterdam Summit, the Prime Minister accepted responsibility for failures on several issues brought forward by Parliament. From a democratic perspective, we would hope to see the Dutch Parliament and delegation reach such a high standard of public accountability more often. However, it can be concluded that the Dutch delegation is publicly accountable, even though sometimes minimally, for the powers bestowed on it by the Dutch Parliament. Nevertheless, we need to be reminded that this conclusion is only valid for the Dutch delegation's accountability towards Parliament regarding its role in the European Council as a *national* representative. In that sense, it relates only to the democratic deficit caused by European integration on the national level. If national parliaments are to be a remedy for the European democratic deficit, we should also expect there to be public accountability by the national delegation regarding the European Council as a collective body.

Accountability Associated with the Dutch Delegation's European Hat

The parliamentary sessions regarding the Haider crisis are the only occasions in which the Dutch delegation is held accountable as a member of a collective and during which it provides accountability from the perspective of its European hat. This is also the only issue in the case selection that did not have any immediate repercussions for the Netherlands. In all the other sessions, accountability is mainly or solely demanded by the Parliament from the perspective of the Dutch delegation's individual responsibility as a national representative. The main issues brought forward in the BSE sessions concerned the relation between the Dutch measurements to contain BSE and the decisions made in Brussels. Among the main issues in the session after the summit on the constitution were the rules for the EU's budget (explicitly linked to the position of the Netherlands as a net payer) and the composition of the Commission (i.e. the Dutch being entitled to 'their own' commissioner). After the Amsterdam Summit, the Dutch delegation even discussed with two opposition MPs its role as a Dutch representative and as Presidency. The first opposition MP demanded that the Minister of Foreign Affairs step outside the role of holding the Presidency. The MP understood the high spirits of the Minister as Presidency but from a national perspective could not understand his joy about the plans presented in Parliament. Later, a second opposition MP continued along this line of thought: 'With whom is the House debating, with the Dutch government or with the European Presidency? . . . in the relationship between House and government, the House does not examine the actions of the

European Presidency but those of the Dutch government, and thus addresses [the Dutch delegation] for the Dutch commitment and contribution.' In other words, the fact that the Dutch delegation occasionally rendered account as a member of the European Council with a responsibility for the collective is not what the forum wants the actor to do.

The conclusion is that we should not expect MPs to hold national delegations accountable to the European Council as a collective body. MPs represent European citizens as nationals of a member state. The task of an MP is to have a national perspective on the EU and on the performance of their national delegation in the European Council. National parliaments are the venue for holding the national delegation to account for its national hat. That is difficult enough as it is.

Implications for other National Parliaments

We have already seen that whether a national parliament is able to hold a national delegation to account depends on the interplay between opposition and majority, and the need felt by the national delegation to be forthcoming. In those parliaments in which majority MPs support requests from the opposition less often than in the Dutch Parliament, we can expect fewer sessions in which public accountability is present. The effect of a majority that is focused more on protecting a common (governmental) position than on seeking a public parliamentary debate on European issues can be seen in Austria and Germany. In both these member states, the extensive parliamentary rights to influence the national delegation's position before going to Brussels are hardly used, because majority MPs usually do not team up with the opposition (Holzhacker, 2002; Pollak and Slominski, 2003; Benz, 2004; Auel and Benz, 2005).

In other words, in those national parliaments in which the executive has more control over the work of the legislative via its majority than in the Dutch Parliament, public accountability will less often be present. Besides the German and Austrian Parliaments, we could think of the Spanish Parliament in which a single party controls the whole of the parliament. Those parliaments that lean more towards monism than the Dutch Parliament does could be expected to find it more difficult to hold their national delegations to account on European Council decision-making.

For several of the twenty-seven parliaments, it may already be too much to hold their own national delegations accountable as a national representative.

Expecting the European national parliaments to demand accountability from their national delegations for the European Council as a collective body is unrealistic. In order to hold the members of the European Council to account as a collective body, the EP with its European mandate is a better candidate than the twenty-seven national parliaments.

Accountability in Practice: The EP

We know from the de jure accountability arrangement that the Presidency is only obliged to *inform* the EP every six months on the progress made by the European Council. The Presidency kept to this minimal obligation in the session of 6 June 1996 on BSE. In this session, the Presidency made an opening statement in which it informed the EP of the last meeting on the BSE crisis, but it refrained from making a closing statement. During that session, the MEPs did not receive any reaction from the Presidency on the comments they had made. The Presidency is not obliged to react to the comments made by the MEPs. On all other occasions, the Presidency did more than it was obliged to do.

However, even when the Presidency did more than fulfil its obligation by making not just an opening but also a closing statement, this did not mean that the Presidency provided accountability. As an example of a session in which the Presidency was not really held accountable, the closing statements in the session after the Florence Summit on the BSE crisis will be discussed (See Box 6.4).

Box 6.4 ACCOUNTABILITY IN THE EP (1)

Accountability by the actor was absent: the BSE crisis, July 1996

The Italian Presidency appeared before the EP shortly after the Florence Summit. The Florence Summit officially dealt with employment policy. However, before the Summit, the major issue was BSE and the United Kingdom's decision to obstruct all EU decision-making if the measurements made by the Commission and the Council against the United Kingdom's meat industry were not lifted. The Italian Presidency was represented by Prime Minister Prodi and Minister of Foreign Affairs Dini. Both made an opening and a closing statement. Prime Minister Prodi had already made his closing statement after the first nine MEPs (i.e. mainly the spokespersons of the party groups) had spoken. In other words, Prodi was not able to take the statements made by the thirteen MEPs who spoke afterwards on the BSE crisis into account in his closing statement.

The actor hardly mentioned any of the central issues raised by the forum and did not provide any answer. All spokespersons, apart from the spokesman from the

European People's Party (an Italian), criticized the European Council for the measures taken to contain BSE, for the United Kingdom's obstruction politics, and for having lost sight of the main purpose of the Florence Summit, that is, employment. The Italian Presidency's reaction to the MEPs' explicitly phrased criticism was to use the closing statement mostly to sing his own praise. Prime Minister Prodi:

> At this point I want to say that the Italian Presidency succeeded in resolving one of the most serious crises that has ever blocked the progress of Europe. It is easy to underestimate the BSE crisis now that it has been resolved. It is easy to say, like Mrs Green, that a political and institutional solution has been found. Certainly, Mrs Green, a political and institutional solution has indeed been found, and it deeply respects consumer safety and the right of the European countries not to submit to vetoes on issues quite different from the specific problem they are intended to resolve. A crisis which could have had devastating consequences for Europe has been ended. In my opinion, that is an important achievement, and I am convinced that there will be far fewer repetitions of such crises in Europe, because the solution the Italian Presidency found gave no satisfaction to those using the veto for unrelated objectives. . . . So within these institutional limits, the limits of the framework we operate in, we have made a huge contribution to overcoming one of the most difficult problems.

This was all that Prime Minister Prodi had to say in relation to the comments made on the BSE crisis. After Prodi left the meeting, thirteen MEPs raised issues in connection with the BSE crisis. The only reply they received from the Italian Presidency was a 'thank you' from Minister of European Affairs Dini: 'Finally, I want to thank honourable Members for having recognized and emphasized, amongst other things, . . . the solution to the political dispute with the United Kingdom affecting European Union business linked to the BSE crisis.'

This case was characteristic of over half the plenary sessions analysed (six out of eleven). In view of the weak de jure accountability arrangement, it could be expected that the Presidency would often use the EP's plenary session more as a platform for his political message than to be accountable in European decision-making. The manner in which the Italian Presidency dealt with central issues raised by the MEPs regarding the BSE crisis fits this picture.

But the glass is also half full. In five out of eleven plenary sessions, the Presidency actually contributed to accountability in the *debate*. It seems best to list these five sessions: the sessions on the Amsterdam Summit, the Haider crisis, and one of the sessions on the Constitution for Europe. These plenary sessions have in common that they all took place at the end of the 1990s or the beginning of this century. Interviews conducted with MEPs and other people working at the EP helped put this finding into perspective. In the interviews, various respondents indicated that something is changing in the manner in which the Presidency relates to the EP. As one respondent put it, Presidencies who respond to the Parliament as if they could be obliged to be accountable established a custom that made it more difficult for other Presidencies to be evasive. This is a form of reputation loss. Perhaps this functioned as a soft sanction.

The turning point in the relation between the EP and the Presidency can possibly be traced to 1997 or 1998. Several respondents from the EP felt that the Presidencies of Luxembourg and the Netherlands (both in 1997) and Austria (in the second semester of 1998) were more often forthcoming and considerate towards the EP than had been the experience under past Presidencies. During the Dutch Presidency, the EP had a plenary session on the Amsterdam Summit. On this occasion, both the forum and the actor contributed to accountability. Regarding the actor, this is the most extensive contribution to accountability out of the eleven sessions analysed (Box 6.5).

Box 6.5 ACCOUNTABILITY IN THE EP (2)

Accountability was present: the session on the Amsterdam Treaty, 1997

The forum was present as an institution and indicated explicitly what it wanted to know. The MEPs used the few minutes at their disposal to give their (positive and negative) opinion on the Amsterdam Summit, held a week before. It is quite remarkable for the EP that almost all statements focused on demanding accountability from the Presidency on the manner in which the European Council had handled the previous summit. The MEPs indicated explicitly what they want to know from the Presidency. Most MEPs listed the issues on which, in their view, the European Council had made some progress, and issues for which the European Council had not been able to come up with what they would consider to be an adequate solution. An example of such an explicitly formulated, balanced statement was made by Green, the spokeswoman of the Party of European Socialists:

> I want to make it clear that my group recognises and welcomes the advances which the Amsterdam Treaty has brought in dealing with a people's Europe.... We respect the fact that some transfer has been made, but I want to repeat the real anxiety we have about the lack of parliamentary control which now exists in these crucial areas of immigration policy, visa controls and asylum.... Perhaps our greatest disappointment is with regard to enlargement. We have grave misgivings about the inability of the Council to agree on any meaningful extension of qualified majority voting. More than any other issue, this puts enlargement at risk.... Therefore my group believes that it is vital that before enlargement the European Council must come together again to address the question of majority voting in the Council as well as the composition of the Commission and the weighting of votes.

The EP laid down its judgement in a resolution that contained all the central issues brought forward in the debate in a manner as explicitly formulated as in the statements.

The actor provided an explicit answer to all central issues raised by the forum. In their closing statements, the Dutch Presidency provided an answer to all central issues brought forward by the MEPs. The central issues for the MEPs were criticism on a lack of institutional reform, positive and negative comments on employment and the social protocol, mostly negative comments on Justice and Home Affairs (JHA) and the Common Foreign and Security Policy (CFSP), and criticism on the co-decision procedure for the EP. Prime Minister Kok of the Presidency replied with a high level of detail to almost all these issues. JHA and CFSP, which received only a short reply from Kok, and the co-decision procedure, which had not received any reply from Kok, were included in the closing statement by State Secretary Patijn for European Affairs.

The actor accepted responsibility for failures. Besides providing a reply that touched on the essence of all of the MEPs' central issues, the Dutch Presidency set an example by providing more accountability than could be expected in relation to a forum with a very weak de jure position. On one occasion in the opening statement, and on several occasions in the closing statement, the Presidency accepted responsibility for failures and acknowledged shortcomings in the agreement reached during the Amsterdam Summit. Prime Minister Kok:

> So I support the outcome as it stands, we have no intention of running away from it, but I really think we should have had the courage to go a little further on majority decision-making than we did.... [The Amsterdam European Council agreed that each member state would be entitled to one Commissioner and the member state that had two would be compensated in the weighting of votes in the Council when the EU was enlarged by six new member states.] This could of course simply be putting off the evil moment, in that we cannot rule out the possibility that the problems we had at Amsterdam will re-emerge when the time comes to decide on enlargement and therefore on the new weighting of votes.... I can assure you that I am all in favour of enlargement as soon as possible.

Still, even if a tradition of accepting accountability towards the EP is developing, having started with the Luxembourg and Dutch Presidencies in 1997, serious accountability cannot be taken for granted. For example, in 2002, the Presidency evaded accountability for the decisions made regarding the *Prestige* disaster. The Presidency explained the actions and decisions made by the Council in reaction to the sinking of the *Prestige*, but in his closing statement he did not mention the most important criticism raised by the EP. The MEPs wondered why the European Council had delayed the adoption of the package prepared by the Commission that should have prevented another *Erica*. What did the Council do in between the sinking of the *Erica* and the *Prestige*? The Presidency left the EP's main question out of his closing statement and got away with doing so.

The EP's contribution to accountability was more often present than the Presidency's contribution (see Table 6.4). The EP's contribution to accountability was present in eight out of eleven plenary sessions. The session on Haider in July 2000 was insufficient, because this was the only session in which the EP was not present as an institution to receive the Presidency's *information*. By the summer of 2000, the Haider crisis had become a pet project of German Christian Democrats, Austrians, and other MEPs with a direct interest in this affair. In the two sessions in June 1996 on BSE, the EP's contribution was insufficient during the *debate*. Other matters were more important than demanding accountability on how the European Council was handling the BSE crisis.

Considering the imperfect formal position of the EP, the correct question to ask is: Is the European Council's Presidency willing to be held accountable by the EP? (Whether there is a de facto accountability arrangement between the European Council and the EP depends largely on the benevolence of the Presidency.) The answer is that half of the time the Presidency was – to different degrees – forthcoming in being accountable to the EP. In spite of a de jure accountability gap, the analysis of eleven plenary sessions suggests that de facto accountability is becoming more regular practice. This would mean that a (thin) line can be drawn in Figure 6.1 that represents a chain of accountability running from the European Council, via the EP, to the European citizens. Of course, the risk with

Table 6.4 Contribution to accountability by the EP and the Presidency of the European Council

Session	EP	Presidency
Maastricht Treaty 1991	Present	Absent ('no' on debate)
BSE crisis 6 June 1996	Absent ('no' on debate)	Absent ('no' on debate)
BSE crisis 19 June 1996	Absent ('no' on debate)	Absent ('no' on debate)
BSE crisis July 1996	Present	Absent ('no' on debate)
Amsterdam Treaty 1997	Present	Present
Haider crisis February 2000	Present	Present
Haider crisis June 2000	Present	Present
Haider crisis July 2000	Absent ('no' on information)	Present
Prestige crisis 2002	Present	Absent ('no' on debate)
Constitutional Treaty March 2004	Present	Present
Constitutional Treaty July 2004	Present	Absent ('no' on debate)

Note: Accountability was coded as being present or absent. For those sessions in which accountability was absent, it is indicated between brackets on which part of the accountability definition the actions of the EP or the Presidency received a 'no'.

interaction practices that have no formal foundation is that they can easily be discontinued by the more powerful in the relationship, in this case the Presidency.

Assessment: An Accountability Deficit?

From a democratic perspective, the accountability practices in the Dutch Parliament and the EP are hopeful. The Dutch delegation to the European Council is held to account on the national level for its responsibility as a national representative, and a practice is emerging of the EP holding the Presidency to account on the European level for the European Council as a collective body (see Table 6.5). The accountability practice for the national delegation's actions at European summits is as could have been expected from a fully equipped national parliament in which majority MPs sometimes team up with the opposition. A similar capability to hold the national delegation to account can probably be found in other national parliaments that lean as much (or more) as the Dutch Parliament does towards dualism – although it must be added that the Dutch Parliament is regularly criticized for being too monistic. As long as national parliaments are able to hold their governments publicly to account on national affairs, this is more than likely to extend towards European issues, such as European Council summits.

Table 6.5 Assessment of de facto accountability arrangements

	National hat: individual	European hat: collective
EP		• Accountability present half the time
	X	• After 1997–8, the Presidency is more often accountable than is to be expected
National parliament	• Opposition MPs need some support from majority MPs	• Accountability for the collective is not usual business. Often absent in demands and in explanations
	• Accountability of the Dutch delegation is a practice	• MPs protested against this type of accountability when it was part of the explanation and justification by the actor
	• Functions reasonably well in the Netherlands	• Not the right venue for this type of accountability

From the perspective of intergovernmentalism, this would suffice. The chain of delegation from the citizens via the national parliament and the government to the European Council is matched with a chain of accountability. However, the other finding from this study is more troublesome from the perspective of intergovernmentalism. The major surprise is the sudden improvement since 1997 in the extent to which the Presidency is forthcoming in rendering account to the EP. Even though the European Council is not the EP's government, several Presidencies have treated the EP during the past decade as if it were a 'normal' parliament. If international politics is seen as a zero-sum game and the European Council as the prerogative of national governments (accountable to national parliaments), then privileges granted to the EP to which it is not entitled may be seen as undermining the position of national parliaments.

On the other hand, supranationalism would only welcome a constellation in which the individual European Council members are held to account for their national responsibility and the European Council as a collective body is held to account via the Presidency by the EP. This may be the constellation towards which we are heading in due course. The assessment of the accountability relation between the EP and the Presidency is tainted positively, because on the basis of the de jure accountability arrangement, one would not expect even a reply to the MEPs comments, let alone an accountability statement. The fact that since 1997, the request for accountability from the EP has been taken more seriously fits with a more general development in which the EP is more often granted the position of a 'normal' parliament (see Chapter 4). In light of these recent developments, it does not matter that a national parliament is unsuitable for holding the European Council delegations to account for their collective, European responsibility. In a supranationalist constellation of democratic European governments, it would be sufficient if the European Council were held to account for its collective responsibility in European decision-making in the EP, and for their national responsibility in the twenty-seven national parliaments.

At this point, a word of caution is called for. Public accountability on European Council decision-making remains fragile. It depends largely on the attitude of individual politicians and the social expectation that they should contribute to public accountability. Rendering account publicly entails risks, especially for the actor, the European Council. De facto public accountability depends on a Presidency who is prepared to give more than an opening statement and who chooses to actually deal with the issues raised by the EP. De facto public accountability depends both on majority

MPs who see the need for demanding accountability and on a national delegation that sees the need for explaining and justifying its actions. A national delegation that is allowed by the MPs from the coalition parties to avoid accountability would probably get away with it. The support of majority MPs is needed for opposition MPs to be able to use the Parliament's formal accountability arrangement in order to exert pressure on the national delegation and back up their demand for accountability. In other words, de facto public accountability depends on executive–legislative relations in a national parliament. Moreover, de facto accountability may depend on the social pressure generated by public attention.

This chapter used the results from analyses of parliamentary sessions on salient cases after European Council decision-making. Would an analysis of public accountability on Council of Ministers decision-making in less salient cases yield the same results? The study by Neuhold, de Ruiter, and Kanen (2009) into British and Dutch parliamentary debate on EU regulation on chemical substances suggests it would. However, more empirical research would be needed to understand the relation between the saliency of cases and general representative–executive relations on the one hand, and public accountability on the other. Public accountability is not an iron-clad rule, but something that has to be created through everyday political actions. It is good for European democracy that de facto public accountability is created more often than could have been expected.

The Future: The Lisbon Treaty and Beyond

The future of the European Council's public accountability looks promising. Increased politicization of EU politics, the Lisbon Treaty, and other recent developments also enhance the chances for public accountability in national parliaments and the EP. The major danger of public accountability to national parliaments is monism, that is, such a close cooperation between the executive and majority MPs that basic parliamentary rights are suffocated. The increased politicization of EU politics may improve the chances that demands for public accountability after European Council summits are placed on those parliaments that tend to monism. Demanding accountability after decision-making has already taken place is one of the least costly strategies for demonstrating to the public that EU decision-making is safe in the hands of the present majority. Moreover, the increased politicization of EU politics may increase the social pressure exerted by the public. Citizens increasingly want their national delegations to explain and justify what they have done in the European Council.

The Maastricht Treaty and the debate on the European democratic deficit were a wake-up call for national parliaments to defend their prerogatives. As Raunio and Hix (2000) put it, national parliaments learnt to fight back. The single national parliaments took action and jointly put their concerns on the political agenda. A first result of this lobby was that Protocol 13 was attached to the Amsterdam Treaty, in which the national parliaments' right to be correctly and timely informed about European decision-making by their respective national delegations was laid down. The Lisbon Treaty contain more rights for national parliaments and an official – if minor – political role on the European scene. Even though national parliaments already had sufficient rights to hold their national delegation to account, the official inclusion of national parliaments in European Treaties may strengthen the awareness of their role and their position. In the future, this may have a beneficial effect on holding the national delegation to the European Council de facto to account.

The major danger for public accountability to the EP is the weak de jure accountability arrangement. The Lisbon Treaty does not contain any provision that improves the de jure accountability arrangement. However, certain changes in the EU's institutional architecture may have a beneficial effect on the de facto accountability arrangement. Upon ratification of the Lisbon Treaty, the European Council officially becomes an EU institution and has its own full-time President with a two-and-a-half-year term of office. For the European Council President, it will be much more important than for the current semi-annual Presidency to have a good working relationship with the EP (Crum, 2009). The sessions of the EP with the President will become a repeated game. This increases the power of soft sanctions. A negative judgement by the EP has more consequences for a permanent President than for the current semi-annual Presidencies who first and foremost are heads of government in one of the member states. The expectation is that the tendency of the Presidency (and the future European Council President) to be more forthcoming in rendering account will continue and become more institutionalized.

How to Further Improve the European Council's Accountability

A subsequent step in making the European Council publicly more accountable would be to codify the practices by bringing the de jure accountability arrangements more in line with the de facto accountability relation. The politically least costly codification would be to oblige the European Council President to make a closing statement after all MEPs have spoken. At present, one of the Treaty provisions only gives the EP the right to be informed. The EP is not entitled to receive a reply to the issues they raise.

A way to improve both the de jure accountability arrangement and de facto accountability is to oblige the Presidency to appear before a parliamentary committee. In the committees, it would be more difficult for the Presidency to evade accountability. As an MEP put it in an interview '[if a Minister of the Presidency were to join a committee discussion] he would be obliged to give information. He could not have a general discourse and say goodbye. He would have to expose himself to possible criticism'. A parallel with the figure of the permanent High Representative teaches us that we can expect a permanent President to appear before the parliamentary committees (Crum, 2009).

In conclusion, if the current situation is extrapolated towards the changes that came into effect with the ratification of the Lisbon Treaty, then the perspective for parliamentary public accountability of the European Council is favourable (see Table 6.6). The most robust de jure accountability arrangement can be found at the national level. Most

Table 6.6 Ideas to improve the parliamentary public accountability of the European Council

	National hat: individual	European hat: collective
EP	N.A.	• The change from a part-time semi-annual Presidency to a full-time permanent President will probably improve the de facto accountability relation
		• Codify the practices. Grant the EP, for example, a right to a reply to their statements
		• It would be an important innovation if the Presidency/President were to render account in the committees, and not only in plenary
National parliament	• No need for changes in the de jure accountability arrangement • Expectation that the de facto accountability relation will improve	N.A.

national parliaments in the EU dispose of an array of formal instruments that can be used to pressure the national delegation into responding to their demand for accountability. De facto, it depends on the political game between majority and opposition MPs as to what extent these formal instruments are used for ex post public accountability.

In view of the rise in public attention for EU politics and the success of Euro-critical and Eurosceptic politicians, it is to be expected that the demand for accountability after European decision-making will improve. This is in line with developments in the past. We have already seen that the debate on a European democratic deficit helped the EP to improve its formal position in the Amsterdam and Lisbon Treaties. The democratic deficit debate has probably also aided the creation of a new tradition in which the Presidency, without any formal obligation, was regularly de facto accountable to the EP. The expectation is that this practice will be strengthened by the change of the semi-annual Presidency held by a head of government (or the French President) into a full-time, permanent President of the European Council. Maybe then we will read in the newspapers, alongside reconstructions of the nightly European Council negotiations on the basis of press conferences and undisclosed sources, some headlines about the EP and national parliaments making it hot for European Council members in public drillings on their conduct behind closed doors.

Notes

1. International relations (IR)-liberal Moravcsik is one of the few voices who go against the current. In his view, direct accountability via the EP is one of the two robust mechanisms for European democratic accountability (Moravcsik, 2002: 611). However, Moravcsik's concept of accountability is one in relation to legislation and elections. His use of accountability is so broad and all-encompassing that it falls outside of the scope of this chapter.
2. The issue selection for the EP does not coincide precisely with the issue selection for the Dutch Parliament. First, in retrospect, the European Council plays a central role in a political EU crisis, but not in crises that are not politicized. For this reason, the BSE crisis was chosen to analyse the European Council's accountability, but the sinking of the *Prestige* was not. The case of the *Prestige* was replaced by the political crisis caused by the 'no' vote in France and the Netherlands in the constitutional referendums. Second, Maastricht was not digitally available for the Dutch Parliament, while all more recent issues were available in an easily accessible digital format. The sessions of the Dutch Parliament were analysed by using MaxQDA (software for qualitative analysis) to improve the quality of the content analysis.

3. The European Council Summits raise much more exposure and publicity than, for example, comitology meetings or the work of European agencies. Moreover, the accountability on a summit takes place within a week after the event. For these two reasons, the forum will already have received much information before the session with the actor from sources such as the media and personal contacts. This makes the provision of *information* from the definition of accountability presented in Chapter 3 different for the European Council than for the actors presented in the other chapters.

4. A reliability test was done. Gijs Jan Brandsma repeated the coding of one parliamentary session. His coding was similar to that of the author of the article who later coded all the debates herself. Thanks to Gijs Jan Brandsma for checking the validity of the coding tree.

7

Accountable Comitology?

Gijs Jan Brandsma

Comitology: Hidden Power

Each day, thousands of national civil servants travel to Brussels from all over the European Union (EU). Sometimes, they are only consulted, for example when the European Commission asks for expert advice before sending a legislative proposal to the Council of Ministers and the European Parliament (Larsson, 2003). In other cases, they are working out agreements among each other before the Council legislates (Fouilleux, De Maillard, and Smith, 2005). And in other cases still, they are discussing implementation measures drafted by the Commission, as in the example in Box 7.1.

The latter type of committee is called 'comitology' in EU jargon. This term refers to a set of roughly 250 committees that are composed of policy experts who represent the member states and are chaired by a 'chef de dossier' from the Commission. A comitology committee's function is to 'assist' the Commission in implementing policy. But it is a powerful form of assistance because the committee participants vote on the implementation measures proposed by the Commission. Depending on the voting procedure used, there can be two outcomes: either the Commission has to adopt the proposed measure or the matter has to be referred to the Council of Ministers. In practice, this means that the Commission cannot implement policies swiftly without the approval of a comitology committee.

Comitology is an implementation device and hence comes into the picture at the end of the policy process, namely when the Council of Ministers (and under co-decision, also the European Parliament) has already adopted basic legislation. But the end of the policy process can

---

Box 7.1 COMITOLOGY IN PRACTICE

Today is a usual day in the usual meeting room in the building of DG Agriculture in Brussels. Policy specialists from all over Europe meet here to discuss the implementation of the Common Agricultural Policy. They know each other quite well, as they generally meet every fortnight, or sometimes even more often. From Holland, experts Patrick van Veen and Frits Bloem[a] agreed to let me join them.

Before lunch, the Commission and the member state experts discuss a large number of technical items related to the price support of a certain agricultural product. The Commission presents its proposals, followed by critical remarks from the member state experts. Sometimes they join each other in their critique towards the Commission. They also take the floor when they believe something should be discussed that is not mentioned on the agenda.

After lunch, it is voting time. 'Mind it,' Van Veen warns me. 'You will not be able to keep up with us now.' And indeed, within only a few minutes the committee rushes through five official votes related to the points discussed before lunch, and the meeting closes instantly. Then, Van Veen turns to me and smiles: 'You saw that? We just spent 50 million here.'

[a] For reasons of anonymity, their real names were replaced.
Source: Observation D. (For the methodology see p. 158 below.)

---

sometimes be lengthy, and it requires a lot of implementation measures to be adopted by the Commission. Table 7.1 shows that around 50 per cent of *all* European acts are handled by comitology committees.

These figures show that comitology is one of the most important governance tools in the EU, measured by the volume of work that it deals with.[1] But in terms of the importance of the acts discussed in the comitology committees, the matters they deal with are much more technical and specific than those discussed in the Council and the European Parliament. The aims of new legislation have thus been decided upon before, and

Table 7.1 Acts adopted by the European institutions between 2004 and 2007

	2004 (%)	2005 (%)	2006 (%)	2007 (%)
Parliament and Council	3.1	2.0	3.5	2.4
Council alone	14.1	12.6	14.8	14.9
Commission:				
Via comitology	49.7	54.4	50.4	49.6
Not via comitology	33.1	31.1	31.4	33.1
Total number of acts	3,093	2,972	2,915	2,313

Note: Commission breakdown made by counting how many times an opinion of a comitology committee was referred to under 'whereas' in all Commission legislative acts (data set compiled from EUR-LEX by Dimiter Toshkov, Leiden University).
Source: EUR-LEX, <http://eur-lex.europa.eu>. Consulted: 5 June 2009.

comitology works out all the fine details. Why, then, would we need to care about its accountability, if comitology is 'only' about the nitty-gritty work of implementation?

This is because seemingly small, technical issues still bear political saliency (Radaelli, 1999). Decisions to exterminate instead of vaccinate all animals in a certain region because of a disease, how personal data stored in the Schengen Information System can be accessed for security purposes, and how hazardous waste is to be treated, and thousands of other issues, are all made in comitology committees. Sometimes, these issues are salient to large groups in society, sometimes only to a small group. In any event, to those who are directly affected by new legislation, the devil is usually not in the objectives of legislation but rather in the details of implementation (Van Schendelen and Scully, 2006: 6).

This also relates to the reason why comitology exists in the first place. The member states recognize the power of implementation measures and do not want to give the Commission an entirely free hand in this. When the first community acts were to be implemented by the Commission in the early 1960s, the Council felt that the Commission should not have too much discretion for implementation. What if this 'new' supranational institution were to act against the preferences of the member states? Comitology was invented as a way out. For legislation for which the Council felt the need to do so, it imposed the condition upon the Commission that it should consult committees of member state representatives before adopting implementation measures. When the committee voiced a negative opinion, the proposed measure was handed back to the Council. This way, the Commission could be controlled in its implementation capacity without jeopardizing the contents of the Treaty (Haibach, 2000; Bergström, 2005; Blom-Hansen, 2008). The Council thus felt a political need to install comitology committees because it saw the implementation of its decisions as a continuation of politics by other means, which was likely to be of continuing interest to the member states.

But at the same time, there are a large number of studies that indicate that the participants to these committees in practice work somewhat detached from their national ties. The participating policy specialists in many cases do not receive instructions, and they deliberate with their colleagues from the other member states and the Commission to find common solutions (Joerges and Neyer, 1997; Wessels, 1998: 225; Dehousse, 2003: 803). Over time, they also internalize European norms so that they become increasingly willing to pursue the common European good, transcending the national interest, even when they still primarily consider themselves

---

Box 7.2 BALANCING NATIONAL AND EUROPEAN INTERESTS

On his way back from lunch, Frits Bloem[a] answers a phone call and takes some steps away. Patrick van Veen[a] explains to me it is a colleague from the Hague, telling Bloem which requests for price support by agricultural businesses were forwarded to the Commission from Holland. The deadline for this passed only moments before, and the Commission works out its subsidy proposal over lunch. This is a matter of routine at every meeting of this committee. The phone call gives Bloem the opportunity to do a last-minute check to see if the Commission got its figures right before the committee votes on the subsidy proposal. 'And', Van Veen adds, 'I don't want to know.'

Van Veen is convinced he should take his position on macroeconomic grounds only, and should not be influenced by any national interest. Otherwise, there could be arguments in the committee if just a bit more subsidies can be awarded to a particular country in order to benefit the national industry. To Van Veen, that is both speculation and preferential treatment, which has nothing to do with the management of the common market.

Therefore, Van Veen and Bloem have divided their tasks. Van Veen is the official Dutch spokesperson and he votes, but he does not know the details of any particular Dutch application. Bloem does, and he checks the data prior to the vote. Only after the meeting closes and millions worth of subsidies are decided upon (cf. Box 7.1), does Van Veen curiously ask his colleague if any Dutch applications were awarded.

[a] For reasons of anonymity, their real names were replaced.
Source: Observation D. (For the methodology see p. 158 below.)

---

to be national representatives (Beyers and Dierickx, 1998; Egeberg, 1999; Trondal, 2002; Egeberg, Schaefer, and Trondal, 2003; Beyers and Trondal, 2004). Their interaction style in committee meetings has in practice little to do with staunchly defending the national interest, whereas defending the national interest was and still is the core motivation underlying the comitology system as a whole. The example in Box 7.2 is a case in point.

Comitology, thus, effectively acts as a decision-maker for a wide range of implementation issues. Its participants are civil servants from the member states, many of whom in practice work somewhat detached from their national ties. To what extent is this power held to account? This chapter argues that comitology is a multilevel governance instrument whose accountability can only be fully understood with an investigation of both the European and the national levels. But the available literature is narrowly focused on accountability at the European level only. Therefore, this chapter presents new quantitative and qualitative evidence collected at the national level among the superiors of the committee participants.

Comitology and Multilevel Accountability

The definition of accountability used in this book is a general one that can be applied to any relationship between an actor and a forum. But in multilevel governance settings such as comitology, there is no single set of actor–forum relationships because of the fusion of different policy levels. Figure 7.1 shows these levels and the corresponding accountability relationships.

The delegation setting can be read in Figure 7.1 from left to right. In basic acts, drawn up by the legislative power, implementation of policies is delegated to the Commission. The legislative power also installs a comitology committee, composed of member state representatives, which needs to give a formal opinion on Commission proposals. The functioning of the committee can be read vertically: the committee functions as a combination of the Commission and delegates from twenty-seven member states.

Figure 7.1 shows that, for comitology, two sets of actor–forum relationships are relevant. On the one hand, there is the institutional set of accountability relationships, with the *comitology committee* as the actor and the *Council of Ministers* and the *European Parliament* as forums.[2] On the other hand, there is the individual set of accountability relationships, consisting of the relationships between each *committee participant* and his own *superior* within his own organization. For a composite political system

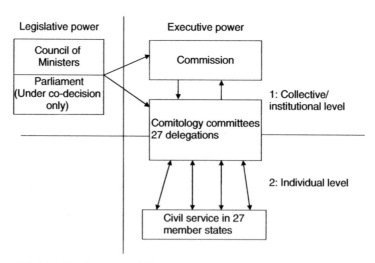

Figure 7.1 Multilevel accountability

like that of the EU, which is characterized by politics at both the national and the European level and interaction between the two, it is essential to take both levels into account (cf. Figure 7.1). But the current body of analysis of accountability in relation to comitology focuses on the institutional set of accountability relationships only, and mainly on the position of the European Parliament.

The European Parliament sees the committees as problematic as they perform executive tasks but are reined in by the Council, which is part of the legislative power. Its long-term goals have always been to be on equal footing with the Council for installing new committees, and to be in a position where it is able to scrutinize the wheeling and dealing of the committees (Neuhold, 2001). It is here that the debate on the institutional level of accountability centres. The available evidence suggests that the European Parliament, acting as a forum in this accountability relationship, is handicapped. In its opinion, it receives little information (Neuhold, 2008) and it cannot rely on others to monitor the committees in its place as little information on the committees is made publicly available (Brandsma, Curtin, and Meijer, 2008). But because its resources are limited, as with any parliament, it partially *needs* to rely on others to keep track of comitology committees (McCubbins and Schwartz, 1984). Given that these third parties (stakeholders, non-governmental organizations, and members of the public) are not in a position to monitor the activities and processes of such committees in a timely and effective fashion, the Parliament is seriously handicapped in its ability to ultimately participate in the process of holding comitology to account.

But even if the European Parliament were well informed, it faces obstacles for debating and sanctioning committee activity. Even though for a limited number of committees it can overturn positive committee opinions (Christiansen and Vaccari, 2006; Bradley, 2008; Neuhold, 2008), in all other cases it can only adopt a resolution condemning a committee for power abuse, but for that it would need to prove that the adopted proposal was not in line with the mandate of that particular committee as set out in the basic act. In this sense, the powers of the Parliament are similar to those of – and add nothing to – the powers of the Court of Justice.[3] However, such a resolution should be adopted within one month after a committee voices its opinion, and since resolutions can only be adopted in the monthly plenary sessions in Strasbourg, this arrangement comes close to being a dead letter.[4]

The *individual level* is conspicuously absent in this debate on accountability. But, given the multilevel nature of comitology, the national level is important to take into account in order to grasp the legitimacy of European policy-making (Schmidt, 2006). There is currently a significant body of studies concerning the behaviour of participants on the comitology committees and their role orientations, for example to what extent they regard themselves to be national representatives, supranational actors, or independent experts (Egeberg, Schaefer, and Trondal, 2003; Beyers and Trondal, 2004). These do not, however, concern the accountability relationship between the actor (i.e. the committee participant) and a forum.

This, however, is a relevant question to ask. As argued before, there is a tension between the intergovernmental design of the comitology system and the actual functioning of the system. Apparently, member states feel that implementation of common policies is important enough to install a system of well over 200 committees in order to control the Commission. But then, the matters these committees discuss are of such a nature that it takes experts to attend these committees, and they do not necessarily bargain on the basis of national preferences. Accountability at the national level can mitigate this: it allows governments to control the wheeling and dealing of their representatives, and also secures the intergovernmental aspect of comitology. The question is to what degree its representatives are actually held to account in practice.

Methods and Data

In order to make a general assessment of the accountability of comitology, new data have been collected at the individual level. These data were obtained by different means: questionnaires and interviews. Questionnaires were sent to the Dutch and Danish representatives on almost all comitology committees that were active in 2006 and to their immediate superiors. This limitation avoided country-specific attributes in the design of the research, giving a clearer picture of the workings of accountability without the need to take account of very different contexts. Further, as the number of comitology committees is relatively low with 250 committees that formally exist, but 225 committees that physically meet, the entire population could be approached. The survey to the committee participants was jointly developed and executed with Jens Blom-Hansen from Aarhus University. The survey to their superiors was not a joint effort, but the team in Aarhus assisted by tracing many respondents and translating the questionnaire into Danish.

For the *survey to the committee participants*, the first challenge was to identify the comitology committees. At the time, no up-to-date list was

available.[5] An initial overview of the existing number of comitology committees was made on the basis of the Commission's 2005 comitology report
(European Commission, 2006). Committees that did not meet during that
year were excluded as 'inactive committees'. New committees discovered
during the data collection process were then subsequently included in the
analysis.

The next challenge was to identify the Dutch and Danish national
representatives. This is no easy task because the member states are free to
choose their representative. This means that a variable number of civil
servants, sometimes from more than one ministry, are attached to the
various committees. Then, they each attend committee meetings depending on what is on the agenda. We handled this problem by contacting the
relevant units in the Dutch and Danish ministries, who helped us find the
most frequent, important, or experienced representative on the individual
committees. This representative was then contacted by phone or email and
asked to fill out a questionnaire.

For the *survey to the superiors*, two strategies were used to identify the
respondents. For Denmark, a list of superiors was provided by Aarhus
University on the basis of publicly accessible government staff registers.[6]
For the Netherlands, the committee participants in the first survey were
asked by email who their actual superior was.[7] Nearly all responded to this
question, but several superiors had meanwhile switched jobs and were not
willing to participate.

For the 225 active committees and two countries, 358 questionnaires
were sent out to the committee participants and 294 were returned, which
gives a response rate of 82 per cent for this group. To the superiors, 261
questionnaires were sent out and 153 were returned. This gives a response
rate of 58.6 per cent for the superiors. Both surveys together cover 34 per
cent of all possible accountability relationships in the population.

Furthermore, the evidence from eight *interviews* with committee participants and sixteen with superiors has been incorporated in order to validate
the survey results. All but one of the interviewed superiors were in the
position of head of unit. Interviews have been conducted both in Denmark
and in the Netherlands, and all were semi-structured. This chapter also
reports four cases in which a committee participant was not only interviewed, but also joined to a committee meeting in Brussels. There, the
committee discussions were observed. When possible, preparatory meetings
at the ministry were attended as well. These *observations*, then, were later
compared to the content of the written reports of the committee meetings
that the participants sent to their superiors.[8] Nearly all respondents wished

to remain anonymous. All names have therefore been replaced, and this chapter will also refrain from making any statements from which persons, committees, or specific organizational units can be identified.

Information: 'Blind Faith'

Both the surveys to the committee participants and their superiors contained a battery of three items on the kinds of information that are, respectively, sent or received: about the content of the discussion in Brussels, about the vote results, and about the input of the agent during the meeting. As it cannot be excluded that information ends up with the superior via a third party rather than directly (McCubbins and Schwartz, 1984), this battery was repeated four times: one time each for information transferred directly from the committee participant to his superior; to or from interest groups; to or from major companies in the sector; and, for the superiors, directly from the European Commission.

It appears that the direct links are strongest. Committee participants report to inform their superiors most often, and vice versa. The involvement of companies and interest groups appears to be limited. They are informed to a lesser extent than the direct superiors; scores differ more than one full point on a five-point scale with those of the direct principals. The superiors, in their turn, are informed even less by those actors than by the committee participants themselves. Here, there is a difference of about two full points. The European Commission has an in-between position here. On average, it keeps the principals informed of the vote results every now and then, but less of the content of the discussion and hardly ever of the committee participant's own input.

This does not mean that interest groups and companies are *always* informed to a lesser extent. The interview material shows clearly that providing information on participation in committees is a routine affair. All interviewed committee participants that were asked about this indicate that they prepare a document and send it to several recipients. Such 'mailing lists' can include both people within the organization and people outside it (CP1, CP5). As one committee participant put it:

> We [committee participants] make the minutes. Officially I make it into a departmental memo, just by putting another header on it, and that is distributed to all interested parties that need to know about it. (CP1)

Informing people, therefore, goes by carbon copy. This is also reflected in the survey results: variation between sending different sorts of information is nearly absent. This means that when an agent sends information on, say, the content of the discussion in Brussels to a recipient, it is almost certain that he also sends information on his own input and the vote results to the same recipient along with it. It also shows that those who inform their principals to a certain extent do not by default inform all others to a *fixed* lesser extent. It can therefore be concluded that committee participants send the same information together in one batch, but to a variable number of recipients – depending on who is on the mailing list.

But still, as the example in Box 7.3 shows, the question of what specific information to put in a report remains a matter of deliberate choice.

Box 7.3 BIG MONEY, LOW ATTENTION

Two days before a committee meeting, I met Sandra Tol and several of her colleagues at a pre-meeting in a Dutch ministry. Lots of specific points were raised about discussion papers that the Commission sent to them, mainly because they are unclear. They resulted in a short list of questions to be asked to the Commission. There were also questions about a budget of €57 billion that the committee was due to approve. Despite the questions, everyone agreed that the Dutch could vote in favour of this budget.

Sandra was joined at the committee meeting by a colleague from another ministry. The meeting consisted mainly of presentations. Two professors who had been contracted by the Commission to do a policy review were invited to give a speech, and there were several points where the Commission gave the member states an update of the latest developments. Finally, there was the official vote. As nobody replied to the question of the chairman 'Do we have unanimity?', this was taken as a vote in favour. The committee just approved €57 billion of spending.

Throughout the meeting, there were discussions between the member states and the Commission, but the Dutch never said a word. Even when issues were discussed on which they had prepared questions, they did not speak. Later on, I was told that those matters could better be asked by telephone, and there was no real necessity to bring these matters up during the meeting itself. After the meeting, Sandra and her colleague briefly discussed what to put in their written report of this meeting. They quickly agreed it would be something of a short list of decisions: there was not much else worthy to report anyway.

A few days later, I visited her head of unit. He had read the report of the meeting, but there was nothing in it upon which he thought he needed to take action. As he deemed other files to be much more important, he did not pay too much attention to it. Committees are only a marginal part of his unit's work.

The report itself was written by Sandra's colleague. It contained a short and factual summary of the proceedings of the committee. It showed no trace of the questions that were asked two days before.

Source: Observation A.

The example in Box 7.3 also illustrates why reports are sometimes left unread or do not get much attention. Heads of unit and policy staff have a different span of control, and sometimes reading a report of a comitology committee meeting is just not a priority:

> If you have something which is very politically sensitive or if there is a big important meeting you are preparing where ministers appear for the parliament... these items may consume all of your day. And therefore when this report from the committee meeting pops up on the inbox, you think: I'll read that later... Another situation might be that the report from the meeting comes in and it is a quiet day, and... you have not spoken to the committee participant for a number of days and is a good reason to call him.   (S1)

> It happened that the international issues were put away because when the minister is calling you have to answer him, and Danish ministers are more nationally oriented than internationally. Because in Denmark he is going to lose his next election.   (S7)

Most superiors also indicated that they were quite satisfied with the information they receive. From the survey it appears that only 5.4 per cent of all superiors were unhappy with the information coming in, 11.4 per cent answered neutrally, and the remaining 83.2 per cent were generally satisfied. They were not being informed about issues other than what they wanted to know about, and they did not feel they received too little information.

Also, they tended to rely on the expert judgement of their staff. When superiors trusted their committee participants to do the right thing, they were happy with receiving relatively little information (S8, S3, S11). Only in two cases were outcomes different: one superior said he always reads everything carefully (S4), and another felt policy specialists should behave less autonomously, but still only wanted to be informed of politically relevant things (S9).

The above results indicate that the superiors are generally informed by the committee participants directly about the participant's own input in the comitology committee, about the content of the discussion in Brussels, and about vote results. Superiors were also relatively satisfied with the amount and content of the information they received: about 83 per cent reported this. But another, not particularly encouraging, finding was that information was not always transferred from agents to principals in the civil service to a consistently high standard. In itself, it is not deplorable that information gets lost *as such* – it is impossible for ministers, government, parliament, or voters to know every detail of what is going on anyway. But what is problematic about this is that the filtering-out of information was not only due to conscious decisions about which important pieces of information should be forwarded to higher management levels. It was also due to less-diligent and selective reading on the part of the principal who had to cope with a high workload, and due to the perceptions of heads of unit about the attitude of their unit staff towards their work that lies at the heart of their working relationship in general. This results in information loss right at the end of the chain of delegation, where the chain of accountability begins.

Debate: Substantive Conversations and Deafening Silence

Whether speaking of debates or of discussions in a more general sense, there is a large variety of practices in this respect. On a five-point scale from low to high discussion frequency, the average score of the committee participants and their superiors is 2.34. They can also appear in various forms. Debates can generally be the straightforward one-on-one meetings in the office (S1), but also unit meetings or phone calls late in the evening (S7), or just popping in with a question or remark (S4, S6, S8, S13).

Debates, therefore, generally take place to a modest extent. Sometimes, there are frequent, organized feedback discussions which are not bilateral between committee participant and superior, but which involve a complete unit (CP4, S7). But there are also instances where hardly any debate takes place at all (CP6). Box 7.4 shows an extreme example of this for a politically salient matter.

Box 7.4 RUBBER-STAMPING SALIENT ISSUES

Margot Kijne works on a policy which is very important to nearly all Dutch farmers, and therefore also to the Dutch parliament. In today's meeting, a Commission proposal is discussed which has been on the agenda for a number of months and for which a vote is due now. The Commission proposal makes it.

On our way back to Holland, I ask Margot if they discuss these seemingly important issues with their managers at all. 'Well,' Margot says, 'as for my own head of unit, I will just tell her that the Commission proposal made it. If necessary there is always the report of the meeting, but so far this has never been necessary. They don't think it is very important.'

There is a paradox in this situation. Political interest in the issue is very high, but interest of the management within the departments is low. The reason for this low bureaucratic interest is that there is not much left to do at the management level. The preferences of parliament and the minister are clear to everyone, so the head of unit only needs to rubber-stamp the proposals of her staff.

Source: Observation C.

Both the survey and the interviews show that the superiors of the committee participants are very much guided by what comes to their desk. The provision of information triggers further discussion, as several superiors also indicated in the interviews (S1, S4). But similarly to the findings on information provision, it appears that superiors who endow their subordinates with a greater degree of autonomy also have fewer feedback discussions ex post. Then, they are available upon request (S11, S12, S13). This even applies on a rare occasion of agency loss:

> It has happened once that I said I was not happy with it, but we would try and make the best of it. Then, he found out too late that he was crossing the lines of his mandate. Things happen, and you don't need to make a big problem out of that. The alternative would be for us to prepare every single meeting together. Then I could just as well go myself. (S11)

But what is actually being said in these discussions? Are they about fundamental aspects of the issue at hand, or rather about small fry? In terms of the intensity of debates, practices are also varied. In about half of the cases, these discussions are, to some or to a greater extent, about basic ideas. In the other half, the opposite applies. This sometimes comes under the guise of *business as usual*. Then, there is hardly any interaction between superior and committee participant because an issue has been dealt with some time ago, and in the meantime the organizational situation has not changed:

> Whether I discuss extensively with my staff what should be said in a meeting or not, the basic idea we have will not be any different from last year's. And luckily we did not have too many staff moving on during the last years, so the people who ran the Council negotiations are now running the committee as well. So they are well-up in this subject. (S10)

The guise of 'business as usual' is a widespread phenomenon. Many respondents believe it does not make sense to revisit key principles time and again when an issue has been handled for quite some time already. Then, debates – including political discussions – have happened before, and there is a group of people who have been working on the issue for several years. In other words, there is an established tradition of behaviour upon which both the committee participant and the superior can fall back (cf. Geuijen et al., 2008). In such situations, committee participants come to see their principals when they believe something should be discussed, and the superiors in their turn believe their subordinates only come to see them about the things the superior deems important (S2, S6, S10, S13, CP2, CP3, CP4, CP7).

Nevertheless, 'business as usual' can be problematic, as it underestimates potential future politicization of issues. Committee participants may thus sometimes mistakenly believe they can vote in favour of a certain proposal as a matter of routine, whereas in fact it is not quite business as usual. Several superiors refer to cell phones and wireless Internet to keep in touch with the capital and to discuss certain items during the meeting, in order to indicate that this problem should not be blown out of proportion (S7, S8, S9). But in itself, this new technology does not solve the main issue. When new issues come up under the guise of 'business as usual', it is not likely that participants will contact their capitals to begin with:

> I have seen many times that people go for a practical solution, but after discussion in the capital they needed to move back. But often there is no way back. (CP3)

Debates, therefore, can serve as a means by which principals and agents – when necessary – can discuss core views and realign the interests they defend. But the evidence suggests that these discussions do not occur frequently.

An experienced committee participant said: 'In general you can say: we can do whatever we want to, as long as you can explain why you did something' (CP4). It looks as if he stated the obvious, but the evidence presented here tells a different story. To put it in similar fashion: they can do whatever they want to, but often nobody asks them why. The superiors of the committee participants are largely guided by what comes to their desks. If no feedback is given about a committee meeting, the odds that past behaviour is being discussed go down. As the previous section argued, the superiors digest the incoming information differently depending on the issue and depending on the person. But this also affects the discussion phase of accountability. The less information comes to the principal, the fewer discussions take place.

Ill-informed principals are thus left uninformed. When principals are convinced their agents are well-intentioned experts, they do not see this as a problem at all. And maybe, had there been a discussion, the superior would have concluded that things are all right as they were. But as long as he shows little interest, he cannot tell. But sometimes, superiors do see it is time for action. What makes them decide to do so, and how do they conclude what sort of measures to take?

Consequences: Carrots and Sticks

The principal–agent literature is geared more towards the instrument of sanctioning than to rewarding. Sanctions are understood in a formal sense: they can include firing the agent, redistributing power, or 'other specific penalties' (Strøm, Müller, and Bergman, 2006: 34–5). There are two dimensions to this, which are central to the discussion from here: *ability* and *actual use*. First, the principal must be physically able to sanction. This ability is reflected by the repertoire of consequences that he can make any of his subordinates face, of which the options have been mentioned before. The second is the extent to which the principals actually do reward or sanction behaviour in the unit for which they are responsible. Do principals actually show their teeth when they have them?

The survey to the superiors shows that nearly all have several formal abilities to sanction or to reward, such as redistributing tasks, firing staff, or giving bonuses. But these formal instruments are rarely used in practice, even though generally principals do have the capacity to use these instruments. This is not without its reasons. Giving someone notice, for example, comes with high transaction costs. As a head of unit mentioned, it shows 'you are really doing something wrong as a manager. It is an outright humiliation, let there be no misunderstanding about that' (S11). The decision to reallocate tasks, then, seems easier and more credible to the staff (CP1, CP8). Sometimes heads of unit do this anyway to avoid tunnel vision among their staff, in which case it is not a sanction for specific behaviour but a more general management instrument (S12). But here too, superiors can have very practical motivations not to reallocate tasks, even in cases where they would prefer to do it:

> If it goes too far, this could mean someone is taken off a file. It is extreme, but possible...But then, nobody may want to do the job instead. Because you have to read a lot and maybe also travel a lot, and there are only few colleagues who really enjoy that. Because you have to get up really early in the morning and you're home really late, or have to stay away for a night. These jobs are not always popular. And it's not always much fun to do. There are committees of which you think: damn, I really don't like it. This can be why sometimes jobs are not reallocated because the others would rather do without it themselves. (S9)

This does not mean that the job of participating in a committee is always the least preferred job in a unit. It is more a matter of finding the right jobs for the right people. Sometimes, anyone could be made familiar with a particular subject easily (S5, S7), while in other cases a particular specialist is needed to cover the European aspects of a particular issue (S3, S11). In such cases, a reallocation of tasks is not the most suitable incentive to steer their future behaviour, even when a committee participant does his job in a way that his superior is not particularly pleased with:

> This person really knows the ropes! He knows more about it than anybody else. I want to keep making use of that. And it would not be very motivating for someone to be moved to a less interesting file. (S3)

In short, the evidence shows that the formal incentive of dismissal is only used in exceptional circumstances. The transaction cost of using this instrument is high, and therefore it is not a credible option to policy specialists. Task reallocation is a more credible threat to policy staff. But here too, the superiors of the committee participants face transaction costs in applying this incentive. Some individual committee participants may be indispensable on a certain position because of their expertise, or other people may not be interested in doing the job instead.

But whereas formal sanctioning instruments seem to be doing more harm than good, there is also a wide array of more subtle measures that superiors can resort to, and that are also generally more effective:

> Committee participant X did a marvellous job. He drafted a new directive, convinced the Commission to adopt it, and shepherded it through the committee. So I gave him a bonus and took him out for dinner. (S14)

The bonus instrument this respondent refers to is one of many ways in which principals can reward their agents. It also appears to be a quite 'organized' way of rewarding. Many heads of unit have a small budget available for bonuses, which is distributed among the staff in a certain predefined way. There can be many criteria by which someone's performance is judged. According to the superiors it is 'very small money', usually about one per cent of the salary, but the staff members are very eager to get it (S1, S15, S16). The trick, therefore, for heads of unit is to find out what committee participants *perceive* to be positive and negative incentives. This goes beyond a list of possible positive and negative formal incentives.

In any event, acting upon the behaviour of a committee participant shows that they are 'being watched'. But being watched can also be experienced as a sanction in its own right. Closer supervision schemes can have a huge impact on the performance of individual people:

> Some people may find it dreadful that they are being supervised more closely and will go and look for another job. (S9)

Box 7.5 REPRIMANDS

A few minutes before the chairman opens an agricultural committee meeting, I ask Gerard de Vries and Berend Groot about the accountability instrument of imposing consequences. What do they experience as a punishment? Groot's grin could not be bigger: 'Well, Gerard, you know everything about that, don't you?'

It turns out De Vries pushed the limits many years ago in another committee, for which he got an official reprimand. And despite the joyful atmosphere this day, De Vries is not willing to share his experience with me.

Source: Observation B.

> Especially thinking of [committee participant X], he is a person who can deal with bigger responsibilities. There is no better way of punishing him than to hold him on a leash. And that is exactly what you can tell him: you get the room for manoeuvre to do things, but in the confidence you are doing it well. If I find out things don't fit, this room will get smaller. So it's up to you.   (S11)

Supporting someone in making a career move, or rather putting someone on a dead track, is a further step down this path. This is also a highly credible instrument in the eyes of committee participants (CP1). And people can indeed be set back or promoted on the basis of committee activity:

> The guy who used to do committee X is our EU-coordinator now. He was doing an absolutely excellent job, he knew about *all* the files, coordinated everything... And then this vacancy came, and it was a true promotion, also in the sense that he got to a higher salary level.   (S3)

In contrast to the more formal incentives presented above, it appears from these results that the less formal incentives are considered to be more effective, and the instruments can be tailored to fit certain people (see Box 7.5).

Ascertaining Accountability: A Three-dimensional Perspective

Thus far, the three dimensions of accountability have been discussed: information transfer, debates, and consequences. Before drawing conclusions on the extent to which comitology committee participants are held to account by their immediate superiors, these three dimensions must first be brought together.

The *accountability cube*, as presented in Figure 7.2, will be used as a tool for this. The elements of information, debate, and consequences can each be

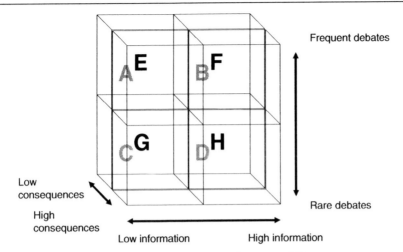

Figure 7.2 A three-dimensional measurement of accountability

scored ranging from 'low' to 'high'. This gives eight possible outcomes for a general measurement of the extent to which committee participants are held to account by their immediate superiors. Figure 7.2 shows these eight possible outcomes.

The eight outcomes shown in Figure 7.2 together constitute one three-dimensional space. Within this cube, empirical results can be plotted at any point. The eight blocks within the accountability cube show in how many cases information transfer, debates, and abilities to impose consequences are high or low, respectively frequent or rare, and in which specific combination on the three dimensions the results occur.

Block C, for example, represents a situation of low accountability. The relationships between committee participants and their superiors that are found within this block are all characterized by relatively little information transfer, few debates, and few opportunities of imposing consequences. In block F, by contrast, all elements are well developed. Relatively, much information is transferred, debates are frequent, and the superior is able to sanction or to reward. The other blocks represent in-between situations.[9]

Figure 7.3 displays the results of the survey by means of the accountability cube. No systematic differences between Danish and Dutch respondents were found.

The figure shows that the block containing least accountability (block B) is rather empty. Only 0.8 per cent of all results are found in this block. The other blocks at the rear of the cube are about equally empty.

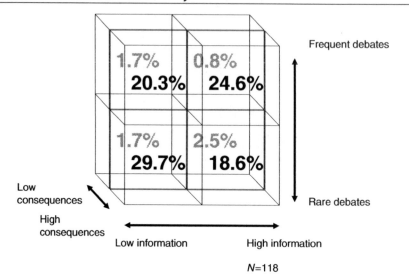

Figure 7.3 The accountability cube

Only 6.7 per cent of all relationships appear to contain three or fewer possibilities of making the committee participant face consequences, either in a positive or in a negative way. This is not a too surprising figure given the hierarchical setting that is investigated here. Nevertheless, there are a small number of cases where a hierarchical superior is not in a position to make the committee participant face consequences. This, though, is a result that is entirely based on the number of formal sanctioning options as captured by the survey. As the paragraph on consequences has shown, there are many more subtle ways of imposing consequences available as well. One can thus safely conclude that, in so far as accountability is underdeveloped, this is not particularly due to lack of sanctioning or rewarding capacities.

But there are also many cases where sanctioning capabilities are high, but where relatively little information is transferred, or where relatively few debates take place. This refers to blocks E, G, and H. Together, 68.6 per cent of all findings fall within these blocks. Only in 24.6 per cent of the cases (block F) does the bureaucratic principal receive relatively much information, and engage in regular debates. In sum, the results show that the superiors of the committee participants are quite able to impose consequences, but that practices with respect to information and debates are much more varied. The previous paragraphs point to several factors that are at the root of these practices: expertise, political salience, and the degree of autonomy of the committee participant.[10]

Holding Comitology Members Accountable Back Home

Comitology committees place their mark on around 50 per cent of all European directives, regulations, and decisions. Implementation decisions on air pollution norms, animal health, research funding, safety at sea, water quality, and many other things finally go through a comitology committee. Because of comitology, the Commission is not in a position to pursue its own policies without sufficient approval from the member states, but in turn the member states cannot cast an official vote in the committees without the Commission tabling a draft measure. The Commission and the member states, therefore, are interdependent and comitology is the arena where their points of view converge on specific measures. This makes comitology a key actor in the European policy process.

Its democratic accountability is a pressing matter, because comitology is responsible for such a high proportion of European acts. Several concerns regarding this have been raised before, but as this chapter has demonstrated, most of these concerns refer to the lack of democratic accountability vis-à-vis the European Parliament.

This chapter argues that an assessment of the democratic accountability of comitology cannot be limited to the positions of the European institutions only. Comitology is a form of multilevel governance, and this means that democratic accountability needs to be ensured at both the institutional *and* the national level. At the institutional level, comitology must be accountable to a forum at the European level, while at the same time at the individual level each individual participant must be accountable to an (ultimately) democratically elected forum in the national administration.

Past studies that relate to the democratic accountability of comitology all focused on the institutional level. These have shown time and again that it is hard to call the committees themselves to account – even if it were for the outcomes of their meetings alone. Only for a minority of committees – those that deal with adapting existing basic legislation – are the Council and the European Parliament able to revoke positive committee opinions. In all other cases, the Council only comes into the picture if the vote result in the committee does not allow the Commission to adopt an implementation measure straight away. The European Parliament has fought a long uphill battle in order to gain more powers of scrutiny. But still, it is only equipped to adopt resolutions in plenary if a committee has given an opinion on matters that are beyond its reach. It also faces very strict deadlines for this which makes it effectively impossible to adopt such resolutions (Bradley, 2008). Further, public information about the wheeling and dealing of comitology committees is not complete. Many documents in the public document register of comitology are not available, and when they are they are often not very informative. This, too, seriously handicaps the European Parliament in holding comitology to account (Brandsma, Curtin, and Meijer, 2008).

For the individual level, this chapter has presented new evidence on the extent to which comitology committee members are held to account at the national level for their input in committee meetings. All evidence indicates that, generally, there is no lack of sanctioning measures, available to the superiors of the committee participants. However, in terms of information transfer and frequency of debates, cases differ a lot more. When little information is transferred and behaviour is not being discussed, superiors know little about the wheeling and dealing of their staff. A well-developed capacity of imposing consequences does not make any difference to that. What appears is that already in the first link in the chain of accountability – the link where accountability is most likely – some elements in practice are developed to a lesser extent.

The study also shows that in the eyes of their superiors, there is a tendency of the committee participants to look for political cues that suggest appropriate behaviour. This, however, is derived at their own initiative. To a great extent, we now observe that democratic accountability has become supply-driven instead of demand-driven: the initiative for sending information rests with the committee participant, and the superior may take this information both as a cue and as a basis for discussion.

These findings do not seem to differ from the way in which modern bureaucracies function in general (cf. Dunsire, 1978; Page and Jenkins, 2005). Participation in a comitology committee does not seem to induce substantially different behaviour than handling domestic issues. For the democratic accountability of comitology, this does however produce a severe problem. This study has shown that in a significant number of instances the immediate superiors of the committee participants do not keep track of their behaviour, mainly because the initiative of accountability lies with the committee participant. Therefore, also given the little public information that is available on committee matters (cf. Türk, 2003; Brandsma, Curtin, and Meijer, 2008), it is not likely that higher management levels, let alone a minister, cabinet, or parliament, are aware of the wheeling and dealing of comitology (cf. Damgaard, 2000: 168; Larsson and

Trondal, 2005). But it should also be noted that a properly functioning accountability regime, which has also been found in a significant number of instances, is no safeguard from agency losses because further steps in the chain of accountability have to be made before political actors or the public at large are reached (Lupia, 2003; Strøm, 2003). In sum, the accountability arrangements at the European level are not optimal, and at the national level the chain of accountability is broken. Nevertheless, there is some cause for optimism as some of the deficiencies at the national level can be fixed, and because the democratic accountability arrangements of comitology at the European level are improving. The final section of this chapter provides a brief look into the future.

Making Comitology More Accountable

This study shows how all the many, seemingly trivial, details about the behaviour of national civil servants in the end add up to a risk of accountability deficits at the national level. To some extent, there is accountability by accident – committee affairs are being discussed because a committee participant happens to send a memo to his superior, who also happens to have read it. This haphazardness is dangerous, especially for comitology. Because of its multilevel character, no single entity can justifiably be held responsible for its outcomes. The Commission depends on the member states and vice versa, and within the member states the national parliaments are supposed to scrutinize their respective government.

For a democratically accountable comitology, efforts must be made to improve its accountability at both the national and at the European level. To begin with the national level, it is evident that no single minister can justifiably be held individually responsible for the formal opinions of committees that consist of twenty-seven member state representatives. But for the contribution of his own state to the committees' deliberations he may be, and as binding agreements are worked out in such comitology committee meetings, accountability for input in this must be safeguarded. The good news is that there are no European Treaty reforms necessary to make changes at the national level. The bad news is that it may prove to be very hard to improve current accountability practices because these are bread and butter to the everyday behaviour within the civil service. Most policy specialists are better informed in a subject than their masters; in fact that is a part of their job as well. Also, a higher priority is often attached to national matters than to comitology affairs.

For a healthy democratic accountability of comitology, all involved actors need to make the most of it, even for issues that will not make a national politician lose an election. Managers within the civil service are therefore advised to spend more systematic effort on holding committee participants to account for their input to comitology committees. The evidence presented in this chapter shows that often other – national – files are deemed to be more salient and thus receive more attention, but this reflex in the end causes an accountability problem. At minimum, one may expect autonomously working policy specialists to engage in fundamental discussions on a more abstract level, even if they do so irregularly. It would certainly be helpful if a general policy towards European issues was made more explicit, which the committee participant can use as a cue for his behaviour.

But there are also ways to address the accountability of comitology at the European institutional level. In the past, we have seen many changes in the formal rules of the functioning of comitology, most notably with respect to voting rules within the committees and the formal position of the European Parliament with respect to democratic accountability (Haibach, 2000; Bergström, 2005; Christiansen and Vaccari, 2006). Upon its implementation, the Lisbon Treaty significantly affects the accountability structure at the institutional level again. In cases where the executive amends basic legislation, comitology committees will cease to be. Then, the Commission will send its proposal to the Council and the European Parliament directly, which can be seen as a significant improvement in the position of the European Parliament vis-à-vis the executive. But for implementing measures that do not involve changes in basic legislation, which is the bigger category, formal consultation of committees of member state representatives will continue to exist. Article 291 (3) of the Treaty of Lisbon explicitly envisages mechanisms for control by the member states of the Commission's implementing powers. A role for the European Parliament in this, however, is neither mentioned nor ruled out (Craig, 2008; Ponzano, 2008; Hofmann, 2009). Specific procedures for this have not been agreed upon yet. But it is evident that this new, or modified, form of comitology will again involve both the Commission and member state administrations.

Despite this loose end, it is thus safe to conclude that on the whole the democratic accountability of comitology is slightly improving, albeit from a low baseline position. The improvement, moreover, occurs fully at the institutional level. At the national level, deficiencies will continue to exist well after the Lisbon Treaty has been implemented.

Notes

1. In a strict legal sense, it is only the Commission adopting acts after consulting a comitology committee. Nevertheless, it has to take notice of the committee's opinion in such a way that comitology in practice acts as a decision-maker.
2. From a constitutional perspective, the Courts can also be seen as forums (cf. Türk, 2000). This chapter, however, focuses on the democratic perspective on accountability because, from a constitutional perspective, the issue of comitology is more or less settled. The legality of comitology has been accepted by the Court of Justice since 1970 (European Court of Justice, Case 25/70), and because in 1997 the Court of First Instance ruled that for access to documents, the Commission is responsible for the committees (Court of First Instance, Case T-188/97). This shows that the Courts have found ways to address the committees without calling the committees themselves to account (Dehousse, 2003).
3. See Article 263 TFEU; Türk (2000); Council Decision 1999/468/EC.
4. See Bradley (2008) and the inter-institutional agreement between Commission and Parliament on procedures for implementing Council Decision 1999/468/EC, OJ L 256/19, 10.10.2000.
5. Such an up-to-date list is now provided by the Commission in the online comitology register <http://ec.europa.eu/transparency/regcomitology/registre.cfm?CL=en>.
6. Based on the yearly published *Hof & Statskalendern* which is only available in Danish. This list proved to be partly outdated, which led to a lower response rate in Denmark (see further below).
7. This question was not asked together with the survey to the committee participants to avoid coordination between them and their superiors as much as possible.
8. Discussions between committee participants and their superiors were not observed, as these can occur at random which makes it impossible to plan such observations ahead. In one case, the superior was only informed orally. In the remaining cases, the written reports matched the content of the respective meetings.
9. For an explanation as to how these dimensions were constructed, see Brandsma (2010).
10. For a more detailed and systematic analysis that traces back the causes of this variance, see Brandsma (2010).

8

The Real World of EU Accountability: Comparisons and Conclusions

Mark Bovens, Deirdre Curtin, and Paul 't Hart

From Assertions to Assessments

In this study, we set out to describe and assess the accountability rules and practices surrounding four key European Union (EU) bodies: the European Council, the European Commission, comitology committees, and European agencies. The principal aim of this exercise was to inject some much needed empirical rigour into the largely fact-free academic and practical debates on the accountability of the EU. Specifically, our study aimed to assess the empirical validity of the oft-voiced assertions that EU governance suffers from an accountability 'deficit' or, more insidious, an 'illusion' of accountability (Gustavsson, Karlsson, and Persson, 2009). This claim is generally made by people concerned about the broader democratic quality of EU governance. Their line of argument is that low levels of public accountability diminish the EU's democratic authenticity, which in turn depresses its public legitimacy (Beetham and Lord, 1998; Follesdal, 2006; Bogdanor, 2007; Hix, 2008). We cannot, in other words, hope to secure more public support for EU institutions if we do not make their modus operandi more open to scrutiny and sanction by (a range of) forums which in some form or other are democratically elected or authorized.

This assertion is certainly not undisputed. As we noted in Chapter 2, some contest whether making the EU more democratic is desirable to begin with (Majone, 1996, 2005; Moravcsik, 2002, 2004). Others question whether enhancing the accountability of EU institutions – among others by a series of treaty provisions adopted since Maastricht – will actually serve to convince citizens of the democratic quality of the Union (Puntscher Riekmann, 2007;

Abromeit, 2009; Gustavsson, Karlsson, and Persson, 2009). Yet others claim that it is 'too early' to aim for a fully developed democratic accountability regime, and that existing checks and balances within the current EU system can do most of the job until the population is 'ready' for the next step (Hix, 2008: 3–7, 89–109).

While this study was not designed to provide a fully fledged test of these competing assertions, it does address an essential link in the argumentative chain by systematically assessing current accountability regimes surrounding pivotal EU bodies. It also shows how these assertions, and the likely assessments their adherents would make of EU accountability practices, are premised on two different types of underlying theoretical commitments: about the nature and purposes of the EU and the nature and rationale of public accountability (cf. Curtin and Wille, 2008; Philp, 2009).

Gustavsson, Karlsson, and Persson (2009) urge scholars to 'tell it like it is' when it comes to the state of public accountability, and who can disagree with that? But the 'truths' they urge us to speak to power are themselves the product of the particular conceptual and normative tools that scholars bring to the design and purposes of both the EU and public accountability projects. In Chapters 2 and 3, we have presented two trios of analytical perspectives, one set reflecting the main currents of thought in European integration theory and the other in the study of public accountability. In this concluding chapter, we draw on these to present and interpret the findings of the empirical studies.

First, we juxtapose, compare, and contrast the results with regard to the four EU institutions singled out for in-depth study. Then, we identify some more general patterns and trends that appear to be driving the dynamics of these and other EU institutions' accountability mechanisms and regimes. Having thus revisited and interpreted the empirical evidence, we are able to address the competing claims about the accountability, democracy, and legitimacy nexus in EU governance and answer the main question with which this study began.

In the final section of this chapter, we look to the future, in terms of both future research and future institutional reform. In it, we speculate about likely and desirable futures for accountable EU governance. Our empirical studies show that accountability has progressed well beyond the status of an illusion, a fata morgana sustained by self-serving transnational power elites. It is starting to gain footholds and make inroads. The long-term challenge, we argue, is therefore to get EU accountability right, that is, to reduce remaining accountability deficits while avoiding looming accountability overloads.

Changing Rules and Practices: Observing EU Accountability

How are (key actors within) EU institutions held to account for their acts? We examined four cases and took pains to adopt a uniform approach to observing and assessing their accountability practices. The conceptual framework we employed has been presented in detail in Chapter 3 and will not be repeated here. We applied it consistently to address both de jure (rules) and de facto (practices) dimensions of accountability. In each case study, we first presented the formal rules, focusing on the powers of relevant accountability forums to (*a*) extract performance *information* from the actor, (*b*) engage it in *debate* regarding its performance, and (*c*) create non-trivial *consequences* for the actor depending on the forum's judgement about the adequacy of the performance accounts given by the actor. What composite picture can we draw from these four exercises?

Expansion and Proliferation of Accountability Regimes

It is clear that in recent times the black letter law of EU-level accountability forums has not stood still. There are more of them now than even ten years ago (proliferation) and some of them have a markedly increased potential to critically engage with executive actors (expansion). Expansion of formal powers and prerogatives was evident in three of the four cases selected (the exception being the comitology case, where the focus was solely on a single managerial accountability mechanism at the national level). In particular, the European Parliament (EP) has been accruing formal means to investigate, demand information from, debate with, and sanction EU office-holders and agencies across a range of areas. It has also acquired formal powers to scrutinize and even veto draft comitology decisions (Bradley, 2008). Likewise, the European courts' expansive interpretation of their mandates has been as conspicuous as it has been unstoppable (Slaughter, Stone Sweet, and Weiler, 1998; Arnull, 1999; Gormley, 2002). Second-guessing possible appeals and future court rulings constraining executive powers, nullifying executive decisions, or forging executive action has become an essential component of prudent policy-making by member state and EU-level executive actors alike (not to mention the time spent on actual court cases).

Evidence of proliferation of accountability forums and mechanisms is also particularly clear in the areas of financial and managerial accountability instruments. This is evident throughout the public sector worldwide (Power, 1994; Pollitt and Bouckaert, 2000; Flinders, 2001; Bouckaert and

Halligan, 2008) and the trend has not bypassed the EU system. Both the Commission and the agencies now have to manage a wide array of reporting and interaction requirements imposed upon them by a variety of accountability forums (as well as other forms of transparency and performance assessment that are not fully developed accountability mechanisms).

How to explain the proliferation and expansion of accountability forums' powers? We think there are a number of reasons. Firstly, there was the *natural reflexivity of democratic political systems* at work, in this case the growing awareness that where executive powers in EU governance proliferate, accountability should do likewise. In particular, the 1992 reforms produced by the Maastricht Treaty have served as a wake-up call to oversight bodies such as the EP that the nature of the European governance game was changing fast, with the Commission and later the Council gaining considerable momentum. In response, the EP successfully sought to increase its role as a co-legislator, but in parallel to this it has also made important strides in increasing its remit as an accountability forum, as Chapter 4 amply illustrates.

Secondly, the fact that the EU has no written constitution, yet a viable system of judicial appeal to *courts with steadfastly activist role conceptions,* is significant. Through case law, an organic expansion of the scope of EU-level legal accountability has been able to take place. A striking example is provided by case law filling a gap in the formal legal provisions and enabling the binding acts of some European agencies to be the subject of judicial review. The broad application of the 'rule of law' in the context of the evolving European legal order is the cement used to bind together – in advance of explicit treaty-level provisions – an unwritten but yet tangible constitution.

Thirdly, *institutional crises*, in particular the implosion of the Santer Commission, have prompted a flurry of support – indeed a political necessity – for a rapid upgrading of the system of checks and balances surrounding the emerging EU executive (Curtin and Wille, 2008; Curtin, 2009). At least on paper and to some extent in practice, this new system now covers not just its most conspicuous core (the Commission and its Directorates-General), but also extends towards its hitherto largely unnoticed outer reaches (the committee system and the European agencies). Some may write this off as a largely symbolic, knee-jerk response to an acute crisis, but the evidence presented here suggests that the Santer Commission crisis to a large extent served as a window of opportunity for managerial reformers within the Commission as well as for political entrepreneurs seeking a strengthening of the EP's stature as an oversight body. The new Commission both needed to restore its institutional legitimacy (hence the Kinnock reforms) and was temporarily powerless to put a stop to the constitutional agenda-setting of the EP. This confluence of forces has produced a series of reforms in both institutions that have changed their relationship, probably for ever.

Finally, it is important to realize that the expansion and proliferation of formal accountability mechanisms in the EU system has not just been the product of assertive accountability forums forcing the hand of reluctant executive actors. Chapter 5 shows that the *proactive stance of some executive leaders*, particularly within the EU agencies, was a contributing factor. They read the writing on the wall, and understood that beefing up and diversifying the accountability regimes of their organizations would not just be seen as bowing to the inevitable, but could in fact serve some of their own purposes. Particularly, the reformers among them seem to have welcomed opening up to public scrutiny by various accountability forums, since that may help them modernize and professionalize their organizations. Accountability helps them spot and stigmatize pockets of inefficiency, nepotism, and corruption. Absorbing a few critical reports and succumbing to negative sanctions from external forums can be part and parcel of their changing management strategies.

Also, some agency leaders keenly appreciate the by-product of more elaborate accountability regimes: increased visibility for their organizations in the broader EU political arena. Agency-building entrepreneurial senior executives seeking to lift their organizations from the unseen and unloved outer reaches of the Eurocracy welcome being monitored by 'many eyes' as an opportunity rather than a problem (until the sheer variety and density of accountability mechanisms starts to impose significant opportunity costs). To the extent, for example, that the EP insists on monitoring agency performance and forges more direct interaction with agency heads as part of that process, rendering account to it also provides agency leaders with opportunities to lobby and forge political networks they hitherto lacked. A caveat applies, though. While it is true that agency heads have even initiated accountability procedures particularly vis-à-vis the EP and lobbied the EP as they have come to realize that accountability is good for business, at the same time some are clearly frustrated by the lack of institutional feedback they receive as part of the process (see Chapter 5) and with the growing administrative burdens of informing and debating with often multiple accountability forums (see Busuioc, 2010).

Evolving Accountability Practices

Following the assessment of formal rules, we used a variety of data-gathering methods to obtain insight into how these formal powers are actually being used by forums and responded to by the actors, and what accountability practices result from this interplay. This allowed us to examine whether and how the growing array of formal powers that hold EU actors to account and have fallen to various national- and EU-level forums translate into observable accountability practices. Do they remain 'dead letter law', or have they provided the wedges needed to open up the hitherto opaque structures of executive power in Europe?

The empirical record of this study provides mixed evidence. Clearly, some forums do not vigorously pursue the cause of scrutinizing the behaviour of key EU actors. In the comitology study presented in Chapter 7, for example, the percentages in different corners of the accountability cube suggest that many supervisors of national comitology participants do not want to know, or feel they do not have time to know, what their junior colleagues are up to when they engage with their professional peers on the EU circuit. Likewise, Chapter 5 on European agencies reveals that most management boards come nowhere near to wielding the full extent of their formal accountability powers. Some boards are simply too big and unwieldy to make for an effective scrutineer of the agency bosses. Many board members, moreover, suffer from considerable 'double-hat' problems and are more interested in using their seats on the board to protect their national agency's interests than in discharging their duties as members of an EU-level accountability forum.

On the other hand, the case studies also provide some indications that sometimes the de facto accountability practices reach well beyond the formal powers of the relevant forum. Chapters 4 and 5 suggest that an activist forum such as the European Court of Justice (ECJ) has repeatedly stretched its mandate and opened up more expansive lines of inquiry, debate, and sanctioning concerning the Commission's and agencies' use of their powers. Likewise, Chapter 6 provides tentative indications that both the EP and at least some national parliaments are pushing for more intensive scrutiny of the Council Presidency and relevant heads of government when it comes to the 'big decisions' of the European Council, for example concerning institutional reform and crisis management.

Half Full or Half Empty? Assessing EU Accountability

Now we move from observation to assessment. We now ask: how adequately are EU institutions being held to account for their exercise of executive powers? In doing so, we return to the main puzzle with which this study began: does EU governance suffer from an accountability deficit? In Chapters 2 and 3, we made clear that answering this question inevitably involves acknowledging that there is no single, universally embraced Archimedean point for making that call. The two strands of scholarship upon which this study draws – accountability studies and European integration studies – both offer multiple, distinct, and partly competing sets of normative principles and evaluation criteria that are pertinent here.

Assessment 1: Through the Lens of European Integration Perspectives

From European studies, we have derived the trio of intergovernmental, supranational, and regulatory perspectives on the nature and purposes of EU governance (see Chapter 2). Each of them translates into a set of principles for the design and performance of public accountability of EU institutions (cf. Tallberg, 2009; Wiener and Diez, 2009). To recapitulate briefly:

- The *intergovernmental* perspective favours strong national-level accountability forums and opposes giving strong powers and capacity to EU-level forums, although some checks and balances at the European level may be appropriate.

- The *supranational* perspective favours strong accountability practices at the EU level where the decisions are taken, although some complementary mechanisms at the national level may also be considered appropriate.

- The *regulatory* perspective is even-minded about the level at which accountability is organized, but strongly favours administrative, professional, and to some degree social accountability over political and, to some degree, legal accountability types (as the latter tend to get in the way of dispassionate, expertise-driven modes of governing).

The question now is to what extent the observed accountability practices conform to these various visions. Table 8.1 provides a set of schematic answers. To interpret the scores, take the example of the *European Commission's* developing accountability regime (see also Tallberg, 2009). Intergovernmentalists like their Commission small to begin with, but to the extent that its scope and powers are considerable they would prefer it to be checked and counterbalanced by a strong Council and assertive national parliaments, rather than the current trend towards strengthening the EP as the principal accountability forum (hence the score). In contrast, the supranationalists rate the deepening of the Commission's various accountability

Table 8.1 Assessing emerging EU accountability rules and practices: a first iteration

	Case 1 Commission	Case 2 Agencies	Case 3 European Council	Case 4 Comitology
Intergovernmental	−	+ / −	+	+ / −
Supranational	+	+	+ / −	+ / −
Regulatory	+ / −	+ / −	N.A.	+ / −

regimes as positive: EU-level political and administrative forums have 'woken up' and put themselves forward to effectively curb Commission autonomy. From a regulatory perspective, the growth of political accountability of the Commission to the EP would also count as a negative, whereas the enhanced administrative and emerging social accountability mechanisms count as a positive development.

Secondly, the developing financial, managerial, and political accountability regimes surrounding *European agencies* will be judged differently when employing the three perspectives. Intergovernmentalists, one assumes, do not like the EP's growing interest in the agencies, nor the encroachment of the ECJ's jurisdiction over them. Yet though they do not welcome the role of those two forums, they do favour agency accountability vis-à-vis management boards composed of member state representatives and accountability arrangements vis-à-vis the Council structures.

Supranationalists, in contrast, welcome the growing remit and role of ECJ and EP and may at some point in the future be able to admit that one can no longer speak of an accountability deficit as such with regard to many agencies (although there will certainly still be gaps). At the same time, supranationalists must still be unhappy with the existing arrangements vis-à-vis Europol and Eurojust, where the Court does not have a role and the EP lacks co-decision powers and cannot exert influence for more supranational accountability arrangements (it will change when the Lisbon Treaty enters into force – on a still optimistic reading during the course of 2010). Proponents of the regulatory perspective welcome the growing use of professional and administrative accountability mechanisms. However, they would be concerned that the even more markedly expanding grip of political and legal accountability forums risks robbing the agencies of the very thing they had going for them: the capacity to do their business in a depoliticized, 'non-majoritarian' climate.

Thirdly, let us look at the *European Council*. From an intergovernmental perspective, the fact that the powers of the EP are still pretty limited in being able to hold the President and members of the European Council to account is probably a welcome state of affairs. In their perspective, the European Council is an arena for interstate bargaining and persuasion. Its members should be held accountable by their national constituencies and not by the European-level EP as a matter of principle. On this view, only the national level can be considered a possible accountability forum. In the event, it emerged from this case study that the Dutch parliament had the formal powers to oblige the prime minister to provide information about his input into European Council deliberations and their outcomes, debate his European Council performance in the chamber, and be bound by the Dutch parliament's opinion. It was also found that the parliament invokes these powers selectively, and that accountability following major European Council summits is patchy, but can be relatively intense at times (depending upon a range of often ad hoc considerations).

This composite picture suits adherents of the intergovernmental perspective nicely. In contrast, applying the supranational perspective to this same set of facts leads to a different appreciation: the limited powers of the EP in this domain are seen as a clear sign of an accountability deficit, while welcoming strong national parliamentary accountability practices even more than its intergovernmental counterpart (cf. Karlsson, 2009). However, the fact is that with the entry into force of the Lisbon Treaty in 2009 the European Council acquires a formal status as an institution of the EU and will almost inevitably find itself in an evolving and living accountability relationship with the EP at the European level of governance. Finally, the regulatory perspective has no preference either way, since the Council as a political entity is beyond its preoccupation with non-majoritarian actors and technocratic rather than political forms of collective decision-making.

Regarding the accountability of *comitology* participants, supranationalists clearly lament the relative weakness of EU-level forums in checking this important cluster of the 'many' and 'invisible' administrative hands, although some progress has been made in recent years (Curtin, 2009). They likewise lament the similar findings of studies concerning the lack of accountability of national public servants stationed at the Permanent Representation in Brussels. While intergovernmentalists may not (yet) be up in arms over the relative (and not very visible until this study) lack of interest and activity of the national bureaucratic principals of comitology participants, they will note that neither do national parliaments appear to be exercising much of a grip on member state governments. At the end of the day though, intergovernmentalists are likely to explain this away as part of the larger implicit delegation bargain that national parliaments have struck with their governments when agreeing to membership and subsequent deepening of the European integration process. Finally, from a regulatory perspective the relative weakness of hierarchical accountability is considered to be largely irrelevant, but the dearth of more institutionalized professional accountability mechanisms of self-regulation and monitoring is probably deplored.

Assessment 2: Through the Lens of Public Accountability Perspectives

From accountability studies, we have extracted three philosophies of accountable governance that equally contain three distinct criteria sets to assess the adequacy of accountability practices (see Chapter 3). The *democratic* perspective emphasizes popular control of the executive, the *constitutional* perspective emphasizes checks and balances around and within the executive, and the *learning* perspective emphasizes the extent to which accountability contributes to intelligent reflection and re-examination of existing governance practices.

Table 8.2 reports the outcomes of this second logic of assessment. Note that the marks indicate an assessment of the observed trends rather than an absolute assessment of the present state of affairs. If we take the *democratic* perspective first – which to some scholars, like Gustavsson (2009), is really the *only* relevant way of assessing accountability (within the EU or otherwise) – there is good news to tell, certainly more than these same authors imply when they conclude their study by stating that EU governance labours under an 'illusion' of accountability. Three of the four cases we studied revealed relatively robust trends towards the increasing scope and strength of parliamentary control mechanisms. Two of them directly concerned an evolving accountability relationship with the EP as the salient accountability forum (the European Council and the Commission). Particularly noteworthy has been the ascendance of the EP in holding the Commission accountable (see Chapter 4), notwithstanding the fact that democratic theorists practically rule out the current EP as a credible accountability forum, given the continuing insignificance of European issues in the European electorate's mind (second-order elections) and the lack of a well-developed EU party system and public sphere (cf. Schmidt, 2006; Hix, 2008; Mair, 2008; Gustavsson, Karlsson, and Persson, 2009).

While the EP itself continues to be viewed as a democratic work in progress by some, there can be little doubt that its exploitation of the Santer Commission crisis has given it significant momentum in its desire to become a more effective check on the Commission. At the same time,

Table 8.2 Assessing EU accountability practices: a second iteration

	Case 1 Commission	Case 2 Agencies	Case 3 European Council	Case 4 Comitology
Democratic perspective	+	+	+	− / +
Constitutional perspective	+ +	+	−	+ / −
Learning perspective	+	−	− −	− −

Chapter 6 shows that the EP is more constrained in any attempt to likewise 'normalize' its control relationship with the European Council, given that institution's strongly intergovernmental origins and features. However, in cases in which the European Council acts as the 'ultimate decision-maker or coordinator' of EU policy on pivotal issues such as treaty reform and transnational emergencies, the EP is slowly but surely doing what it can under the present arrangements to hold it accountable (but under present rules it remains dependent upon whoever happens to hold the EU Council Presidency at the time to appear and debate the issues in a sustained and serious fashion).

In the present study, we have only looked at one (i.e. the Dutch) national parliament's role in holding its head of government accountable for his role in European Council decision-making, revealing a mixed picture. We know from other research that there are considerable cross-national variations in these parliaments' desires and capacities to do so – although again the general trend seems to be one of rising ambitions and abilities (Fitzmaurice, 1996; Marquand, 2008; Sousa, 2008). The two trends – increased, and more overtly politicized, forms of parliamentary oversight of European Council inputs and outputs by both national parliaments and the EP – can coexist without too many difficulties, since they target different actors about different aspects of Council decision-making (except perhaps the Council President's own national parliament, whose scrutiny of its head of government may overlap with that of the EP's scrutiny of him or her in his or her role of Presidency).

The sole area covered in this study where democratic accountability forums operate at considerable arm's length is comitology. This may well be an artefact of the study's design, which focused first and foremost on the hierarchical accountability arrangement between comitology participants and their bureaucratic superiors at the national level. But at the same time, other research suggests that it is safe to say that comitology processes remain relatively impervious to direct scrutiny from the EP or national parliaments (Rhinard, 2002; Brandsma, 2007; Brandsma, Curtin, and Meijer, 2008; Neuhold, 2008), although there is certainly some evidence of more legal powers being given to the EP in particular (Bradley, 2008; Curtin, 2009).

The *constitutional perspective* detects even stronger positives. Our studies of both the European Commission and the European agencies clearly report an ongoing 'thickening' of their accountability regimes, at least in the de jure sense: there are now more accountability forums that can hold them accountable on a broader range of subjects employing a wider range of powers of information-gathering, debate, and sanctioning than just ten years ago (see Chapter 4, also Busuioc, 2010). To the extent that these formal possibilities have also been translated into actual accountability practices, this has meant in practice that senior bureaucrats in the European executive branch have had to pay more attention to explaining their past practices to a variety of bodies. Consequently, one may infer, the norms of good public and corporate governance (e.g. transparency, responsibility, actuarial propriety, motivation of decisions, rights of appeal, competence-based recruitment, and career advancement) have become a lot more salient in the way they run their organizations (see also Groenleer, 2009).

There may be differences between the two actors in terms of the formalization – and intensification – of these accountability forums, but one thing is sure: the accountability regime of the other two institutions is very thin by comparison. That of the comitology system may have seen some formal thickening in recent times, but its day-to-day realities are such that it remains a problematic arena of European governance from a checks and balances perspective spanning both the national and the European levels (Neuhold, 2008).

From the *learning* perspective, the picture is more mixed. Of the four studies reported here only one found significant evidence – for example, the Kinnock reforms' emphasis on strengthening professionalism of the European Commission's cadres and organizational cultures – for the existence of the more reflective accountability practices envisioned by deliberative democrats such as Eriksen and Fossum (2000). Some directors of EU agencies, for example, seem to be more concerned by issues of 'overload' instead of welcoming the possibilities for (self-)reflection and performance improvement that the increasingly thick accountability regimes they are embedded in entail. Moreover, to the extent that the observed trends point towards 'normalization' (more comprehensive and more overtly political forms of oversight gaining strength vis-à-vis more technocratic – e.g. managerial, financial, legal – types of checks and balances) of not just the Commission but also the Council and to some extent the agencies, the learning potential of these accountability regimes is more likely to be compromised than it is to be enhanced.

What Deficit? Whose Deficit?

Where does that leave the much-vaunted accountability deficit of the EU? By now, it will come as no surprise to the reader that our answer to this question is 'it depends'. It depends on which accountability mechanism, regime, or cluster of regimes is being assessed. It depends on whether one is judging snapshots or long-term trends. It also depends on who is doing the assessing, as there are marked differences among EU scholars in particular as to what constitute the relevant criteria. And it depends on what implicit or explicit benchmarks or counterfactuals are being used in doing the assessing, even among proponents of one and the same criteria set. For supranational and 'democratic' accountability students, for example, the benchmark issue is whether EU-level accountability rules and practices should be 'as good' as the average (or the 'best') member state's national practices. For intergovernmental accountability theorists, the benchmark issue is whether EU accountability should be more or less elaborate than that of other regional or global international organizations. For adherents to the regulatory perspective on the EU and the 'learning' perspective on accountability, it is how categorically 'non-majoritarian' they like the accountability regimes of each and every EU institution to be. And finally for 'constitutional' accountability scholars, it is how many checks and balances are 'enough' (and, by implication, when they become 'too much').

If we look at the de jure situation, the conclusion can be relatively straightforward. Granted that the picture is diverse and subject to ongoing change, the overall observation that emerges from our studies is that slowly but surely forums have been gaining powers vis-à-vis actors. Depending on vantage points, some might say too much so, others will say not yet enough. Certainly, among the cases studied here, the most obvious example of a continued shortfall in formal powers of forums over actors is that of the political accountability of the European Council. The EP has very little to go on, and in all but a very limited number of national parliaments' mandates there is no special provision (or designated institutional capacity) made for checking the European deal-making activities of heads of governments and ministers.

Turning from formal powers to observable practices, general observations and assessments become progressively more difficult. It is clear that in some cases forums make limited use of their existing powers to hold executive actors accountable. This is the case for national parliaments vis-à-vis heads of government, for management boards in relation to EU agency heads, and most glaringly for the direct superiors of comitology members. But does that in and of itself provide sufficient reason to speak of a deficit? Doing so would imply that in each of those three accountability relationships at the national level, forums are more energetic, proactive, or tenacious – which we know from other research is certainly not always the case (Müller, 1994; Schillemans, 2007). In fact, there is considerable reason to claim, as many 'democratic auditors' do, that in any case many national political accountability practices are equally deficient (Weir and Beetham, 1999; Sawer, Abjorensen, and Larkin, 2009), in which case the European deficit looks somewhat less conspicuous. That does not, of course, make it any less real and problematic, certainly not in the eyes of adherents to the 'democratic' school of accountability assessment (Lord, 2007).

How different the picture becomes when one switches towards a more 'constitutional' perspective. In doing so, the alleged deficit shrinks considerably, at least for visible actors frontstage and backstage. What one sees instead is a proliferation of perhaps still weak, but clearly nascent administrative accountability norms and practices in most nooks and crannies of EU governance – coming on top of already well-developed financial and often outright strong legal accountability mechanisms. If, as 'monitory democrats' (Keane, 2009), what we care about most is that executive power is being effectively checked by (a set of) forums or principals, then the developments of the last decade regarding both the Commission and the EU agencies are most gratifying. To the extent that deficits remain, we find them around the political actors comprising the Council (and its growing administrative apparatus; Curtin, 2009) and the administrative actors of comitology committees. Perhaps not coincidentally, both are right at the interface between national and supranational levels of governance, falling as it were between the cracks of multilevel governance. Both are consequently subject to relatively 'thin' and one-dimensional accountability regimes. There is little besides (weakly developed) national political accountability checking heads of government in their roles as EU architects and policy-makers. Likewise, there is little besides (mostly weakly developed) national hierarchical accountability checking technical experts and their EU-level 'epistemic communities' of comitology committees.

Also, we find that learning-based accountability mechanisms are generally underdeveloped in the EU system. We know from prior research (Bovens, 2007; Schillemans, 2007) that horizontal (professional and social) mechanisms have greatest learning potential, but as far as we can tell on the basis of our limited study they appear to be underutilized (see also Parks, 2009; Persson, 2009). This may be an artefact of the lack of direct citizen exposure/contacts of many EU institutions, and the many difficulties of organizing effective interest representation at the European level. That said, research also suggests that such horizontal mechanisms are not very strong (or ultimately are overshadowed by learning-unfriendly vertical ones) at the national level of government (see e.g. Bovens, 't Hart, and Schillemans, 2008; Schillemans, 2008).

To add insult to injury for supranationalists and democrats, there is even the occasional whisper of 'accountability overload' encroaching upon the EU system – and our study offers some food for thought in this regard too. The whispers come, of course, from among the accountors: Commission bureaucrats and agency officials deploring the growing number of accountability obligations they are coming under, as well as the inordinate amount of time and energy consumed by meeting all these obligations. Chapters 4 and 5 in particular paint a picture in which senior EU bureaucrats are not all that far removed any more from having to spend as much time reporting and justifying what they and their colleagues have been doing as they can devote to actually doing things. This is, of course, the natives' point of view, which accountability assessors may choose to discount as self-serving and mandarinesque. But in our view, these voices too are legitimate contributions to the debate. If these voices increase in number and intensity in years to come, their lived experiences of 'doing accountability' deserve to be taken as seriously as those of the vociferous, concerned democrats riding the deficit bandwagon. It is up to assessors to not dismiss either's claim out of hand, but rather to provide relevant and systematic empirical evidence needed to arrive at a more balanced and almost inevitably actor-specific assessment of both the 'bite' and the 'burdens' of the accountability rules and practices that impinge upon them.

From Accountable to Legitimate EU Governance?

So, to what extent does the observed gradual beefing up of accountability regimes contribute to enhance EU legitimacy? This way of framing the question presupposes a two-pronged set of expectations: (*a*) better accountability mechanisms and regimes lead to better (more responsive, more virtuous, and more clever) governance in the EU system as well as anywhere and (*b*) better governance will be seen and appreciated, and thus lead to higher levels of public and political support – and even trust – for the EU and its institutions. Yet, as asserted in Chapters 2 and 3, the various theoretical perspectives on EU integration and on public accountability harbour significantly different understandings of what 'better' accountability regimes consist of and just how they may enhance EU legitimacy:

- To both EU supranationalists and accountability 'democrats', the argument means that strong political accountability mechanisms at both the national and EU level should foster strong political legitimacy for the EU as such.

- To EU intergovernmentalists, it means that strong domestic political accountability mechanisms alone should have 'trickle up' effects towards a certain (minimally required) domestic legitimacy for EU involvement.

- To both EU regulatory and accountability as well as 'learning' proponents, it means that strong peer/professional and social accountability mechanisms should produce smarter governance, yielding higher public value and therefore creating more contented citizens ('happy customers').

- To accountability constitutionalists, this means that a general thickening of accountability regimes surrounding EU actors should help to make the exercise of European executive power cleaner and therefore more publicly palatable.

The problem we have at this point is that there is very little evidence supporting in any hard and fast way the above propositions. The easiest, perhaps because it is the most familiar, is the intergovernmental chain of reasoning. Stronger national accountability mechanisms, especially the political/democratic ones, feed into national political legitimacy in a way that can almost only be self-reinforcing and not terribly contested in itself. This too is the assumption of the *Bunderverfassungsgericht* in its judgment dealing with the Lisbon Treaty. It is downright dismissive about any possible democratic legitimacy flowing from the role of the EP in the EU political system. Its harsh verdict, despite all the advances that have been made in recent years in constitutionalizing and increasing its powers, is that as the EP is 'not a body of representation of a sovereign European people', it cannot (as yet?) be considered legitimate democratically. All the efforts that have been made to reinforce the supranational democratization arenas have been premised 'as if' the EU was a sovereign state, which it is not. The problem for the supranationalists and the EU democrats is that institutional tweaking and reinforcement of accountability mechanisms and regimes will probably never be enough to cause citizens and political actors in various national settings to shift their loyalties, expectations, and political activities to the supranational centre. Indeed, such empirical evidence as there is indicates the contrary. This shifting of allegiance, acceptance, and trust has definitely not happened, nor do recent debates in the context of ratification of the Lisbon Treaty (and indeed various of its predecessors) provide much food for hope in the foreseeable future. But how realistic is it to expect that to happen in a short time frame? We can recall at this point just how long it took for systems of bureaucratic accountability to develop in the national parliamentary systems, not to mind how long it took for allegiances to switch, for example, from regions to more centralized and unitary nation states.

Balancing and Integrating Perspectives

What this volume, however, does show is that both the rules and the practices of democratic accountability are developing in a dynamic and incremental fashion but at different governance levels (European and national) and also in ways that overlap. It is thus not an 'either/or' approach but an accumulation. The EP as an imperfect repository of democratic legitimacy at the European level is nonetheless engaging with new and less than fully visible actors at the European level and finding ways and means, often informal, to put and keep them under the spotlight. We see that not only with the obvious frontstage example of the European Commission but also with the more backstage example of European agencies. The point the *Bundesverfassungsgericht* missed is that in spite of the theoretically perfect democratic legitimacy of the German parliament under the inalienable core of the German constitution, it simply cannot reach any of what happens at the collective supranational level, and nor can any of the national parliaments. In effect, this kind of purely intergovernmentalist attitude is the equivalent of the ostrich with its head in the sand, choosing to ignore the realities around it that it does not wish to see or engage with.

That said, at the national level too we see an intensification in the role being asserted at least de jure by national parliaments and an increasing realization that they constitute the appropriate democratic forum to hold political actors such as (prime) ministers (and national civil servants) to account. So to start understanding democracy in Europe and the way it will most probably continue to develop in the coming decade, we need to put both levels together in a composite fashion, even if huge problems remain in terms of the meta parameters of the political system. The absence of a viable European public sphere and of genuine European political parties who compete for the votes of European citizens on the basis of European issues platforms, continue to be considered as major deficits in the realm of representation in Europe. Yet in the realm of accountability practices this volume shows that substantial progress has been made.

Still, the notion of a more composite form of democracy in Europe leaves plenty of scope for development but factors in that there is no one 'right' answer or level but rather that the very complexity and multilevel nature of European decision-making dictates the input of multilevel democratic accountability forums. So the vision of neither intergovernmentalists nor supranationalists on their own can suffice. They need, somehow, to be put together. Even so, institutionalizing more democratic accountability at multiple levels is not necessarily the 'solution to the legitimacy problems of the European Union' (Puntscher Riekmann, 2007). The unfinished democratization of Europe requires more: ultimately that the citizens can approve or reject the laws they are subject to (Eriksen, 2009).

When it comes to a more constitutional perspective, then the same picture of the composite nature of the evolving constitution – also composite in nature and in level – emerges (Besselink, 2007). Such 'checks and balances' are largely under construction by European and national courts. This chapter has already highlighted the activist role of the European courts in constructing an unwritten constitution, case by case, actor by actor, practice by practice. Their approach is rarely holistic and depends to a large extent on the actual cases brought before them for judicial review (with all the inherent access to justice problems). But at the same time, national courts – and especially national constitutional courts – also consider that they are engaged in this constitution-defining exercise, in particular regarding the boundaries with their own national constitutions (e.g. the aforementioned judgment of the German *Bundesverfassungsgericht* on the Lisbon Treaty). This multilevel trend of engagement, activism, and boundary control is one that no doubt will continue and perhaps intensify, and in doing so supersede and blur hitherto separate intergovernmentalist and supranationalist perspectives on European integration. Whether it will actually lead to a feeling among European citizens that the composite polity as a whole is more acceptable remains an open question. There is no evidence showing that it will.

The regulatory perspective also transcends the idea of separate spheres of government at national, European, and indeed international or global levels. Its emphasis on governance as collective problem-solving, the pivotal role of (transnational) professional expertise, and more learning-oriented forms of accountability is one that both transcends levels and requires them to be put together. The jury is still out on the impact that the higher effectiveness of European governance that such practices allegedly bring may have on citizen perceptions of the EU.

Tracking the Future of Accountability in EU Governance

The Dynamics of EU Accountability

Let us conclude by suggesting a few implications for both the study and the (re)design of European accountability practices. One lesson learnt about describing, explaining, and assessing accountability relationships and regimes is that these should not be treated as static structures but rather as dynamic, evolving practices. Rather than focusing all the analytical energy on actors, the evolution of their powers, and the extent to which all of these are 'covered' by adequate accountability provisions (as most accountability studies tend to do), this volume has shown the benefit of applying such a dynamic approach to study of forums. Some of the case studies clearly document how forums over time renegotiate their powers and generally try to broaden the scope of their control or the 'bite' of their powers of investigation, debate, and sanctioning – however imperfect they may initially have been and, depending upon one's perspective, still are.

Secondly, in terms of a broader research agenda on accountability in the EU, there are clearly new, horizontal, diagonal, professional, networked accountability regimes and practices emerging within the EU that can also be factored into further empirical study. A key analytical (as well as practical) challenge in this regard is that of how to deal with the many hands in multilevel, networked governance settings that are so common in the EU: how to track accountability practices without involving a simple 'billiard ball' model of one actor accounting to one forum, but involving instead a complex cast of actors, only some of which are fully 'public sector', operating at European, national, and subnational levels of governance, accounting in a range of ways to a whole cast of accountability forums. Crime fighters and counterterrorism experts are fond of saying that it takes a network to catch a network, but from an accountability perspective the simultaneous dispersal of both actors and forums into networks creates a whole new set of challenges.

Thirdly, future studies should investigate to what degree and how trends towards multilevel policy-making and implementation that in-volve EU actors beyond the EU have been matched by corresponding changes and innovations in accountability regimes and practices. They should examine the (limits of) holding to account EU actors who operate in networked, sometimes largely informal, cooperation involving both other EU and non-EU actors in larger transnational settings. The EU is not an island, and its structures and processes are partially and perhaps increasingly intertwined with those of larger international regimes, creating the kinds of 'networks of networks' that are perhaps the most elusive targets for democratic accountability designers and scholars alike.

The Saliency of Supranationalist Accountability

As this chapter has made clear, we are not convinced that there is a gaping, let alone a growing, accountability deficit in contemporary governance. There are clear gaps in the fabric however, which we have pointed out in the various case studies. Therefore, we do feel a case can be made for a selective strengthening of accountability with respect to some actors, networks, and the power and practices of some forums. This is particularly the case for the political and the horizontal forms of accountability operating within the EU. Which of the various lenses on EU governance and accountability that we have utilized in this volume are suited to help us conceptualize such changes?

This volume clearly shows that the real world of accountability in EU governance is not confined to neat single-level interactions. In almost every case we have studied, there is a plurality of actor–forum interactions at a plurality of levels. This has to do partially with the fact that EU governance is in large part no longer a matter of pure intergovernmental relations (e.g. the powers of the European Commission, comitology committees, and EU-level agencies networking with their national counterparts in a disaggregated fashion); it is also supranational and also regulatory in ways that cannot be neatly cordoned off.

At the end of the day, therefore, we feel the intergovernmental lens offers too limited a field of vision. It is least in line with the empirical practices of how EU-level governance takes shape and evolves. Even in a field supposedly on the fringes of EU governance with a profoundly intergovernmental rhetoric, EU common foreign and security policy, experts more and more point to the fact that autonomous EU-level actors are being created and empowered, so that a simple intergovernmental analysis no longer captures a more complex reality (Sjursen, 2007). The same point emerges in other fields too (Eriksen, 2009). At the end of the day, we incline more towards acceptance of (a version of) the supranational perspective as being more in line with what happens in practice, and therefore also a more salient normative yardstick for assessing EU accountability. At the same time, we are not dogmatic or visionary supranationalists (let alone federalists) claiming that, come what may, a fully supranational or even post-national model of democracy has to emerge (but see Eriksen, 2009). Our preferred view of supranationalism retains a strong dose of intergovernmentalism, particularly in its emphasis on the need for thick political forums at the national level. And it includes an express acknowledgement of the importance of the explicitly 'regulatory' phenomena such as networks and agencies, which, after all, have long been part of the normal fabric of governance at the national level too, and are on the increase in many sectors of international governance.

Reinforcing the Role of Parliaments

As regards the three accountability perspectives, we feel a mixture of democratic and constitutional perspectives is the most appropriate tool to adopt. It is not possible to get to grips with and hold complex multilevel and multifaceted actors to account without having a combination of political forums at both national and supranational levels. We favour a further reinforcement of this approach, which is already emerging in practice, bit by bit. At the national level there is a welcome trend from national parliaments to reinforce their own powers vis-à-vis their own national executives, as indeed there should be. No one else can hold national (prime) ministers and national civil servants to account on an individual basis for the performance of the role of representing the 'national interest' but the apex of the national political (and democratic) hierarchy: the national parliament. At the same time, they are confronted with the impossibility of holding the collective executive actor in whatever shape or form (from the Commission to the European Council to comitology committees) to account.

It is here that we see a deepening of the role that the EP has begun to claim and assert for itself: as an accountability forum with some political powers and considerable (financial) sanctioning powers. The power of the purse has traditionally been the way that most parliaments (including the EP) have acquired a more powerful role. In addition, it is likely (and desirable) that the EP will take a more assertive role as interlocutor of various actors and networks and will insist on the need for publicity and openness in substantiating this role. This has not always been the case in the past, where the EP has allowed itself to be too much influenced by the aura and culture of diplomatic negotiations in intergovernmental organs (such as the Council of Ministers in particular).

That said, we also care about transaction costs and unintended effects of accountability: more is not better, and we have to be careful that accountability overload in some settings does not become as much of an issue as deficits traditionally have been. It is about getting the balance right. The quality of the accountability regimes and arrangements studied in this volume will not be strengthened per se by giving more formal powers to the forums in question. What many of them need instead is better institutional capacity to act as credible, constructive accountability players. In the case of management boards of European agencies, for example, this would involve: augmentation or reduction of forum size, more time to process information provided by actors prior to meetings/debate, more staff capacity, and elimination of blatant conflict of interest in modes of selecting forum members. In other areas, for example both the European Council and the Council of Ministers, there is still plenty of scope for enhancing the de jure regime: more scrutiny powers for the EP vis-à-vis the European Council chair (similar to what has now been put in place with regard to the Commission). That would represent real progress and may be some time coming but the EP will no doubt push this agenda and incrementally scale up its own practices in this direction. With regard to national parliaments, the picture is probably more scattered: some parliaments need more legal powers, others have got them already, but nearly all of them need more organizational capacity to be a credible control player. Most of all, however, national parliaments need to embrace the realities: if they do not link into what their own national executives are up to at the European level, they marginalize themselves (also as a matter of national constitutional relationships). And if it 'takes a network to catch a network', then part of the future lies with networking (European and national) parliaments to mirror and keep pace with their networking national and European executives, who have long ago jumped the fence of national constitutional systems.

The Complexity of Executive Power in the EU

This brings us right back to where we started this volume. Why bother about EU accountability? The answer we gave in Chapter 1 was simple and straightforward: because the nature and reach and intensity of EU governance. Now, at the end of the volume, a second part to the answer is clear for all to see: because of the institutional complexity of the executive power that is being exercised. For a long time, the focus of constitutional lawyers, international relations scholars, and indeed (comparative) political scientists has been on the legislative power of the EU level and its interaction with the national level of government. The current volume broadens this scope. It accepts the premise that so-called non-legislative power at the EU level is growing at an accelerated pace, both formally and informally. Such EU executive power is paradoxically both autonomous and dependent. It is autonomous for some EU-level actors exercising power conferred formally at the EU level; it is dependent because many of the executive actors at the EU level are in fact composed of members of the national executive power, wearing different hats. This complexity breeds opaqueness, indeterminacy, and creates incentives for executive improvisation, negotiation, and entrepreneurship. It creates an executive system that is well and truly a world of many, many hands. To keep such a system in check, keep it smart, and provide it with public legitimacy is a key and urgent challenge. Designing and managing appropriate accountability regimes is a crucial part of meeting this challenge.

All four of the institutions/actors studied empirically in this volume bear witness to the complexity and plurality of the nature of executive power in the EU. The European Council is the informal 'newcomer' to the original EU institutional design. Its formalization in the Lisbon Treaty explicitly states that its powers are 'not legislative'. Its members, except for the new European-level President provided for in the Lisbon Treaty with a clearly autonomous role, all wear two hats. The Commission has long proclaimed its mission to be the sole executive power of the EU. In recent years, it has seen its dream trodden on – heavily – by the member states (in the Council, the European Council, and at successive intergovernmental conferences including the two that ultimately led to the Treaty of Lisbon). Both of the 'backstage' actors studied (agencies and comitology) have moved in orbit around the core political actors (Commission and Council) but at the same time share the characteristic that they, to a very significant extent, include member state bureaucrats in their core institutional design (committees and management boards).

Many of the multifarious actors and institutions at the EU level are constantly engaged in two-level, sometimes multilevel 'games'. They are embedded in an institutional design that is more complex than that which exists at the level of national political and constitutional systems. The issue of their accountability is urgent and is unlikely to go away for the foreseeable future. A core message emerging from the empirical studies in this volume is that the roles and practices (as well as the internal organization) of accountability *forums* are absolutely key. Given the fact that we cannot realistically expect more grand designs or constitutional big bangs at the European level after the entry into force of the Lisbon Treaty in 2009, we will need to work with what we have already. We need viable parliamentary, judicial, and other forms of institutional reflexivity, both European and national. We need these forums to continue to adapt in order to provide checks on these evolving and potentially elusive forms of executive power.

The present real word of EU accountability is imperfect, but it can no longer be adequately characterized as a clear and gaping deficit on all fronts. Yet this does not guarantee that the future world of EU accountability will bring a steady and benign reduction of remaining deficits. The reality is more complicated and ambiguous. To be sure, Europe needs vigilant, dynamic accountability forums; it also needs to guard against overshooting the target. Where once was a deficit, no overload may be allowed to grow either. Such is the challenge for executive actors as well as the designers and managers of forums alike: though they ostensibly sit on separate sides of the fence, at the end of the day they need to collaborate in making accountability of EU governance work.

Bibliography

Aarts, K. and Van der Kolk, H. (2005). *Nederlanders en Europa. Het referendum over de Europese grondwet.* Amsterdam: Bert Bakker.

Abbott, A. (1988). *The System of Professions: An Essay on the Division of Expert Labor.* Chicago, IL: University of Chicago Press.

Abromeit, H. (2009). 'The Future of the European Accountability Problem', in S. Gustavsson, C. Karlsson, and T. Persson (eds.), *The Illusion of Accountability in the European Union.* London: Routledge, 23–34.

Ackrill, R., Kay, A., and Morgan, W. (2008). 'The Common Agricultural Policy and Its Reform: The Problem of Reconciling Budget and Trade Concerns'. *Canadian Journal of Agricultural Economics/Revue canadienne d'agroeconomie,* 56/4: 393–411.

Adelberg, S. and Batson, C. D. (1978). 'Accountability and Helping: When Needs Exceed Resources'. *Journal of Personality and Social Psychology,* 36: 343–50.

Allison, G. (1971). *Essence of Decision: Explaining the Cuban Missile Crisis.* Boston, MA: Little, Brown.

Andeweg, R. B. (1992). 'Executive-Legislative Relations in the Netherlands: Consecutive and Coexisting Patterns'. *Legislative Studies Quarterly,* 17/2: 161–82.

Anechiarico, F. and Jacobs, J. B. (1996). *The Pursuit of Absolute Integrity: How Corruption Control Makes Government Ineffective.* Chicago, IL: University of Chicago Press.

Armstrong, K. and Kilpatrick, C. (2007). 'Law, Governance or New Governance? The Changing Open Method of Coordination'. *Columbia Journal of European Law,* 13/3: 649–78.

Arnull, A. (1999). *The European Union and Its Court of Justice.* Oxford: Oxford University Press.

—— and Wincott, D. (eds.) (2002). *Accountability and Legitimacy in the European Union.* Oxford: Oxford University Press.

Aucoin, P. and Heintzman, R. (2000). 'The Dialectics of Accountability for Performance in Public Management Reform'. *International Review of Administrative Sciences,* 66/1: 45–55.

—— and Jarvis, M. D. (2005). *Modernizing Government Accountability: A Framework for Reform.* Ottawa: Canada School of Public Service.

Auel, K. and Benz, A. (2005). 'The Politics of Adaptation: The Europeanisation of National Parliamentary Systems'. *Journal of Legislative Studies,* 11/3: 372–93.

Ban, C. (2008). 'The Challenge of Linking Organizational and Individual Accountability in the European Commission'. Working Paper. Available at: <http://
carolynban.net/>

Barberis, P. (1998). 'The New Public Management and a New Accountability'. *Public
Administration*, 76/1: 451–70.

Bauer, M. W. (2007). 'Introduction: Management Reforms in International Organizations', in M. W. Bauer and C. Knill (eds.), *Management Reforms in International
Organizations*. Baden-Baden: Nomos, 11–24.

Beetham, D. and Lord, C. (1998). *Legitimacy and the European Union*. London:
Longman.

Behn, R. D. (2001). *Rethinking Democratic Accountability*. Washington, DC: Brookings
Institution Press.

Benz, A. (2004). 'National Parliaments in the EU'. *West European Politics*, 27/5:
875–900.

Bergman, T. and Damgaard, E. (eds.) (2000). *Delegation and Accountability in the
European Union*. London: Frank Cass.

—— Müller, W. C., and Strøm, K. (2003). 'Democratic Delegation and Accountability: Cross-national Patterns', in K. Strøm, W. C. Müller, and T. Bergman (eds.),
Delegation and Accountability in Parliamentary Democracies. Oxford: Oxford University Press.

Bergström, C. F. (2005). *Comitology: Delegation of Powers in the European Union and the
Committee System*. Oxford: Oxford University Press.

Besselink, L. F. M. (2007). 'A Composite European Constitution/Een samengestelde
Europese constitutie'. Inaugural Address Jean Monnet Chair European Constitutional Law, University of Utrecht, 10 January. Groningen: Europa Law Publishing.

Besson, S. and Martí, J. L. (eds.) (2006). *Deliberative Democracy and Its Discontents*.
Aldershot: Ashgate.

Beyers, J. and Dierickx, G. (1998). 'The Working Groups of the Council of the
European Union: Supranational or Intergovernmental Negotiations?' *Journal of
Common Market Studies*, 36: 289–317.

—— and Trondal, J. (2004). 'How Nation States "Hit" Europe: Ambiguity and Representation in the European Union'. *West European Politics*, 27: 919–42.

Bickel, A. (1962). *The Least Dangerous Branch: The Supreme Court at the Bar of Politics*.
Indianapolis, IN: Bobbs-Merrill.

Blom-Hansen, J. (2008). 'The Origins of the EU Comitology System: A Case of
Informal Agenda-Setting by the Commission'. *Journal of European Public Policy*,
15: 208–26.

Boer, M. den (2002). 'Towards an Accountability Regime for an Emerging European
Policing Governance'. *Policing and Society*, 12/4: 275–89.

Bogdandy, A. von (2000). 'The EU as a Supranational Federation: A Conceptual
Attempt in the Light of the Amsterdam Treaty'. *Columbia Journal of European
Law*, 6: 27–52.

Bogdanor, V. (2007). *Legitimacy, Accountability and Democracy in the European Union*. A Federal Trust Report, London.

Bohman, J. (2007). *Democracy Across Borders: From Dêmos to Dêmoi*. Cambridge, MA: MIT Press.

Boin, A. (2001). *Crafting Public Institutions: Leadership in Two Prison Systems*. Boulder, CO: Lynne Rienner.

Boström, M. and Garsten, C. (eds.) (2008). *Organizing Transnational Accountability*. London: Edward Elgar Publishing.

Bouckaert, G. and Halligan, J. (2008). *Managing Performance: International Comparisons*. London: Routledge.

Bovend'Eert, P. and Kummeling, H. (2004). *Het Nederlandse parlement*. Deventer: Kluwer.

Bovens, M. (1998). *The Quest for Responsibility: Accountability and Citizenship in Complex Organisations*. Cambridge: Cambridge University Press.

—— (2006). 'Analysing and Assessing Public Accountability: A Conceptual Framework'. *European Governance Papers* (EUROGOV), C-06-01. Available at: <www.connex-network.org/eurogov/pdf/egp-connex-C-06-01.pdf>

—— (2007). 'Analysing and Assessing Accountability: A Conceptual Framework'. *European Law Journal*, 13/4: 447–68.

—— Schillemans, T., and 't Hart, P. (2008). 'Does Public Accountability Work? An Assessment Tool'. *Public Administration*, 86/1: 225–42.

—— 't Hart, P., Dekker, S., and Verheuvel, G. (1999). 'The Politics of Blame Avoidance: Defensive Tactics in a Dutch Crime-Fighting Fiasco', in H. K. Anheier (ed.), *When Things Go Wrong: Failures and Breakdowns in Organizational Settings*. Thousand Oaks, CA: Sage, 123–47.

Bradley, K. (2008). 'Halfway House: The 2006 Comitology Reforms and the European Parliament'. *West European Politics*, 31: 837–54.

Braithwaite, J. (1989). *Crime, Shame, and Reintegration*. Cambridge: Cambridge University Press.

—— and Drahos, P. (2002). 'Zero Tolerance, Naming, and Shaming: Is There a Case for It with Crimes of the Powerful?' *The Australian and New Zealand Journal of Criminology*, 35/3: 269–88.

Brandsma, G. J. (2007). 'Accountability Deficits in European "Comitology" Decision-Making'. *European Integration Online Papers*, 11. Available at: <http://www.eiop.or.at/eiop/index.php/eiop/article/view/2007_004a/51>

—— (2010). 'Backstage Europe: Holding Comitology Committees to Account'. Ph. D. thesis, Utrecht University.

—— Curtin, D. M., and Meijer, A. J. (2008). 'How Transparent are EU Comitology Committees in Practice?' *European Law Journal*, 14/6, 819–38.

Burgess, M. (2004). 'Federalism', in A. Wiener and T. Diez (eds.), *European Integration Theory*. Oxford: Oxford University Press, 25–43.

Busuioc, M. (2009). 'Accountability, Control and Independence: The Case of European Agencies'. *European Law Journal*, 15/5: 599–615.

—— (2010). *The Accountability of European Agencies: Legal Provision and Ongoing Practices* Delft: Eburon.

—— and Groenleer, M. (2008). 'Wielders of Supranational Power? The Administrative Behaviour of the Heads of European Union Agencies'. Paper presented at the ECPR Standing Group on Regulatory Governance, 5–7 June, Utrecht.

Christiansen, T. (1997). 'Tensions of European Governance: Politicized Bureaucracy and Multiple Accountability in the European Commission'. *Journal of European Public Policy*, 4/1: 73–90.

—— (2001). 'Intra-institutional Politics and Inter-institutional Relations in the EU: Towards Coherent Governance?' *Journal of European Public Policy*, 8: 747–69.

—— (2005). 'Towards Statehood? The EU's Move Towards Constitutionalisation and Territorialisation'. *ARENA Working Paper*, 21. Available at: <http://www.arena.uio.no/publications/working-papers2005/papers/05_21.xml>

—— and Gray, M. (2004). 'The European Commission in a Period of Change: A New Administration for a New European Union?' *Eipascope*, 3: 20–4.

—— and Vaccari, B. (2006). 'The 2006 Reform of Comitology: Problem Solved or Conflict Postponed?' *Eipascope*, 3: 9–17.

CIE (Committee of Independent Experts) (1999). First Report on 'Allegations regarding Fraud, Mismanagement and Nepotism in the European Commission'. 15 March.

Cini, M. (2000). 'Organizational Culture and Reform: The Case of the European Commission under Jacques Santer'. *EUI Working Papers*, European Forum Series, RSC No 2000/25.

Cohen, J. and Sabel, C. F. (1997). 'Directly-Deliberative Polyarchy'. *European Law Journal*, 3/4: 313–40.

Considine, M. (2002). 'The End of the Line? Accountable Governance in the Age of Networks, Partnerships and Joined-up Services'. *Governance*, 15/1, 21–40.

Craig, P. (2008). 'The Role of the European Parliament under the Lisbon Treaty', in S. Griller and J. Ziller (eds.), *The Lisbon Treaty: EU Constitutionalism Without a Constitutional Treaty?* Vienna: Springer, 109–34.

Cram, L. (2002). Introduction to Special Issue on the Institutional Balance and the Future of EU Governance: 'The Future of the Union and the Trap of the "Nirvana Fallacy".' *Governance*, 15/3: 309–24.

Crum, B. (2009). 'Accountability and Personalisation of the European Council Presidency'. *Journal of European Integration*, 31/6: 685–701.

Cruz, J. (2007). 'The Role of the European Commission'. Discussion Paper 4. Federal Trust Working Group on Democracy, Legitimacy and Accountability in the EU. Federal Trust.

Curtin, D. (1997). *Postnational Democracy: The European Union in Search of a Political Philosophy*. The Hague: Kluwer Law International.

—— (2004). 'European Union Executives Evolving in the Shade?', in A. E. Kellermann (ed.), *The European Union: An Ongoing Process of European Integration*. The Hague: T. M. C. Asser Instituut, 97–110.

Curtin, D. (2005). 'Delegation to EU Non-Majoritarian Agencies and Emerging Practices of Public Accountability', in D. Geradin, R. Munoz, and N. Petit (eds.), *Regulation through Agencies in the EU: A New Paradigm of European Governance*. Cheltenham: Edward Elgar, 88–119.

—— (2007). 'Holding (Quasi-)Autonomous EU Administrative Actors to Public Account'. *European Law Journal*, 13/4: 523–41.

—— (2009). *Executive Power of the European Union. Law, Practices and the Living Constitution*. Oxford: Oxford University Press.

—— and Egeberg, M. (2008). 'Tradition and Innovation: Europe's Accumulated Executive Order'. *Western European Politics*, 31/4: 639–61.

—— and Wille, A. (eds.) (2008). *Meaning and Practice of Accountability in the EU Multi-Level Context*. Mannheim: CONNEX.

Dalton, R. (2004). *Democratic Challenges, Democratic Choices: The Erosion of Political Support in Advanced Industrial Democracies*. Oxford: Oxford University Press.

Damgaard, E. (2000). 'Conclusion: The Impact of European Integration on Nordic Parliamentary Democracies', in T. Bergman and E. Damgaard (eds.), *Delegation and Accountability in European Integration*. London: Frank Cass, 151–69.

Day, P. and Klein, R. (1987). *Accountabilities: Five Public Services*. London: Tavistock.

De Clerck-Sachsse, J. and Kaczyński, P. M. (2009). 'The European Parliament: More Powerful, Less Legitimate? An Outlook for the 7th Term'. CEPS Working Document, 314.

Decker, F. (2002). 'Governance Beyond the Nation-State: Reflections on the Democratic Deficit of the European Union'. *Journal for European Public Policy*, 9/2: 256–72.

Dehousse, R. (2002). 'Misfits: EU Law and the Transformation of European Governance'. *Jean Monnet Working Paper*, 2/02, New York University School of Law.

—— (2003). 'Comitology: Who Watches the Watchmen?' *Journal of European Public Policy*, 10: 798–813.

—— (2008). 'Delegation of Powers in the European Union: The Need for a Multi-Principals Model'. *West European Politics*, 31/4: 789–805.

Dekker, I. and Wessel, R. (2004). 'Governance by International Organisations: Rethinking the Normative Force of International Decisions', in I. Dekker and W. Werner (eds.), *Governance and International Legal Theory*. Dordrecht: Martinus Nijhoff, 215–36.

Deutsch, K. (1963). *The Nerves of Government*. New York: The Free Press.

Dinan, D. (1999). *Ever Closer Union: An Introduction to European Integration*. Houndmills: Palgrave Macmillan.

Dowdle, M. (2006). 'Public Accountability: Conceptual, Historical, and Epistemic Mappings', in M. Dowdle (ed.), *Public Accountability: Designs, Dilemmas and Experiences*. Cambridge: Cambridge University Press, 1–26.

Dubnick, M. (2002). 'Seeking Salvation for Accountability'. Paper presented at the Annual Meeting of the American Political Science Association.

—— (2005). 'Accountability and the Promise of Performance: In Search of the Mechanisms'. *Public Performance and Management Review*, 28/3: 376–417.

—— (2007). 'Sarbanes-Oxley and the Search for Accountable Corporate Governance', in J. O'Brien (ed.) *Private Equity, Corporate Governance and the Dynamics of Capital Market Regulation*. London: Imperial College Press, 226–54.

Dunsire, A. (1978). *Control in a Bureaucracy: The Executive Process*, vol. 2. Oxford: Martin Robertson.

Easton, D. (1953). *The Political System: An Inquiry into the State of Political Science*. New York: Albert Knopf.

—— (1965). *A Systems Analysis of Political Life*. New York: Wiley.

Eberlain, B. and Grande, E. (2005). 'Beyond Delegation: Transnational Regulatory Regimes and the EU Regulatory State'. *Journal of European Public Policy*, 12/1: 89–112.

Ebrahim, A. and Weisband, E. (eds.) (2007). *Global Accountabilities*: *Participation, Pluralism, and Public Ethics*. Cambridge: Cambridge University Press.

Edwards, C. and Cornforth, C. (2003). 'What Influences the Strategic Contribution of Boards?', in C. Cornforth (ed.), *The Governance of Public and Non-Profit Organisations: What Do Boards Do?* London: Routledge, 77–96.

Edwards, G. (2006). 'Introduction: The European Commission in Perspective', in D. Spence (ed.), *The European Commission*. London: John Harper Publishing, 1–24.

Egeberg, M. (1999). 'Transcending Intergovernmentalism? Identity and Role Perceptions of National Officials in EU Decision-Making'. *Journal of European Public Policy*, 6: 456–74.

—— (2003). 'The European Commission', in M. Cini (ed.), *European Union Politics*. Oxford: Oxford University Press, 131–47.

Egeberg, M. (ed.) (2006). *Multilevel Union Administration: The Transformation of Executive Politics in Europe*. Basingstoke: Palgrave Macmillan.

—— Schaefer, G. F., and Trondal, J. (2003). 'The Many Faces of EU Committee Governance'. *West European Politics*, 26: 19–40.

Elchardus, M. (2002). *De Dramademocratie*. Lannoo: Tielt.

Ellinas, A. and Suleiman, E. (2008). 'Reforming the Commission: Between Modernization and Bureaucratization'. *Journal of European Public Policy*, 15/5: 708–25.

Eriksen, E. (2009). *The Unfinished Democratization of Europe*. Oxford: Oxford University Press.

—— and Fossum, J. E. (eds.) (2000). *Democracy in the European Union: Integration Through Deliberation?* London: Routledge.

European Commission (2001). *European Governance: A White Paper*. COM(2001) 428 final. Brussels, 25 July.

—— (2003*a*). *Report from the Commission on European Governance*. Luxembourg: Office for Official Publications of the European Communities.

—— (2003*b*). Budget Directorate General, 'Meta-Evaluation on the Community Agency System', 15 September. Available at: <http://ec.europa.eu/budget/library/documents/evaluation/eval_review/meta_eval_agencies_en.pdf>

Eriksen, E. (2006). *Report from the Commission on the Working of Committees During 2005*. COM(2006) 446. Brussels, 9 August. Available at: <http://eur-lex.europa.eu/LexUriServ/site/en/com/2006/com2006_0446en01.pdf>

—— (2007). 'Competition: Commission Fines Members of Beer Cartel in the Netherlands over €273 Million'. Press Release IP/07/509, 18 April. Available at: <http://europa.eu/rapid/pressReleasesAction.do?reference=IP/07/509&guiLanguage=en>

—— (2008). Communication from the Commission to the European Parliament and the Council: 'European Agencies – The Way Forward'. COM(2008) 135 final, Brussels, 11 March.

European Court of Auditors (2008*a*). 'The European Union's Agencies: Getting Results'. Special Report, no 5. Luxembourg: Office for Official Publications of the European Communities.

—— (2008*b*). 'Report on the Annual Accounts of the European Agency for Safety and Health at Work for the Financial Year 2007 Together with the Agency's Replies'. *Official Journal of the European Union*, 2008/C 311/08. Available at: <http://eca.europa.eu/portal/pls/portal/docs/1/1879627.pdf>

—— (2008*c*). 'Report on the Annual Accounts of the European Police College for the Financial Year 2007 Together with the College's Replies'. *Official Journal of the European Union*, 2008/C 311/20. Available at: <http://eca.europa.eu/portal/pls/portal/docs/1/1883569.pdf>

European Ombudsman (2009). *Overview: The European Ombudsman, 2008*. Luxembourg: Office for Official Publications of the European Communities.

European Parliament (2007*a*). Working Document on Governance in the European Commission, part 1. PE 392.252v02-00. Committee on Budgetary Control, 29 August.

—— (2007*b*). Committee on Budgets: 'Working Document on a Meeting with the Decentralised Agencies on the PDB for 2008'. DT\666715EN.doc. Rapporteur: J. Haug and K. Virrankoski, 23 May.

—— (2008). Committee on Constitutional Affairs: 'Report on a Strategy for the Future Settlement of the Institutional Aspects of Regulatory Agencies'. 2008/2103(INI). Rapporteur: G. Papastamkos, Rapporteur for opinion: J. Haug.

Europol, Management Board (2006). 'Draft Minutes of the 50th Management Board Meeting: 15–16 May 2006'. The Hague, 11 July. 5500-20060515MI(Draft) #176889 (on file with author).

Everson, M. (1995). 'Independent Agencies: Hierarchy Beaters?' *European Law Journal*, 1/2: 180–204.

Finer, S. E. (1970). 'Almond's Concept of the Political System'. *Government and Opposition*, 5/1: 3–21.

Fisher, E. (2004). 'The European Union in the Age of Accountability'. *Oxford Journal of Legal Studies*, 24/3: 495–515.

Fitzmaurice, J. (1996). 'National Parliamentary Control of EU Policy in the Three New Member States'. *West European Politics*, 19/1: 88–96.

Flinders, M. (2001). *The Politics of Accountability in the Modern State*. Aldershot: Ashgate.

—— (2004). 'Distributed Public Governance in the European Union'. *Journal of European Public Policy*, 11/3: 520–44.

Follesdal, A. (2006). 'The Legitimacy Deficits of the European Union'. *Journal of Political Philosophy*, 14/4: 441–68.

Fouilleux, E., De Maillard, J., and Smith, A. (2005). 'Technical or Political? The Working Groups of the EU Council of Ministers'. *Journal of European Public Policy*, 12: 609–23.

Freidson, E. (2001). *Professionalism: The Third Logic*. Cambridge: Polity Press.

Friedman, L. M. (1985). *Total Justice*. New York: Russell Sage.

Frink, D. D. and Ferris, G. R. (1998). 'Accountability, Impression Management, and Goal Setting in the Performance Evaluation Process'. *Human Relations*, 51/10: 1259–83.

Fung, A., Graham, M., and Weil, D. (2008). *Full Disclosure: The Perils and Promise of Transparency*. New York: Cambridge University Press.

Gallie, W. B. (1962). 'Essentially Contested Concepts', in M. Black (ed.), *The Importance of Language*. Ithaca, NY: Cornell University Press, 121–46.

George, A. L. and Bennett, A. (2004). *Case Studies and Theory Development in the Social Sciences*. Cambridge, MA: MIT Press.

Geradin, D., and Petit, N. (2004). 'The Development of Agencies at EU and National Levels: Conceptual Analysis and Proposal for Reform'. *Jean Monnet Working Paper*, 1/4, New York.

Geuijen, K. P., 't Hart, P., Princen, S., and Yesilkagit, K. (2008). *The New Eurocrats: National Civil Servants in EU Policy-Making*. Amsterdam: Amsterdam University Press.

Gormley, L. W. (2002). 'The Judicial Architecture of the European Union after Nice', in A. Arnull and D. Wincott (eds.), *Accountability and Legitimacy in the European Union*. Oxford: Oxford University Press.

Grant, R. and Keohane, R. (2005). 'Accountability and Abuses of Power in World Politics'. *American Political Science Review*, 99/1: 29–43.

Green, M., Visser, P., and Tetlock, P. E. (2000). 'Coping with Accountability Cross-Pressures: Attitude Shifting, Self-Criticism, and Decision Evasion'. *Personality and Social Psychology Bulletin*, 24: 563–74.

Groenleer, M. (2006). 'The European Commission and Agencies', in D. Spence (ed.), *The European Commission*. London: John Harper Publishing, 156–72.

—— (2009). *The Autonomy of European Union Agencies: A Comparative Study of Institutional Development*. Delft: Eburon.

Gustavsson, S. (2009). 'Putting Limits on Accountability Avoidance', in S. Gustavsson, C. Karlsson, and T. Persson (eds.), *The Illusion of Accountability in the European Union*. London: Routledge, 35–47.

—— Karlsson, C., and Persson, T. (eds.) (2009). *The Illusion of Accountability in the European Union*. London: Routledge.

Haas, E. B. (1958). *The Uniting of Europe: Political, Social and Economic Forces, 1950–1957*. Stanford, CA: Stanford University Press.

Haas, P. M. (1992). 'Introduction: Epistemic Communities and International Policy Coordination'. *International Organization*, 46/1: 1–35.

Habermas, J. (1976). 'Legitimationsprobleme im modernen Staat', in *Zur Rekonstruktion des Historischen Materialismus*. Frankfurt: Suhrkamp.

Haibach, G. (2000). 'The History of Comitology', in M. Andenas and A. Türk (eds.), *Delegated Legislation and the Role of Committees in the EC*. The Hague: Kluwer, 185–216.

Halachmi, A. (2002). 'Performance Measurement, Accountability, and Improved Performance'. *Public Performance and Management Review*, 25/4: 370–4.

Hardacre, A. (2008). 'Better Regulation: What is at Stake?' *Eipascope*, 2: 5–10.

Harlow, C. (2002). *Accountability in the European Union*. Oxford: Oxford University Press.

Hayes-Renshaw, F. and Wallace, H. (1997). *The Council of Ministers*. Basingstoke: Macmillan Press.

Hearit, K. M. (2005). *Crisis Management by Apology: Corporate Response to Allegations of Wrongdoing*. London: Taylor & Francis.

Hix, S. (2000). 'Parliamentary Oversight of Executive Power: What Role for the European Parliament in Comitology?' in T. Christiansen and E. Kirchner (eds.), *Europe in Change: Committee Governance in the European Union*. Manchester: Manchester University Press, 62–78.

—— (2005). *The Political System of the European Union*, 2nd edn. The European Union Series. Basingstoke: Palgrave Macmillan.

—— (2008). *What's Wrong with the European Union and How to Fix It*. Cambridge: Polity Press.

—— and Noury, A. (2009). 'After Enlargement: Voting Patterns in the Sixth European Parliament'. *Legislative Studies Quarterly*, 34/2: 159–74.

Hoffman, S. (1995). *The European Sisyphus: Essays on Europe, 1964–1994*. Boulder, CO: Westview Press.

Hofmann, H. (2009). 'Legislation, Delegation and Implementation under the Lisbon Treaty: Typology Meets Reality'. *European Law Journal*, 15: 482–505.

Holzhacker, R. (2002). 'National Parliamentary Scrutiny over EU Issues: Comparing the Goals and Methods of Governing and Opposition Parties'. *European Union Politics*, 3/4: 459–79.

Hood, C. and Heald, D. (eds.) (2006). *Transparency: The Key to Better Governance*. Oxford: Oxford University Press.

—— Jennings, W. and Hogwood, B., with Beeston, C. (2007). 'Fighting Fires in Testing Times: Exploring a Staged Response Hypothesis for Blame Management in Two Exam Fiasco Cases'. London School of Economics/ESRC Research Centre Discussion Paper, 42. Available at: <http://www.lse.ac.uk/collections/CARR/pdf/DPs/Disspaper42.pdf>

House of Lords (2008). European Union Committee, 'Europol: Co-ordinating the Fight Against Serious and Organised Crime', 29th Report of Session 2007–08, Report with Evidence.

Houses of the Oireachtas, Sub-Committee on Ireland's Future in the European Union (2008). *Ireland's Future in the European Union: Challenges, Issues and Options*. November. Available at: <http://www.oireachtas.ie/documents/committees30thdail/j-europeanaffairs/sub_cttee_eu_01122008-3.pdf>

Joerges, C. and Neyer, J. (1997). 'From Intergovernmental Bargaining to Deliberative Political Processes: The Constitutionalisation of Comitology'. *European Law Journal*, 3: 273–99.

Judge, D. and Earnshaw, D. (2002). 'The European Parliament and the Commission Crisis: A New Assertiveness?' *Governance*, 15/3: 345–74.

—— —— (2008). *The European Parliament*, 2nd edn. London: Palgrave Macmillan.

Karlsson, C. (2009). 'Holding Treaty Reformers Accountable: Any Progress?', in S. Gustavsson, C. Karlsson, and T. Persson (eds.), *The Illusion of Accountability in the European Union*. London: Routledge, 67–82.

Kassim, H. (2004). 'A Historic Accomplishment? The Prodi Commission and Administrative Reform', in D. G. Dimitrakopoulos (ed.), *The Changing European Commission*. Manchester: Manchester University Press, 33–62.

—— (2008). '"Mission Impossible", But Mission Accomplished: The Kinnock Reforms and the European Commission'. *Journal of European Public Policy*, 15/5: 648–68.

Katz, R. (2001). 'Models of Democracy: Elite Attitudes and the Democratic Deficit in the European Union'. *European Union Politics*, 2: 53–78.

Kay, A. (1998). *The Reform of the Common Agricultural Policy: The Case of the MacSharry Reforms*. Wallingford: CABI International.

Keane, J. (2009). *The Life and Death of Democracy*. New York: Simon & Schuster.

Keleman, D. (2002). 'The Politics of "Eurocratic" Structure and the New European Agencies'. *West European Politics*, 25/4: 93–118.

Kohler-Koch, B. and Rittberger, B. (eds.) (2007). *Debating the Democratic Legitimacy of the European Union*. Lanham, MD: Rowman & Littlefield Publishers.

Koopmans, T. (1992). 'Federalism: The Wrong Debate'. *Common Market Law Review*, 29: 1047–52.

—— (2008). 'Confederalisme: Van de "Articles of Confederation" naar het Verdrag van Maastricht', in F. Judo and G. Geudens (eds.), *Confederalisme?* Ghent: Larcier, 1–18.

Koppell, J. (2005). 'Pathologies of Accountability: ICANN and the Challenge of "Multiple Accountabilities Disorder"'. *Public Administration Review*, 65/1: 94–107.

Kroon, M. B. R. (1992). *Effects of Accountability on Groupthink and Intergroup Relations: Laboratory and Field Studies*. Amsterdam: Thesis Publishers.

Laffan, B. (2003). 'Auditing and Accountability in the European Union'. *Journal of European Public Policy*, 10/5: 762–77.

Larsson, T. (2003). *Precooking in the European Union: The World of Expert Groups*. Stockholm: Expert Group on Public Finance (ESO).

—— and Trondal, J. (2005). 'After Hierarchy? Domestic Executive Governance and the Differentiated Impact of the European Commission and the Council of

Ministers'. *European Integration Online Papers*, 9/14. Available at: <http://eiop.or.
at/eiop/texte/2005-014a.htm>

Lenaerts, K. (1998). 'Federalism: Essential Concepts in Evolution – The Case of the
European Union'. *Fordham International Law Journal*, 21: 746–98.

Lerner, J. S. and Tetlock, P. E. (1999). 'Accounting for the Effects of Accountability'.
Psychological Bulletin, 125: 255–75.

Lijphart, A. (1984). *Democracies: Patterns of Majoritarian and Consensus Government in
Twenty-One Democracies*. New Haven, CT: Yale University Press.

Lindberg, L. and Scheingold, S. (1970). *Europe's Would-Be Polity: Patterns of Change in
the European Community*. Englewood Cliffs, NJ: Prentice-Hall.

Lindblom, C. E. (1965). *The Intelligence of Democracy*. New York: Free Press.

Lord, C. (1998). *Democracy in the European Union*. Sheffield: Sheffield Academic Press.

—— (2000). 'Legitimacy, Democracy and the EU: When Abstract Questions become Practical Policy Problems'. Available at: <http://www.mcrit.com/scenarios/
visionsofeurope/>

—— (2004). *A Democratic Audit of the European Union*. Basingstoke: Palgrave
Macmillan.

—— (2007). 'Contested Meanings: Democracy Assessment and the European
Union'. *Comparative European Politics*, 5/1: 70–86.

—— and Beetham, D. (2001). 'Legitimizing the EU: Is There a "Post-parliamentary
Basis" for its Legitimation?' *Journal of Common Market Studies*, 39/3: 443–62.

Luhmann, N. (1966). *Theorie der Verwaltungswissenschaft: Bestandsaufnahme und
Entwurf*. Cologne: Grote.

Lupia, A. (2003). 'Delegation and its Perils', in K. Strøm, W. Müller, and T. Bergman
(eds.), *Delegation and Accountability in Parliamentary Democracies*. Oxford: Oxford
University Press, 33–54.

Magnette, P. (2003). 'Between Parliamentary Control and the Rule of Law: The
Political Role of the Ombudsman in the European Union'. *Journal of European
Public Policy*, 10/5: 677–94.

—— (2005). *What Is the European Union? The Nature of the European Union*. Basingstoke: Palgrave Macmillan.

—— and Papadopoulos, Y. (2008). 'On the Politicization of the European
Consociation: A Middle Way Between Hix and Bartolini'. *Eurogov Working
Paper*, no. C-08-0. Available at: <http://www.connex-network.org/eurogov/pdf/
egp-connex-C-08-01.pdf>

Mair, P. (2005). 'Popular Democracy and the European Union Polity'. *Eurogov Working
Paper*, no. C-05-03. Available at: <http://www.connex-network.org/eurogov/>

—— (2008). 'Popular Democracy and the European Union Polity', in D. Curtin and
A. Wille (eds.), *Meaning and Practice of Accountability in the EU Multi-Level Context*,
Connex report series no. 7. Mannheim: University of Mannheim, 19–62.

Majone, G. (1996). *Regulating Europe*. London: Routledge.

—— (2000). 'The Credibility Crisis of Community Regulation'. *Journal of Common
Market Studies*, 38/2: 273–302.

Majone, G. (2002). 'The European Commission: The Limits of Centralization and the Perils of Parliamentarization'. *Governance*, 15/3: 374–92.

—— (2005). *Dilemmas of European Integration: The Ambiguities and Pitfalls of Integration by Stealth*. Oxford: Oxford University Press.

—— (2009). 'The Mutation of the EU as a Regulatory Regime'. Keynote paper presented at the RECON project midterm conference. Prague, 9–10 October.

Malena, C. with Forster, R. and Singh, J. (2004). 'Social Accountability: An Introduction to the Concept and Emerging Practice'. *Social Development Papers*, no. 76. Washington, DC: World Bank.

Malkopoulou, A. (2009). 'Participation in EU Elections and the Case for Compulsory Voting'. *CEPS Working Document*, no. 317.

Manin, B., Przeworski, A., and Stokes, S. C. (1999). 'Elections and Representation', in A. Przeworski, S. C. Stokes, and B. Manin (eds.), *Democracy, Accountability, and Representation*. Cambridge: Cambridge University Press, 29–54.

March, J. and Olsen, J. (1989). *Rediscovering Institutions: The Organizational Basis of Politics*. New York: Free Press.

—— —— (1995). *Democratic Governance*. New York: The Free Press.

Markman, K. D. and Tetlock, P. E. (2000). 'Accountability and Close-Call Counterfactuals: The Loser Who Almost Won and the Winner Who Almost Lost'. *Personality and Social Psychology Bulletin*, 26: 1213–24.

Marquand, J. (2008). 'Spatial Change and Economic Divergence in the EEC'. *Journal of Common Market Studies*, 19/1: 1–20.

Maurer, A. (2002). 'National Parliaments in the European Architecture: Elements for Establishing a Best Practice Mechanism'. Paper presented to Working Group IV of the European Convention entitled 'The Role of National Parliaments'.

—— and Wessels, W. (eds.) (2001). *National Parliaments on Their Ways to Europe: Losers or Latecomers?* Baden-Baden: Nomos.

McCandless, H. E. (2001). *A Citizen's Guide to Public Accountability: Changing the Relationship Between Citizens and Authorities*. Victoria, BC: Trafford.

McCubbins, M. and Schwartz, T. (1984). 'Congressional Oversight Overlooked: Police Patrols Versus Fire Alarms'. *American Journal of Political Science*, 28: 165–79.

Meijer, A. (2002). *De doorzichtige overheid: Parlementaire en juridische controle in het informatietijdperk*. Delft: Eburon.

—— and Schillemans, T. (2009). 'Fictional Citizens and Real Effects: Accountability to Citizens in Competitive and Monopolistic Markets'. *Public Administration and Management*, 14/2: 254–91.

Moe, T. M. (1987). 'Interests, Institutions and Positive Theory: The Politics of the NLRB'. *Studies in American Political Development*, 2: 236–99.

Molle, W. (2006). *The Economics of European Integration: Theory, Practice, Policy*. Aldershot: Ashgate.

Moore, M. H. (1995). *Creating Public Value: Strategic Management in Government*. Cambridge, MA: Harvard University Press.

Bibliography

Moravcsik, A. (1993). 'Preferences and Power in the European Community: A Liberal Intergovernmental Approach'. *Journal of Common Market Studies*, 31/4: 473–524.

—— (2002). 'In Defence of the Democratic Deficit: Reassessing Legitimacy in the European Union'. *Journal of Common Market Studies*, 40/4: 603–24.

—— (2004). 'Is there a "Democratic Deficit" in World Politics? A Framework for Analysis'. *Government and Opposition*, 39/2: 336–63.

Moynihan, D. (2005). 'Goal-Based Learning and the Future of Performance Management'. *Public Administration Review*, 65/2: 203–16.

Mulgan, R. (2000). ' "Accountability": An Ever-Expanding Concept?' *Public Administration*, 78/3: 555–73.

—— (2003). *Holding Power to Account: Accountability in Modern Democracies*. Basingstoke: Palgrave Macmillan.

Müller, E. (1994). *Terrorisme en politieke verantwoordelijkheid: Gijzelingen, aanslagen en ontvoeringen in Nederland*. Gouda: Quint.

Neuhold, C. (2001). 'Much Ado About Nothing? Comitology as a Feature of EU Policy Implementation and Its Effects on the Democratic Arena'. Working Paper. Vienna: Institut für höhere Studien.

—— (2008). 'Taming the "Trojan Horse" of Comitology? Accountability Issues of Comitology and the Role of the European Parliament'. *European Integration Online Papers*, 12.

—— de Ruiter, R., and Kanen, M. (2009). 'Out of REACH? Parliamentary Control of EU Affairs in the Netherlands and the UK'. Paper presented at the Politicologen-etmaal, May.

Neunreither, K. (1994). 'The Democratic Deficit of the European Union: Towards Closer Cooperation Between the European Parliament and the National Parliaments'. *Government and Opposition*, 29/3: 299–314.

Nugent, N. (2001). *The European Commission*. Basingstoke: Palgrave.

O'Connell, L. (2005). 'Program Accountability as an Emergent Property: The Role of Stakeholders in a Program's Field'. *Public Administration Review*, 65/1: 85–93.

O'Donnell, G. (1999). 'Horizontal Accountability in New Democracies', in A. Schedler, L. Diamond, and M. F. Plattner (eds.), *The Self-Restraining State: Power and Accountability in New Democracies*. London: Lynne Rienner Publishers, 29–51.

Ooik, R. van (2005). 'The Growing Importance of Agencies in the EU: Shifting Governance and the Institutional Balance', in D. M. Curtin and R. A. Wessel (eds.), *Good Governance and the European Union: Reflections on Concepts, Institutions and Substance*. Antwerp: Intersentia, 125–52.

Page, E. (1997). *People Who Run Europe*. Oxford: Clarendon Press.

—— and Jenkins, B. (2005). *Policy Bureaucracy: Government with a Cast of Thousands*. Oxford: Oxford University Press.

Parks, L. (2009). 'Accountability and Legitimacy in the Eyes of Brussels Activists: Evidence from Research on EU Social Movements', in S. Gustavsson, C. Karlsson, and T. Persson (eds.), *The Illusion of Accountability in the European Union*. London: Routledge, 155–69.

Peers, S. (2005). 'Governance and the Third Pillar: The Accountability of Europol', in D. M. Curtin and R. A. Wessel (eds.), *Good Governance and the European Union: Reflections on Concepts, Institutions and Substance*. Antwerp: Intersentia, 253–76.

Persson, T. (2009). 'Accountability and Expertise in the European Union', in S. Gustavsson, C. Karlsson, and T. Persson (eds.), *The Illusion of Accountability in the European Union*. London: Routledge, 141–54.

Peterson, J. (2004). 'The Prodi Commission: Fresh Start or Free Fall', in D. G. Dimitrakopoulos (ed.), *The Changing European Commission*. Manchester: Manchester University Press, 15–32.

—— (2006). 'Where Does the Commission Stand Today?', in D. Spence (ed.), *The European Commission*. London: John Harper Publishing, 502–19.

Philp, M. (2009). 'Delimiting Democratic Accountability', *Political Studies*, 57/1: 28–53.

Pollack, M. (2003). *The Engines of European Integration: Delegation, Agency and Agenda-Setting in the EU*. Oxford: Oxford University Press.

Pollak, J. and Slominski, P. (2003). 'Influencing EU Politics? The Case of the Austrian Parliament'. *Journal of Common Market Studies*, 41/4: 707–29.

Pollitt, C. (2003). *The Essential Public Manager*. London: Open University Press/ McGraw-Hill.

—— and Bouckaert, G. (2000). *Public Management Reform: A Comparative Analysis*. Oxford: Oxford University Press.

—— and Summa, H. (1997). 'Reflexive Watchdogs? How Supreme Audit Institutions Account for Themselves'. *Public Administration*, 75/2: 313–36.

Ponzano, P. (2008). '"Executive" and "Delegated" Acts: The Situation After the Lisbon Treaty', in S. Griller and J. Ziller (eds.), *The Lisbon Treaty: EU Constitutionalism Without a Constitutional Treaty?* Vienna: Springer, 135–41.

Power, M. (1994). *The Audit Explosion*. London: Demos.

—— (1997). *The Audit Society: Rituals of Verification*. Oxford: Oxford University Press.

Przeworski, A., Stokes, S. C., and Manin, B. (eds.) (1999). *Democracy, Accountability, and Representation*. Cambridge: Cambridge University Press.

Pujas, V. (2003). 'The European Anti-Fraud Office (OLAF): A European Policy to Fight Against Economic and Financial Fraud?' *Journal of European Public Policy*, 10/5: 778–97.

Puntscher Riekmann, S. (2007). 'The Cocoon of Power: Democratic Implications of Interinstitutional Agreements'. *European Law Journal*, 13/1: 4–19.

Radaelli, C. (1999). 'The Public Policy of the European Union: Whither Politics of Expertise?' *Journal of European Public Policy*, 6: 757–74.

Raunio, T. and Hix, S. (2000). 'Backbenchers Learn to Fight Back: European Integration and Parliamentary Government'. *West European Politics*, 11: 142–68.

Reinalda, B. and Verbeek, B. (1998). *Autonomous Policy Making by International Organizations*. London: Routledge.

Rhinard, M. (2002). 'The Democratic Legitimacy of the European Union Committee System'. *Governance*, 15/3: 185–210.

RMO (Raad voor Maatschappelijke Ontwikkeling) (2003). *Medialogica: Over het krachtenveld tussenburgers, media en politiek*. The Hague: SDU.

Robertson, C. (2008). 'Impact Assessment in the European Union'. *Eipascope*, 2: 17–20.

Roch, S. G. and McNall, L. A. (2007). 'An Investigation of Factors Influencing Accountability and Performance Ratings'. *Journal of Psychology: Interdisciplinary and Applied*, 141: 499–523.

Romzek, B. (1996). 'Enhancing Accountability', in J. L. Perry (ed.), *Handbook of Public Administration*, 2nd edn. San Francisco, CA: Jossey Bass.

—— and Dubnick, M. (1998). 'Accountability', in J. Shafritz (ed.), *International Encyclopaedia of Public Policy and Administration*, vol. 1. Boulder, CO: Westview Press.

Sartori, G. (1970). 'Concept Misformation in Comparative Politics'. *American Political Science Review*, 64/4: 1033–53.

Sawer, M., Abjorensen, N., and Larkin, P. (2009). *Australia: The State of Democracy*. Annandale, NSW: Federation Press.

Scharpf, F. (1999). *Governing Europe: Effective and Democratic?* Oxford: Oxford University Press.

Schendelen, R. (2002). *Machiavelli in Brussels: The Art of Lobbying the EU*. Amsterdam: Amsterdam University Press.

Schermers, H. G. and Blokker, N. M. (2003). *International Institutional Law: Unity Within Diversity*, 4th rev. edn. Leiden: Martinus Nijhoff.

Schillemans, T. (2006). 'Horizontal Accountability of Agencies as Extensions of Control and Instruments for Autonomy'. Paper on file with author.

—— (2007). *Verantwoording in de schaduw van de macht: Horizontale verantwoording bij zelfstandige uitvoeringsorganisaties*. The Hague: Lemma.

—— (2008). 'Accountability in the Shadow of Hierarchy: The Horizontal Accountability of Agencies'. *Public Organization Review*, 8/2: 175–94.

—— (2009). 'Horizontal Accountability. A Partial Remedy for the Accountability Deficit of Agencies'. Paper presented at 5th Transatlantic Dialogue: The Future of Governance. Washington, DC, 11–13 June.

—— and Bovens, M. (2004). 'Horizontale verantwoording bij zelfstandige bestuursorganen', in S. van Thiel (ed.), *Governance van uitvoeringsorganisaties: Nieuwe vraagstukken voor sturing in het publieke domein*. Apeldoorn: Kadaster, 27–37.

Schimmelfennig, F. (2004). 'Liberal Intergovernmentalism', in A. Wiener and T. Diez (eds.), *European Integration Theory*. Oxford: Oxford University Press.

Schmidt, V. (2006). *Democracy in Europe: The EU and National Polities*. Oxford: Oxford University Press.

Schmitter, P. (2000). *How to Democratize the European Union . . . and Why Bother?* Lanham, MD: Rowman & Littlefield.

Schön-Quinlivan, E. (2007). 'Administrative Reform in the European Commission: From Rhetoric to Relegitimization', in M. W. Bauer and C. Knill (eds.), *Management Reforms in International Organizations*. Baden-Baden: Nomos, 25–36.

Scott, C. (2000). 'Accountability in the Regulatory State'. *Journal of Law and Society*, 27/1: 38–60.

Seidenfeld, M. (2001). 'The Psychology of Accountability and Political Review of Agency Rules'. *Duke Law Journal*, 51: 1051–95.

Selznick, P. (1957). *Leadership in Administration: A Sociological Interpretation*. New York: Harper & Row.

Shapiro, M. (1997). 'The Problems of Independent Agencies in the United States and the European Union'. *Journal of European Public Policy*, 4/2: 276–91.

—— (2005). 'A Deliberative "Independent" Technocracy v. Democratic Politics: Will the Globe Echo the EU?' *Law and Contemporary Problems*, 68: 341–56.

Shore, C. (2000). *Building Europe: The Cultural Politics of European Integration*. London: Routledge.

Sinclair, A. (1996). 'The Chameleon of Accountability: Forms and Discourses'. *Accounting, Organisations and Society*, 20: 219–37.

Sjursen, H. (2007). *Civilian or Military Power? European Foreign Policy in Perspective*. London: Routledge.

Slaughter, A-M. (2004). *A New World Order*. Princeton, NJ: Princeton University Press.

—— Stone Sweet, A. and Weiler, J. (eds.) (1998). *The European Court and National Courts – Doctrine and Jurisprudence: Legal Change in Its Social Context*. Oxford: Hart Publishing.

Sousa, M. (2008). 'Learning in Denmark? The Case of Danish Parliamentary Control over European Union Policy'. *Scandinavian Political Studies*, 31/4: 428–47.

Stevens, A. and Stevens, H. (2001). *Brussels Bureaucrats? The Administration of the European Union*. Basingstoke: Palgrave.

Stevens, H. and Stevens, A. (2006). 'The Internal Reform of the Commission', in D. Spence (ed.), *The European Commission*. London: John Harper Publishing, 454–80.

Stie, A. (2009). 'Co-decision: The Panacea for EU Democracy?' Ph.D. thesis, Department of Political Science, University of Oslo, Oslo, Norway.

Strøm, K. (2000). 'Delegation and Accountability in Parliamentary Democracies'. *European Journal of Political Research*, 37/3: 261–89.

—— (2003). 'Parliamentary Democracy and Delegation', in K. Strøm, W. C. Müller, and T. Bergman (eds.), *Delegation and Accountability in Parliamentary Democracies*. Oxford: Oxford University Press, 55–108.

—— Müller, W. C., and Bergman, T. (eds.) (2003). *Delegation and Accountability in Parliamentary Democracies*. Oxford: Oxford University Press.

—— Müller, W. C., and Bergman, T. (2006). 'The (Moral) Hazards of Parliamentary Democracy', in D. Braun and F. Gilardi (eds.), *Delegation in Contemporary Democracies*. Abingdon: Routledge, 27–51.

Tallberg, J. (2009). 'Executive Politics and Accountability', in S. Gustavsson, C. Karlsson, and T. Persson (eds.), *The Illusion of Accountability in the European Union*. London: Routledge, 111–25.

Tetlock, P. E. (1983). 'Accountability and the Perseverance of First Impressions'. *Social Psychology Quarterly*, 46: 285–92.

Tetlock, P. E. (1985). 'Accountability: A Social Check on the Fundamental Attribution Error'. *Social Psychology Quarterly*, 48: 227–36.

—— Skitka, L., and Boettger, R. (1989). 'Social and Cognitive Strategies for Coping with Accountability. Conformity, Complexity, and Bolstering'. *Journal of Personality and Social Psychology*, 57: 632–40.

Thatcher, M. (2002). 'Regulation after Delegation: Independent Regulatory Agencies in Europe'. *Journal of European Public Policy*, 9/6: 954–72.

—— (2005). 'The Third Force? Independent Regulatory Agencies and Elected Politicians in Europe'. *Governance: An International Journal of Policy, Administration, and Institutions*, 18/3: 347–73.

—— and Stone Sweet, A. (2002). 'Theory and Practice of Delegation to Non-Majoritarian Institutions'. *West European Politics*, 25/1: 1–22.

Thomassen, J. and Schmidt, H. (2004). 'Legitimacy and Democracy in the EU'. Available at: <http://www.mzes.uni-mannheim.de/publications/papers/Schmitt_26_1_04.pdf>

Thompson, D. F. (1980). 'Moral Responsibility of Public Officials: The Problem of the Many Hands'. *The American Political Science Review*, 74/4: 905–16.

Tilly, C. (2007). *Credit and Blame*. Princeton, NJ: Princeton University Press.

Toonen, T., Steunenberg, B., and Voermans, W. (2005). 'Saying No to a European Constitution: Dutch Revolt, Enigma or Pragmatism?' *Zeitschrift für Staats- und Europawissenschaften*, 3: 594–619.

Trondal, J. (2002). 'Beyond the EU Membership–Non-Membership Dichotomy? Supranational Identities Among National EU Decision-makers'. *Journal of European Public Policy*, 9: 468–87.

Tsakatika, M. (2005). 'Claims to Legitimacy: The European Commission Between Continuity and Change'. *Journal of Common Market Studies*, 43/1: 193–220.

Türk, A. (2000). 'The Role of the Court of Justice', in M. Andenas and A. Türk (eds.), *Delegated Legislation and the Role of Committees in the EC*. London: Kluwer Law International, 217–53.

—— (2003). 'Transparency and Comitology', in C. Demmke and C. Engel (eds.), *Continuity and Change in the European Integration Process*. Maastricht: EIPA.

Van de Steeg, M. (2009). 'Public Accountability in the European Union: Is the European Parliament Able to Hold the European Council Accountable?' *European Integration Online Papers (EioP)*, 13. Available at: <http://econpapers.repec.org/article/erpeiopxx/p0169.htm>

—— (2010). Accountability of European Summits to National Parliaments: The Dutch Case, forthcoming.

Van Gerven, W. (2005). *The European Union: A Polity of States and Peoples*. Stanford, CA: Stanford University Press.

—— (2007). 'Legal, Ethical, Political and Financial Responsibility of EU Commissioners'. Paper presented for Committee on Budgetary Control, European Parliament, 4 October.

Van Schendelen, M. C. P. M. (2006). 'The In-sourced Experts'. *The Journal of Legislative Studies*, 8/4: 27–39.

—— and Scully, R. (2003). *The Unseen Hand: Unelected EU Legislators*. London: Frank Cass.

—— —— (2006). 'Introduction'. *The Journal of Legislative Studies*, 8/4: 1–13.

Van Twist, M. (2000). 'Organizing Accountability: From Best Practices to Dilemmas in Design', in H. Wagenaar (ed.), *Government Institutions: Effects, Changes and Normative Foundations*. Dordrecht: Kluwer, 217–33.

Virally, M. (1981). 'Definition and Classification of International Organisations: A Legal Approach', in G. Abi-Saab (ed.), *The Concept of International Organization*. Paris: UNESCO, 50–66.

Vos, E. (2000). 'Reforming the European Commission: What Role to Play for EU Agencies?' *Common Market Law Review*, 37/5: 1113–34.

Weiler, J. H. H. (1991). 'The Transformation of Europe'. *Yale Law Journal*, 100/8: 2525–36.

Weir, S. and Beetham, D. (1999). *Political Power and Democratic Control in Britain: The Democratic Audit of the United Kingdom*. London: Routledge.

Werner, W. and Wessel, R. (2005). *Internationaal en Europees Recht: Een verkenning van grondslagen en kenmerken*. Groningen: Europa Law Publishing.

Wessels, W. (1998). 'Comitology: Fusion in Action. Politico-administrative Trends in the EU System'. *Journal of European Public Policy*, 5: 209–34.

Wiener, A. and Diez, T. (2009). *European Integration Theory*. Oxford: Oxford University Press.

Williams, G. (2005). 'Monomaniacs or Schizophrenics? Responsible Governance and the EU's Independent Agencies'. *Political Studies*, 53/1: 82–99.

Williams, S. (1990). 'Sovereignty and Accountability in the European Community'. *Political Quarterly*, 60: 299–31.

Witte, B. de (1994). 'Rules of Change in International Law: How Special is the European Community?' *Netherlands Yearbook of International Law*, 25: 299–333.

Witteveen, W. (1991). *Evenwicht van machten*, Inaugural Address Katholieke Universiteit Brabant. Zwolle: Tjeenk Willink.

Index

The letter n indicates a footnote and t a table.